INDIA'S FORGOTTEN ROCKET PIONEER

STEPHEN H SMITH - PIGEON MAIL TO
ROCKET MAIL

GURBIR SINGH

Copyright © 2020 by Gurbir Singh

All rights reserved. No part of this publication may be reproduced, distributed or transmitted in any form or by any means, including photocopying, recording, or other electronic or mechanical methods, without the prior written permission of the publisher, except in the case of brief quotations embodied in critical reviews and certain other noncommercial uses permitted by copyright law.

Front and back cover images from the Dr Robert Paganini Collection, Museum of Communication, Bern Switzerland.

Ordering Information:

Quantity sales: Special discounts are available on quantity purchases by corporations, associations, and others. For details, please contact the editor via an email to info@astrotalkuk.org.

India's Forgotten Rocket Pioneer. Stephen H Smith From Pigeon Mail to Rocket Mail. Gurbir Singh - 1st edition.

ISBN: 978-1-913617-01-1

For permission requests contact the publisher at the email address below.

Gurbir Singh/Astrotalkuk Publications

www.astrotalkuk.org

info@astrotalkuk.org

CONTENTS

Title	7
Foreword	11
About the Author	13
Introduction	15
1. Origins	23
2. Postal Services and Philately in India	41
3. Mail Transport	53
4. Airmail	65
5. Rocket Mail	83
6. Rocket Mail in India	105
7. Special Event Rocket Mail	125
8. Global Connections	137
9. Prelude to Space	151
10. Legacy	177
11. Appendices	195
Glossary	197
Published and Unpublished Works	201
Brief Timeline	203
Rocket Launch Log	207
End Notes	219
Also by Gurbir Singh	241

India's Forgotten Rocket Pioneer

Stephen H Smith - From Pigeon Mail to Rocket Mail

Professor U. R. Rao

As a scientist, humanist and the chairman of the Indian Space Research Organisation, he helped realise Stephen Smith's vision of using rocket power to improve the quality of lives of ordinary Indians.

FOREWORD

Technological advancements and innovative use of technologies to convey information and materials from one place to another have been the hallmark of progress in human society. Pigeons, bullock carts, mules and horses have provided mankind with the means of communication and transport from the earliest human settlements. As the transport technologies started developing with the use of boats, ships, motor vehicles, locomotives, balloons and aircrafts the activity of transport of information through surface mail, sea mail and airmail become integral part of modern civilisation. Today's high-speed digital communication allows us to see, hear and communicate with each other anytime, anywhere, almost instantaneously.

This book titled 'India's Forgotten Rocket Pioneer Stephen H Smith - From Pigeon Mail to Rocket Mail' written by Mr Gurbir Singh celebrates the untiring efforts of Mr Smith taming rocket technology for transporting mail and parcels that was otherwise primarily used in warfare. The author has through his painstaking efforts brought out the trials and tribulations of Mr Stephen Smith (1891-1951) in demonstrating the ability of rockets in delivering essential supplies of food and medicines especially during extreme events such as earthquakes, floods and storms. He supported his experiments through the sale of commemorative covers/stamps of the rocket mail flights. It is through the international philatelic community that preserved records of his work that his story can be told.

The author has brought out vividly the efforts of an individual by interacting with people and institutions associated with Mr Smith and his activities. This book will serve as a great tribute to Mr Stephen Smith who had conducted early experiments with rockets as a tool for novel applications in delivering information and material. While the development of rockets took place primarily to gain upper hand in warfare, there were attempts made to use rockets for initiating transport of information and materials.

India is now a major player in space with significant assets in space for remote sensing, communication and navigation. There is also a spacecraft orbiting Mars, another in lunar orbit and a space telescope in Earth orbit. Rockets are now playing a key part providing the support and services for ordinary Indians as Smith had hoped rockets would in his lifetime.

A. S. Kiran Kumar

Chairman of the Indian Space Research Organisation (2015 - 2018)

Bangalore

India

ABOUT THE AUTHOR

Gurbir Singh is the publisher of www.astrotalkuk.org and the author of *Yuri Gagarin in London and Manchester* published in 2011 to mark the 50th anniversary of humanity's first journey into space. His second book, *The Indian Space Programme* was published in 2017. A former college lecturer, since 1999 he has worked in the private sector in IT and cyber security. He has a science and an arts degree.

Once keen on flying, Gurbir holds a private pilot's license for the UK, US and Australia. He was one of the 13,000 unsuccessful applicants responding to the 1989 advert "Astronaut wanted. No experience necessary" to become the first British astronaut, for which Helen Sharman was eventually selected and flew on the Soviet space station MIR in 1991.

He is married with a 11-year-old daughter, and lives in Lancashire in England.

INTRODUCTION

The practical development of rockets that has made spaceflight possible and now routinely supplies and astronauts to the International Space Station, started at around the late 1920s. Individuals such as Herman Oberth, Robert Goddard and Sergei Korolev were working independently of each other in Europe, USSR and the USA. Their contemporary in India was Stephen Smith. Although known within the philatelic community for his air and rocket mail activities, the larger picture of his origin, inspiration and ambitions has remained obscure until now.

Through recently uncovered letters, Smith can now be assessed as a humanitarian and a tenacious champion of developing rockets as a means of transport to deliver mail, food and medicine. Given his limited skills, access to funds and resources, in the end his work did not result in a significant technical contribution to rocketry. Today he remains India's only rocket mail experimenter. In April of 1946, five years before he died, he thought he had finally made a breakthrough but the opportunity was lost in the aftermath of World War Two and the chaos of Indian independence.

The development of rockets in India is commonly accepted to have ended with Tipu Sultan in 1799 and started again in 1963 with what is now called the Indian Space Research Organisation. However, in the intervening period, rockets were built, and championed by one man, working alone in Calcutta. Between 1934 and 1944 he conducted almost 300 rocket experiments. He was born in India in Assam to a father from Brigg in Lincolnshire and a mother of mixed heritage in India. He was an Indian, and his name was Stephen Hector Taylor Smith.

Delivery of messages is usually the first use of any new form of transport. The rocket pioneers of the 1920s and 30s developed postal rockets to speed up postal delivery or deliver it where no other means existed. At this time, individuals and amateur rocketry groups emerged around the world including in Europe, USSR, Australia and the USA to help develop rocket technology. In India, it was just one man, Stephen Smith. He was the first to demonstrate that rockets could also be used for the transport of medicines, food and livestock, and not just mail.

As an ordinary Indian, Smith appears to reach out well above his station. As a subject of the vast British Empire he made direct contact with King George V in Buckingham Palace, the King of Sikkim in Gangtok, a member of Parliament in London and eventually India's first Prime Minister - Jawaharlal Nehru. His rocket mail covers are still highly sought after today. They form treasured items in private philatelic collections around the world. His documents, notes and correspondence are found in private and public collections in the Museum of Communication in Bern, Switzerland, the Royal Archives in Buckingham Palace in London, the London Postal Museum, National Archives in Sikkim, a substantial private collection in Liverpool and the National Air and Space Museum in Washington, DC.

I first came across Stephen Smith when researching my book, The Indian Space Programme. I published my first piece about him in 2014 and based on what I knew then, I concluded, "he was doing not much more than lighting the blue touch-paper of a traditional firework and then standing back". How wrong I was. I knew, as his name hinted, that he was an Anglo Indian. I knew where and when he was born and whilst the philatelic community documented in meticulous detail his activities in airmail and rocket mail, I did not know much about him as an individual, his motivations or his primary objective. A chance discovery of a large archive of his personal correspondence was a revelation.

During the 1930s and 1940s, he was India's preeminent rocket mail experimenter. His work acquired greater international recognition than he had within India. Whilst there is a significant philatelic content in the following pages, this book is not about philately.

Do you know who Stephen Smith was? That was a question I frequently asked many senior people working in India's space agency, Indian Space Research Organisation. Invariably, the answer was no. Whilst some names have gone down in the annals of history, the name of Stephen Smith is almost entirely forgotten. This book is one small attempt to address that omission. Between 1934 and 1944, he was working alone and unsupported in Calcutta experimenting with rockets as a means of transport. He was the first to demonstrate the use of rockets to transport food and medicine at times of emergency. He chose a small hen and a chick to show that rockets could transport living creatures using only rocket power. He experimented with powering his rockets with solid propellant, compressed air and gas. He tested rockets with multiple compartments and stages, using gliding vanes, fins, rudders and parachutes.

Pictures of him in the public domain were generally tiny, old and faded. The details about him as a person were just as ghostly and out of reach. He had been dead for more than half a century when my search started, so there were not many left who had any personal experiences of meeting him.

I had believed that contact with his descendants would result in a fuller understanding of his life and work. In 2016, I did make contact with his London-based granddaughter and great-granddaughter. They did not expressed interest in discussing his unique role in history or in meeting me. I respected their privacy. Besides, they indicated they did not have any documentary or photographic records that may have been useful to me. If I wanted to learn about him, I would have to find another source. That came in early 2019 when I visited the archive of Dr Robert Paganini in the Museum of Communication in Bern, Switzerland.

In a letter dated 25 October 1925, Smith asked Paganini to join as an honorary member of the Indian Aerophilatelic Club of India which he had just founded in Calcutta. On Christmas Eve 1925, he expresses his delight that Paganini has accepted and so started a correspondence that lasted until 1950 when Paganini died. During this quarter of a century of correspondence they develop a long, deep and sincere relationship despite being anchored in profoundly different cultures separated by thousands of miles.

The letters from Paganini to Smith have long been lost. Perhaps one day they will emerge in a private collection. The letters in Paganini's collection are letters only from Smith to Paganini. So here was a source where I could finally hear Smith in his own words speaking about his motivations, ambitions, hopes, obstacles and fears. This collection threw a new light not only on Smith's rocket mail experiments but the unique time that Smith lived through. The period between 1925 and 1950 coincided with one of India's most tumultuous periods in its long and rich history. The letters capture the harsh and brutal conditions of the struggle for independence, a World War, famine, post-independence riots and the civil unrest that accompanied partition.

Paganini's archive illustrates their initial and evolving relationship. In the beginning, it was in pursuit of their mutual interest in philately. Smith frequently sent Paganini unique and special airmail covers. He had mail on the first official airmail flights from India to England, mail on the first airplanes to fly over the summit of Mount Everest and covers flown on his numerous rocket mail experiments. As the only one testing rocket mail in India, his flown covers were in high demand then and continue to be so today.

The objective of this book was to help bring the life and work of

Stephen Smith out of the shadows. The numerous illustrations include stamps and cachets of his own design along with people, places and technology of the time. Extracts from his letters paint a vivid picture of his struggles, frustrations and occasional triumphs. However, many questions remain; for example, why did no one else in India step up and work with him or even compete? What happened to the collection of his notes, documents and letters that were sent to the USA in December 1945? What was behind the mysterious offer for his services that he was not permitted to tell anyone about? What happened to the collection of his correspondence, the letters he received from Paganini, Leslie Johnson and many others from around the world? In the following pages, much is revealed about him for the first time but there is more yet to be discovered.

ACKNOWLEDGEMENT

Almost all of what is known about Stephen Smith's life and achievements in the public domain has been chronicled by the global philatelic community. It is this community that deserves the primary credit for keeping his name and work in the public imagination. They include organisations such as The India Study Circle, The American Airmail Society, Philatelic Congress of India and numerous local philatelic societies around the world. It was the face to face meetings with numerous individuals from these organisations that helped me to home in on the story of Stephen Smith and also understand it in the proper context. Some of these individuals include Piyush Khaitan, David Hudson, Kenneth Knight, Bruce Gillham, Max Smith, Markand Dave, Brian Lythgoe, Pradip Jain and Terry Hare-Walker. Some of the information and pictures included here come from the private collections of individuals including Markus Wydera, Walter Hopferweiser, Eric Winter, Piyush Khaitan, Markand Dave, Neil Donan, Ramu M Srinivasa and Pam Reid.

I would also like to acknowledge the assistance of institutions, archivists and individuals including Barry Attoe at the Postal History Museum London, Brian Riddle the Chief Librarian at the National Aerospace Library, Grif Ingram and Gill Norman from the British Interplanetary Society, Alistair Lawson and Giles Camplin from the Airship Heritage Trust and Pam Reid who made her father, Leslie Johnson's correspondence with Stephen Smith available to me Beatrice Bachmann in Austria who shared her personal correspondence with Friedrich Schmiedl, the Royal Archives at Windsor Castle who shared some of Smith's correspondence with King George V.

I also benefited from the support of several individuals on-line who I never met in person including Ohsin from Reddit, Brian Birch, Vedant Sukhani, Jeremy Argyll Etkin and Duncan Crewe. In the final weeks before publications I was contacted by auctioneer Stéphane

Cloutier who told me about the Leon Victor Pont collection that had recently surfaced in Ottawa, Canada. Whilst in Calcutta, Pont had been a member of the Indian Airmail Society that Smith had founded. These were letters that Smith sent to Pont when Pont returned to England in the early 1930s.

This book would probably not have been written without the help of the archivists at the Museum für Kommunikation in Bern Switzerland. It was in this museum where 25 years of Stephen Smith's correspondence with Dr Robert Paganini was archived. My special thanks to Andrea Tschanz, Barbara Schmutz, Jean-Claude Lavanchy and especially Olivia Strasser.

Historian Frank Winter at the National Air and Space Museum was in personal contact with many of the early rocket pioneers. His published books, articles and notes in the NASM archives provided a vivid insight into the activities and motivations of these early pioneers. Although I did not get to meet him during my visit to Washington, DC, he provided very useful guidance and clarifications via email. There were three individuals who I did meet during my visit to DC and who made my visit a very productive one: Elizabeth Borja at the Steven F. Udvar-Hazy Center gave me access to the unexpectedly large Stephen Smith collection as well as material associated with the British Interplanetary Society and especially the enormous Arthur C Clarke archive. Baasil Wilder who seems to work round the clock and Susan Smith at the National Postal Museum provided me with all the resources I sought and much more besides. There were many others not listed here who have helped me on this journey.

I have benefited from constructive comments to early drafts of this manuscript from accomplished writers including Ken MacTaggart, Bruce Gillham, Terry Hare-Walker and Brian Harvey. A huge thank you to my editors Liza Joseph and Julie Cordiner who have knocked my rough and ready manuscript into shape. I have attempted to contact all the copyright owners of all the pictures that appear in these pages. If you spot any that are incorrectly credited or indeed anything that requires a correction, please let me know.

Despite all the cycles of checking and rechecking, I can only assume that some errors remain. Responsibility for which lay entirely with me. I would welcome your comments or questions.

Gurbir Singh

March 2020

Lancashire, United Kingdom

1
ORIGINS

Stephen Smith - A Life

Stephen H Smith is a familiar name within the philatelic community, not only as a collector and a dealer but especially as a pioneer of rocket mail in India. During the early 1930s, rocket mail testing was popularised in Europe and beyond. Friedrich Schmiedl from Austria is credited with the launch of the first official rocket mail in Austria in 1931. Other nations followed, but Stephen Smith took this further and demonstrated that rockets could be used not only for mail but also to transport food, medicines and livestock. He supported his work by selling flown covers to collectors within India and globally. Almost 70 years after his death, his covers are distributed around the world and are still highly sought after. In a philatelic catalogue published in 2019, one of his covers is valued at $20,000.[1]

The development of trains, cars, airships and airplanes coincided with Smith's coming of age. Rockets were seen as the next breakthrough technology in transportation. Nothing else offered such a huge leap in speed and the potential to transport larger, heavier cargo over a longer distance. Smith had been interested in stamp collecting from an early age. By chance, the world's first official airmail took place in 1911 in India not far from Smith's school. Later, living close to Dum Dum airport in Calcutta (an international transport hub of the British Empire), he must have been drawn in by the sheer magic of airplanes. He founded the Aerophilatelic Club of India in 1925 and invited Robert Paganini from Switzerland to join; Paganini was probably the first systematic collector of airmail.

Schmiedl conducted his rocket mail demonstration in September 1931, at a time when rocketry groups were being established around the world. They were small and self-funded, and many were driven by the realistic pursuit of spaceflight. It was the 1934 test conducted by a German experimenter, Gerhard Zucker in England, that triggered Smith into action in India.[2] Smith was the only one who conducted rocket mail experiments in India over the next decade, longer than anyone anywhere else.

During the height of its popularity in the late 1930s, rocket mail was dubbed Racket Mail because some of the protagonists put profit first. For example, Gerhard Zucker was criticised for being a showman and a charlatan rather than a serious experimenter in rocketry. Many of his rocket mail tests ended in spectacular public failures, undermining public credibility in this new mode of transport. A cloud of mistrust surrounded many in the philatelic community, and inevitably Smith was occasionally tarred with the same brush.[3] He was seen as a chancer, an opportunist and a profit-seeking dealer, and was not taken seriously as a rocket mail experimenter. However, Smith persisted and continued to work alone; his success during the initial stages was limited but sincere.

During the 1920s and 30s, small self-funded rocket societies were established in countries around the world including the UK, USA, Germany, Austria, Australia and the Netherlands. It was from these groups that Sergei Korolev and Wernher von Braun emerged and competed in the epic space race that resulted in Sputnik, Gagarin and Apollo 11. Stephen Smith was their contemporary.

In 1934 Smith joined the British Interplanetary Society, which had been founded in Liverpool a year earlier. He was probably the first member from India. Through the BIS and its regular bulletins, news of his work was spread across the globe. Through journals like the one from the BIS, Smith would have been aware of the very early developments in space, but his goals were modest and terrestrial. In his time, space was well beyond his reach.

It was from the early rocketry societies that in 1950, after a devastating World War but before the advent of the space age, the International Astronautical Congress was formed. Its primary objective was to foster international cooperation. Rocketry societies were established around the world but there was no equivalent organisation in India. Had there been one, or if Smith had been formally supported in his work, he could have been present at the first IAC in Paris in 1950, representing India. Schmiedl was there, representing Austria.[4]

India is now a major player in space with significant assets including operational spacecraft collecting data in orbit around the Moon and one around Mars. Most of India's satellites are in Earth orbit providing navigation, Remote Sensing observation and communication services. Rockets are now playing a key part in providing support and services for ordinary Indians, as Smith had envisaged in his lifetime.

His attempt to work with the military authorities in India during World War II ended in frustration. They did not consider rocket technology viable and did not think highly of the progress Smith had made. But his success was recognised by others. In 1946 he wrote to his friend Robert Paganini in Switzerland lamenting that, 'a prophet is never believed in his own land'. In the same letter he goes on to indicate that he had received an offer for his services 'from quite another quarter, one day when I am permitted I shall tell you'.[5]

In December 1950, after a correspondence lasting a quarter of a century, his mentor and friend in Switzerland Robert Paganini died. He was a widower and had no children. They had never met or spoken to each other but in his will, Paganini left twenty-five percent of his estate to Smith.⁶ Smith himself died two months later in February 1951.

Smith's son Hector did not share his father's deep passion for rockets. Smith's notes, covers, photographs, stamps and rockets were destroyed, lost or sold. Several months after his death, some of his collection came up for sale in the Los Angeles.⁷ Parts of Smith's collection are now distributed around the globe. In 1989, Smith was inducted into the Hall of Fame by the American Airmail Society. In 1992, a year after the centenary of his birth, the Indian government commemorated his achievements by issuing a stamp and a first day cover dedicated to his work.

Most of what is known about Stephen Smith comes from the records of letters, covers and stamps from the global philatelic community of collectors, dealers and writers. His work is recognised elsewhere too. His contacts with the King of Sikkim, King George V and a member of parliament in London are recorded in private collections. His work is documented in a NASA publication and the Smithsonian Institute in Washington, DC. The largest collection of Smith's personal letters is in the private collection of the Swiss philatelist Robert Paganini. It is in the content of these letters, the product of a 25-year-long correspondence, that Smith reveals in his own words his struggle to attain wider recognition and formal support for his work.

Family Origins

Darjeeling and Assam are names familiar to tea drinkers around the world.⁸ The East India Company acquired Assam in the North east of India through a treaty with the Ahom Kings and then annexed the 600-year-old Assam Kingdom in 1838. In the 1920s, vast swathes of land were set aside for large-scale production of tea. The first tea plantations in India were grown from tea brought illegally from China, smuggled via Hong Kong to Calcutta in the autumn of 1848 by the Scottish horticulturalist Robert Fortune. It was commercialised by the East India Company and is now considered an archetypal British beverage.⁹

Stephen Smith's father Charles William Bath Taylor[10] (1865–?) was one of the many attracted to India to manage these huge tea plantations. He came from the market town of Brigg in Lincolnshire to serve as the Superintendent of the Hoolingurie Tea Estate. Charles Taylor married Arabella Nee Martin, the daughter of a tea planter. Given Smith's dark complexion, she was probably of mixed race with a white father and Indian mother.

Charles secured a role as a superintendent in a plantation owned by the Andrew Yule Company. Andrew Yule, a Scottish entrepreneur, had set up the company on arrival in Calcutta in 1863. As the imperial capital, Calcutta was at the heart of action at a time when the postal service, railways and telegraph were transforming the Indian landscape and society. The Andrew Yule Group is still in existence and operating successfully with over 16,000 employees, although now owned by the Government of India.[11]

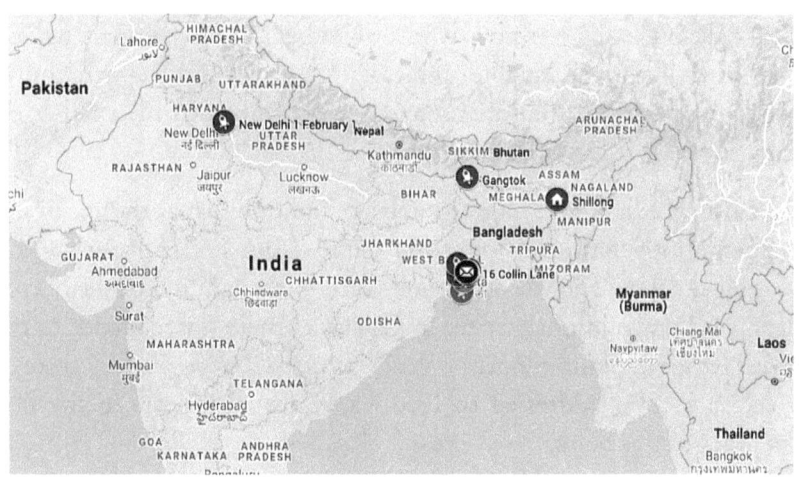

1.1 Parts of India where Smith was born and conducted his rocket experiments. Credit Google

Assam is in the elevated (up to 1,900m) north eastern part of India close to the Himalayas, and benefits from a pleasant temperature with moderate rainfall. The climate in Assam was relatively more comfortable for someone from Lincolnshire. In his new role as a tea plantation superintendent, Charles Taylor settled in Assam with his wife. On Valentine's Day, 14th February 1891, Arabella gave birth to Stephen Smith in the Strawberry Hill region of Shillong.[12]

By then, Shillong was a popular hill station located at 1,500m altitude, with Bhutan to the North and Bangladesh to the South. Its undulating mountainous landscape reminded many in the British Raj of the Scottish Highlands, so much so that Shillong was known by some as the Scotland of the East.[13] Arabella's sister, Millicent Smith, was also married to an English tea planter and acted as Charles' guardian. It was probably in deference to this support that Stephen's parents introduced the surname Smith as part of their son's full name: Stephen Taylor Hector Smith.[14]

Although born in India, Stephen's birth was registered in England, where he had domiciled status. Stephen had one sister, Marjorie, who married an Englishman and moved to southern England by around 1920. Although there is no record of Stephen Smith visiting England as an adult, his granddaughter indicates that as a child Stephen Smith, along with his sister Marjorie, may have 'accompanied their father on home leave on at least one occasion'.[15]

The British India Office marriage records indicate that at the age of 26, Stephen Smith married 19-year-old Gulner Ann Fay Harcourt on 6th November 1918. The wedding took place in the Church of the Sacred Heart on Dhurrumtollah Street in Calcutta. There is a reference to the bride's father in Smith's short book *World Flier's Danger Zone*,[16] printed in 1927: a cover addressed to Fredrick Harcourt appears in the first few pages of this book.

Smith's death is recorded as 15th February 1951.[17] He was buried at the Circular Road Cemetery in Kolkata, not far from Elliot Road where he lived for most of his adult life. Old photographs attest that his grave initially had a headstone at the outset, but none was present in 2014. His wife lived until 1985. In written documents, he is typically referred to as Stephen Smith. He also appears as Stephen H Smith and Stephen Hector Taylor Smith, and was known to his friends as 'Stevie'. The cemetery register records his name as Taylor-Smith, Stephen Hector.

Around 1919, Stephen Smith had a son, Hector. There are several instances of Smith addressing some of his rocket mail covers to his son. Despite this early exposure, Hector appears not to have shared his father's interest in philately or rockets.

There is evidence that much of Smith's work was sold to collectors in and outside India. Much of it ended up with his long-time friend, the eminent philatelist Jal Cooper. A US-based collector, John R. Dilworth, purchased some of Smith's collection directly from his widow.[18] According to his granddaughter, Hector destroyed some of what was left of Smith's work on his death.

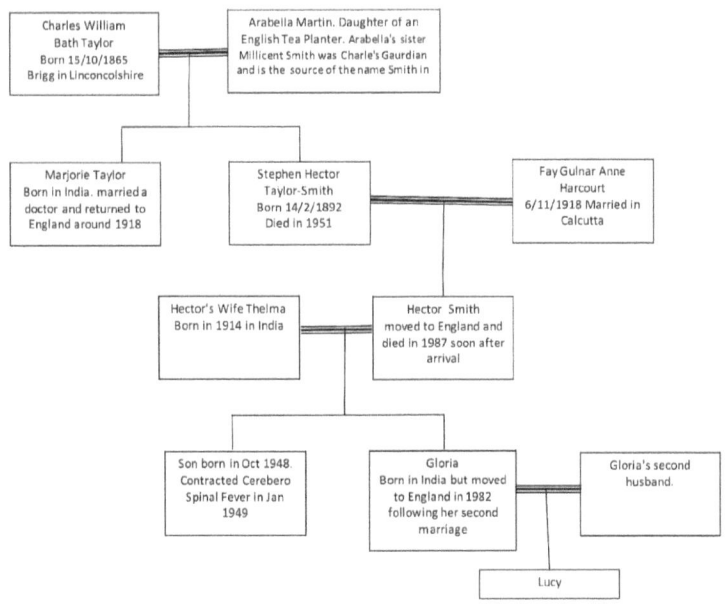

1.2 Stephen Smith's partial family tree. Credit Author

Hector himself went on to have two children, a son and a daughter. There is little known about his son other than that he had contracted cerebrospinal fever on 3rd October 1948, when he was just four months old.[19] Hector's daughter Gloria married in India but that marriage did not work out, and she moved to England with her daughter Lucy in 1982. Hector and his wife Thelma joined them in 1987, but Hector died within a few months of his arrival in England. In 2017, Smith's daughter-in-law Thelma, his granddaughter Gloria and his great-granddaughter Lucy were living in East London, far removed from India and the pioneering work he conducted between 1934 and 1944. In 2016, his granddaughter concluded that her grandfather 'was a very talented man and would have gone very far if he had lived in the twenty-first century.'[20]

Smith's Calcutta

As one of India's large cosmopolitan cities and its capital until 1931, Calcutta was home to wealthy Europeans and a hub for commerce, the arts, film, science, music and education. It was also home to Nobel laureates, including India's first, Rabindranath Tagore.

1.3 Suburb of Calcutta where Stephen Smith Lived. Credit Google

In 1911, King George V announced New Delhi as the new capital of India. However, it would take another two decades before New Delhi was ready. The new capital was eventually inaugurated on 13th February 1931. Calcutta still remains a hub for business and home of the elite.

Smith lived in the vicinity of south central Calcutta, a diverse and vibrant part of the city during the 1920s. Over the next three decades, he experienced the privations, civil unrest and violence that accompanied the Great Depression, riots against British occupation, World War II, famine, and the civil unrest that accompanied India's independence and partition.

Smith lived in four addresses, all of which were within walking distance of the Park Street police station where he worked and Park Street Post Office where he must have been a very familiar face, regularly posting his flown rocket mail covers. The Calcutta Maidan, a large urban park, was probably the launch site for some of Smith's rocket experiments.

There is no indication that Stephen Smith lived anywhere other than Assam and Calcutta. He initially made his home at 16 Collin Lane in the 1920s, before moving to 14 Elliot Road (in 1930), 18 McLeod St (1936), and 25 Elliot Road (1940). He lived his adult life in Calcutta, the centre of one of India's most vibrant Anglo-Indian communities.

Calcutta airport was located just 14 km from Smith's home. Originally known as Dum Dum airport, it was renamed in 1995 as Netaji Subhas Chandra Bose, after an Indian nationalist leader who had made Calcutta his home. Dum Dum airport was India's first large airport and served a strategic role for the British Empire, as a prominent stopover for aircraft making long-haul flights from Europe to South East Asia and Australia. Smith would have visited the airport on many occasions, meeting pilots from around the world to gather information for his writing. He used these opportunities to send and collect special airmail covers to promote airmail philately collections.

The city was also the home of one of India's largest Anglo-Indian communities, of which Smith was a member. That community dwindled following Indian independence in 1947 and migration to UK, Australia, USA and Israel. There are not many alive today who have a personal recollection of Stephen Smith. Living on the same Elliot Road as Smith, in 2014 Melvyn Brown recalled meeting Stephen Smith's son Hector twice in the late 1970s. Brown has been championing and chronicling the achievements of Anglo-Indians. In 1993 he unsuccessfully attempted to have a part of Elliot Road renamed after Stephen Smith.[21]

St. Patrick's Boys School in Asansol

Stephen Smith was privately tutored at home in his early youth but spent time 'dodging his private tutor and dreaming in the pine forests of Shillong'.[22] Those daydreams were mostly about the flight of birds and climbing the hills without using his legs. He attended the boarding school, St Patrick's in Asansol, from 1903 to 1911.

1.4 St Patrick's school where Stephen Smith studied. Credit St Patrick's School

The school for Anglo-Indian boys was established the same year that Smith was born. It is located 200 km to the south of Calcutta in 1891 by the first Irish Christian Brothers. They had arrived in Calcutta in the previous year. Its location close to Calcutta and its more temperate climate ensured it received attention and investment from the colonial administration, which had a significant and growing presence during the early twentieth century.

The school is still present and flourishing. It offers a varied modern secondary school curriculum that includes English language, English literature, Bengali, Hindi, Physics, Chemistry, Mathematics, Biology, Computer Science and History.

Stephen Smith's interest in rockets started while he was still in school. In what may have been his first rocket experiment, he and four schoolmates attempted to transport a live garden lizard over the school's swimming pool using a rocket of their own making. That attempt failed, killing the lizard, but the interest in rockets stayed with him. In 1911 Smith left St Patrick's school in 1911 with a character report declaring he was 'a model boy and a perfect athlete'.[23] In addition, he had an interest in botany, ants and birds. He completed a book entitled *Queer Birds of Aerophilately*, bringing together his interest in philately and birds, but it was never published.[24]

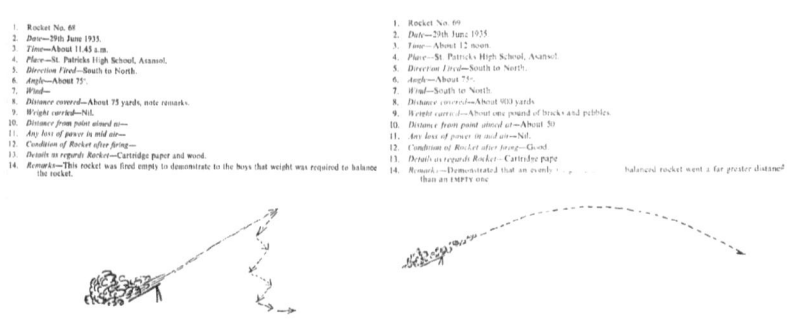

1.5 Sketches of trajectories taken by Rocket 86 and Rocket 87. Credit Stephen Smith

Twenty-five years after leaving St Patrick's, Stephen Smith returned on 29th June 1935 and fired two rockets to demonstrate their utility to staff and students in the school. He launched two in order to prove that a weighted balanced rocket has a longer range than one without any load. Rocket number 68 was empty and fell vertically after travelling about 75 m once the thrust was exhausted. Rocket number

69 was weighed down by about a 'pound of bricks and pebbles' and travelled about 900 m.[25]

His masters at St Patrick's must have left a deep and long lasting impact. Almost two decades after he left school, he acknowledged the close resemblance between Robert Paganini, a Swiss philatelist with whom he corresponded for many years and one of his masters, Rev. Brother Joseph. He regarded his late school master as someone 'honest and upright who feared no man'.[26]

Customs Official, Policeman and Dentist

After leaving school, Smith worked briefly at the customs department in Calcutta, which was then a vibrant hub of early twentieth-century global trade. The port of Calcutta is India's oldest port and was one of the first footholds in India established by the East India Company. It is located on the left bank of the Hooghly River, 200 km from the sea.

On 18th March 1913, Stephen Smith joined the Calcutta police as a round sergeant on a salary of Rs. 100 per month.[27] He was probably based at the Park Street police station close to his home on Elliot Road. His time with the Calcutta police appears to have been uneventful. He resigned on 4th December 1914.

After studying at the College of Physicians and Surgeons, Smith served in World War I as a dental surgeon.[28] He continued in this profession after the war, with a private dental practice based at his home on 25A Elliot Road in Calcutta. At the time of his marriage in November 1918, Smith was a dentist, and this remained his primary and official source of income throughout his adult life. By the mid 1930s, however, he would have supplemented his salary (and perhaps even completely replaced it) by sale of airmail and rocket mail covers, as well as his royalties as an author. By then, his writing duties as the secretary to the Indian airmail Society and the time spent developing and launching rockets would probably not have left him much time to practice his profession as a dentist.

During his lifetime, he wrote several books. In 1927, he authored a small book *The World Flyer's Danger Zone,* covering the hazards of airmail flights in a south-easterly direction from Calcutta across the Bay of Bengal to Burma and Thailand. He dedicated the book and its proceeds to the widow of Arthur B Elliott, a flight engineer accompanying the pilot Alan Cobham. Elliott was killed on 5th July 1926 whilst on the Bagdad leg of a flight from England to Australia. He also published *Indian Airways* in three volumes between 1926 and 1930. A final posthumous publication (and a revised second edition) called *Rocket Mail Catalogue* was published in 1955 under his name, authorised by his wife. It covers details of his rocket mail experiments in India and also rocket mail experiments conducted by others around the world.

Smith's adult life coincided with three of the most dramatic decades in Indian history. During the 1920s, 30s and 40s, living in the heart of Calcutta, the capital of British India until 1931, he could not have escaped experiencing the effects of decisions made thousands of miles away. These decades saw the Great Depression of 1929 and the introduction of protectionist policies from London, resulting in the loss of jobs in India, a rise in nationalism and Gandhi's march against the salt tax. The 1940s brought the tumult of World War II and Indian independence, with civil unrest in the immediate aftermath. These dramatic global events were the backdrop against which Smith worked as a dentist, writer, philatelist and rocket experimenter.

Anglo-Indians

Stephen Smith's father was from England and his mother probably an Anglo-Indian. In pictures Stephen Smith is dark-skinned, indicating an Indian ancestor at some point in his family history, most likely his mother. Despite being domiciled in Britain by virtue of registering his birth in England and his emphatically English sounding name, Smith was neither an Englishman nor an Indian. He was educated in an English-speaking school, practised the Christian faith and inherited his name from a male European forefather, which probably classified him as an Anglo-Indian. In a letter to Robert Paganini in 1949, he asserted "I am Indian by birth".

The definition of the term Anglo-Indian has evolved over time and today is typically used to describe Indians with a male European progenitor, typically British. Many familiar names in the UK share the identity of an Anglo-Indian, including writers such as George Orwell and Rudyard Kipling, actors Joanna Lumley and Ben Kingsley and singers Cliff Richard and Engelbert Humperdinck.

The European traders and soldiers seeking adventure and fortune in India were mostly men. Prior to the opening of the Suez Canal in 1869, it was predominantly men who made the long, arduous journey to India. The Portuguese, Dutch, Danes, French, Spanish and Germans, along with the Chinese and Armenians, had already settled in the towns of Goa, Madras, Bombay, Cochin and Calcutta along India's considerable coastline before the British established colonies in India. The Dutch had established a significant commercial foothold by building factories in several Indian cities by the early seventeenth century.

Just as the first settlers to America and Australia assigned names to the new towns that they established using names of towns from which they came, a similar naming convention unfolded in India. The post office department, founded by India's first Governor-General on 31st March 1774, established the first Anglo-Indian post office in Barrackpore on 16th May 1776.[29] At the time, this region of West Bengal was a centre of settlement for the East India Company and the first British barrack was established a few years earlier, which most likely led to its name. Today, there is a Venice in Florida (USA), Cambridge in Tasmania (Australia) and East London in South Africa. The detailed record of how these places acquired their names is lost in many cases. The names of towns have been frozen in history, hinting at the origins of the early settlers who established them.[30]

The children from relationships between European men and Indian women came to be known as Anglo-Indians, and the European administration in these colonies encouraged such relationships. The directors of the Dutch East India Company gave soldiers, sailors and minor officials bonuses if they agreed to marry local women and stay in Dutch colonies. In 1687, the directors of the British East India

Company encouragement this arrangement by decreeing that any child resulting from the marriage of any soldier and a native woman be paid a small grant on the day of the christening.[31] Later, this evolved into a payment of one guinea towards every child they produced.[32]

The motivation for the East India Company to encourage its employees to take local wives had a hard economic foundation. Anglo-Indian children could be a powerful instrument for political change; they could be used to spread British values amongst the indigenous population, from within families to the wider community.

Despite being the product of an official British policy, the Anglo-Indians were denied British nationality following Indian independence. Some consider this as nothing less than abandonment by the British.[33] With tangible connections to both Indian and British roots, Anglo-Indians, however, belonged to neither. They suffered discrimination from the local Indian communities and racism from the British. The question of identity for the Anglo-Indian community has cast a long shadow over its 400-year long history, and it preoccupies the ever-diminishing community even today.[34]

Anglo-Indians are a distinct community in India, with English as their first language and predominantly following Christianity as a religion. Many Anglo-Indians have fair skin, brown hair and blue eyes, but others have dark skin, brown eyes and black hair. In the few images available of Smith, he appears dark-skinned but with European facial characteristics. He studied in a recognised Anglo-Indian school. His written English is elegant and he probably spoke in a similar manner. He lived at the heart of the Anglo-Indian community in Calcutta. This all points to the strong probability that Stephen Smith was an Anglo-Indian.[35]

Ostracised by their colonial masters and the local communities, Anglo-Indians sought independent political representation. Rights for many of India's minorities, including the Anglo-Indians, were captured in the independent Indian constitution. Their access to central grants, political representation in local and national government and even jobs in government were protected.

During the upheaval leading up to Indian independence, a gifted Anglo-Indian lawyer feared the future of a people with ill-defined roots in India after the British left. Frank Anthony secured from India's first post-independence prime minister Nehru the reservation of two seats in the Lok Sabha (lower House) of the Indian parliament for the Anglo-Indian community. Out of the 545 Lok Sabha seats, only 543 have actually been contested in each of the 18 Indian general elections since independence.

Melvyn Brown, the chronicler of Anglo-Indians who had met Smith's son Hector in the 1970s, recalls the apprehension and even fear of the Anglo-Indian community in the immediate aftermath of independence. He remembers the pre-war years as a golden period for Calcutta, particularly Park Street, which had become the hub of a friendly cosmopolitan community sprinkled with music halls, theatres, night clubs and cinemas. Melvyn Brown still resides close to Park Street. In his assessment, the 'British were very shrewd. They look not only at the present but a 100 years ahead'.[36]

When India became independent in 1947 and the British departed, many in the Anglo-Indian community emigrated to the member countries of the newly created Commonwealth, mainly Australia, Canada, UK and New Zealand. Around 150,000 remained. The last Indian census to record Anglo-Indian numbers was in 1941. No official number for the current size of the community exists. It is estimated to be around 125,000 dispersed across cities in India, with Kolkata (formerly Calcutta) and Chennai (formerly Madras) home to the largest populations.

Like all other disparate groups that make up India's stunning diversity, the Anglo-Indians have played their part in India's development. From their struggle to belong emerged a strong independent Anglo-Indian identity. Anglo-Indian communities were established around local schools, agricultural schemes and churches. During World War I, around 8,000 Anglo-Indians fought alongside the British. In World War II, many Anglo-Indians joined the Indian Air Force (IAF) and 'made a very significant contribution to the growth and successes of IAF—well beyond their proportional representation in the service'.[37]

Despite his personal contacts around the world, Smith spent all his adult life in India. The dramatic shifts of populations at times of war appear not to have affected Smith. He remained firmly rooted in Calcutta until his death in 1951. In 1982, his granddaughter and great-granddaughter moved to England, where they reside today.

2

POSTAL SERVICES AND PHILATELY IN INDIA

Philately

Stephen Smith became a stamp collector or philatelist early in his life and was involved with collecting pigeon mail, balloon mail and airmail long before the advent of rocket mail. It is in the philatelic community that his life's work is remembered, almost 70 years after his death.

Communication has been a hallmark of human civilisations. Archaeological discoveries of seals in stone, metal, clay or resin in Egypt, Persia, Iraq and the Indus Valley civilisations attest to the importance of communicating with people not in their immediate vicinity. This gave rise to the idea of letter writing. Amongst other benefits, the phenomenon of writing has facilitated the communication of ideas and thoughts from one place and time to another.

Stamps are a relatively recent invention but an integral element of the postal system. Stamp collecting, or philately as it came to be known, is much more than the collecting of stamps. It is the study of postal history and of societies and cultures from which they originate. The

English word philately was coined in 1864 by Georges Herpin and derives from the French philo (meaning loving) and ateleia (meaning that the receiver is exempt from paying).

In nineteenth-century Britain, Sir Rowland Hill (1795–1879) introduced profound changes that shaped the present postal service. He introduced the idea that it should be the sender and not the receiver who should pay. Convinced that a significant reduction in cost would substantially increase the demand, he introduced the adhesive postage stamp, the Penny Post. In the process he defined the principles of postage still in use today.

When the overland route to India was being established the Post Office issued a notice that, 'persons wishing to send letters by that route to Australia must address them to "an agent in India", who must pay the postage onward, as otherwise the letters would not be forwarded. It was Sir Rowland Hill who highlighted the 'absurdity' of expecting that everyone writing by that route to Australia would have an agent in India. Within a week, the notice was withdrawn. His work helped to establish the Universal Postal Union in 1874; today it has 192 member nations and facilitates the movement of parcels, postcards and letters using an internationally agreed set of rules, standards, procedures and fees.[1]

Stamps do more than simply fulfil the function of a paid delivery service of an item from the sender to the receiver. Etched on to the walls of the new post office building when completed in 1914 in Washington, DC are the words that define the role of a mail service from Harvard president Dr Charles W. Eliot (reviewed by President Woodrow Wilson): 'Carrier of news and knowledge, instrument of trade and commerce, promoter of mutual acquaintances among men and nations, and hence, of peace and goodwill. Carrier of love and sympathy, messenger of friendship, consoler of the lonely, bond of the scattered family, enlarger of the common life.'[2] The deeper value of a mail service is enshrined in the modern era, as exemplified by the USA's 1971 Postal Reorganisation Act, which dictates that the postal service shall 'have as its basic function the obligation to provide postal services to bind the nation together through personal, educational, literary and business correspondence of the people'.

Postal services capture the artistic and cultural values of the communities of origin and also commemorate individuals, places and events of national and global significance. The American prisoners of war in Vietnam learnt of the landing of Apollo 11 on the Moon through commemorative stamps. The contents of mail were censored, but not the stamps.[3]

Most technological advances and innovations, especially since the industrial revolution, in transport on the ground (trains and automobiles), sea (steamships and submarines) and air (balloons, airships, aircraft and rockets) have been captured in the design of stamps. Their small size, rich international variety, national and international historical significance and ephemeral nature make stamps an ideal collector's item. Philatelic organisations, including local, national and international clubs and societies, have captured these fleeting but profound moments in history through stamps.

It was in Allahabad on 18th February 1911 that the first officially sanctioned mail was transported by air, just 600 km from Smith's school. Smith was twenty years old at the time and he must have been intrigued by the cutting-edge technology that allowed people to fly. Flying machines must have been as revolutionary in his age as spacecraft are in the modern era. Perhaps it was this unique historical event, the first ever airmail, that drew him to philately. It was a tangible way to keep in contact with aviation which was bound to have a profound social impact during his lifetime.

Philately in India

As the jewel of the British Empire, India was strategically placed to serve as a communications hub for South East Asia and Australia. India also holds a unique place in postal history. Calcutta, where Smith lived, was a key transport hub for the British Empire, connecting England with Australia. Calcutta was also where the Philatelic Society of India (PSI) was inaugurated in 1897 and remains active today. Smith was in the right place at the right time to make a contribution in philately.

Initially, the territory occupied by the East India Company was primarily around the presidency towns of Calcutta, Bombay and Madras. By the beginning of the nineteenth century, it acquired huge swathes of India (in 1799, Mysore and Tanjore, in 1801 the area between the Rivers Ganges and Jumna known as the Doab, in 1803 Orissa and in 1815 Hyderabad). The EIC established the initial the first Post Office infrastructure that served as the template for the Post Office in India today. But being a private company rather than a government operation, the early history is not well documented. In the middle of the 19th century there was no single Post Office service, but rather a collection service in every province, each with its own rules and rates. There were no postage stamps, service was limited to a few important towns and the Collectors in districts were responsible for the management of their local post offices.[4]

Prior to 1854 there were 650 post offices across India. Each had a hand struck postage stamps recording place, date and postage paid or due. The public in India were allowed to use the service from 1774 in the Bengal province, although no hand stamps are recorded before 1775.[5] In the following year, radical changes were introduced as the influence of the East India Company grew.[6]

Postage stamps were first introduced in 1854 (with the exception of the district of Scinde in 1852) for a fixed rate irrespective of distance. A more efficient postal system was required to support the British hubs of administration for tax collection spread all over India. A century after Calcutta became the primary British trading hub, a large domed General Post Office building was inaugurated close to the Hooghly River. Stephen Smith's local post office, the Park Street Post Office, was located about 3 km south of the General Post Office. Both are active today, providing postal services to the residents of Kolkata.

As the Company's trade and political power expanded, a structured and swift communication system between the major centres separated by vast distances[7] became essential, laying the groundwork to establish the postal system we are familiar with today.[8]

The Philatelic Society of India was always led by a Briton until 1950 when, for the first time, an Indian became the head. The first local philatelic society or club in India was founded in February 1894 in the then Indian capital Calcutta. Known as The Philatelic Society of Bengal, it was founded by Gordon Jones, F S Gubbay and G J Hynes and supported by the then Deputy Director General of the Post Office in India, G J Hynesa. Initially, it had about 60 members; all but four were men, and all were British. The first Indian was a Mr K C Dutt, who joined in 1897. The Society moved its office around India to Lahore, Bombay, New Delhi and Madras and has been in Bombay since 1955.[9]

The organisation and the work of the post office is mostly mundane and routine. But the effects of that work on the private individual and nations is a bedrock of modern human civilisation. One of the earliest steps to implement a formal postal system across India was the Post Office Act XVII of 1837. It started a fresh chapter in the Indian postal system by repealing Bombay Regulation XI of 1830, which declared that all existing private dawks (local post offices) within the Bombay Presidency were illegal, with a fine of Rs. 50 for each letter found to breach the Act. The Act also conferred on the Governor-General[10] exclusive rights for carrying mail in all the territories occupied by the East India Company. In addition, the Governor-General reserved the power to grant anyone the right to send and receive letters and parcels by post for free.[11]

Indian philately has always attracted interest from philatelists abroad perhaps because it has been at the centre of global historical events. Writing in 1942, Jal Cooper lamented that the 'narrow minded-natives of India have not shown any enthusiasm for this noble hobby'.[12] Out of a population of 350 million, there were fewer than 1000 active stamp collectors. Only 64 of the 177 members of the PSI were Indians. In the Empire of India Philatelic Society that was established in 1941, only 108 of the 200 members were Indian nationals.

The most prominent Indian philately group outside India is The India Study Circle. It was established in 1950 and has over 500 members with a vibrant Facebook group that has more than 800 members. It publishes a magazine in colour called *India Post* four times a year and is probably the most internationally diverse philately organisation that remains active today.[13] A similar but smaller group is located in Germany, The German Study Circle, studies the postal history and philately of the Indian subcontinent and southern Asia (Forschungsgemeinschaft Indien e. V. - FGI). It covers not just India but all countries or areas that have been administered by an Indian postal authority for any time.[14]

Philately was initially championed in India by Europeans. They were in positions of influence and had the wealth. With his Anglo-Indian name and connections, Smith bridged that divide and helped make philately more accessible. It is primarily the work of mostly amateur organisations in and outside India that have preserved the valuable contemporary records of the activities and events, not only of Stephen Smith but of many of his contemporaries.

Indian Airmail Society

The world's first airmail flight had taken off from Allahabad on 18th February 1911, in the same week that Smith had turned 20. Just as steam engine locomotives had inspired enthusiasts in the past and rocket launches into space do today, this flight probably played a part in Stephen Smith and others fostering an interest in airmail. In 1920, the Indian Postal Department set up an internal Bombay to Karachi and return airmail service. It did not last long. Lack of public interest forced its demise after just fourteen trips.[15]

Described as the 'life of the Indian Air Mail Society', Stephen Smith had founded it in 1924 with the original name of the Aero Philatelic Club of India.[16] In the following year, he wrote to Robert Paganini inviting him to become an honorary member of the society. In 1925, the first 'Anglo-Indian Survey flight' by Sir Alan Cobham added to the intense airmail activity in India. It was probably in this dynamic environment that he also started his first writing project, a three-volume work called *Indian Airways*, between 1926 and 1930. His frequent visits to Dum Dum airport allowed him to see first-hand, the evolution of aviation and make personal contact with pilots from around the world flying through Calcutta.

2.1 *First Imperial Airways airmail between England and India. 27 March 1928.*
Credit Sparks Auctions

Founded in 1924, the Aero Philatelic Club of India changed its name to the Indian Airmail Society on 19th January 1930 because two other clubs with identical names had also been established. Smith served as the Society's secretary from the outset to the mid 1930s, during which time he recorded the development of airmail in India in the Society's monthly bulletins. The bulletins recorded news about scheduled airmail flights within India, as well as between India and the rest of the world. He chronicled interesting and mundane details, including information on the first balloon flight in India in 1837 and the number of airmail flights in the first five months of the Karachi-Croydon route. In the society's bulletin he noted prices, timetables, quantities of airmail, individual pilots covering hazardous routes and details of air crashes, as well as the routine business of running the Society.

The first regular airmail service from England to India was flown by Imperial Airways. A biplane Armstrong Whitworth Argosy 'City of Glasgow' (G-EBLF), left Croydon airport on 30th March 1929 and arrived in Karachi on 6th April. On the return flight using a different aircraft on the following day, Smith sent a letter to King George V at Buckingham Palace in London.[17] The King's Private Secretary responded on 19th April acknowledging his letter.

2.2 de Havilland DH 66 Hercules. The first aircraft to fly a regular mail service from England to India in 1929. Credit BAE Systems

As the number and frequency of airmail flights grew, so did the hobby of collecting airmail memorabilia. On 31st December 1925, many people in Calcutta saw for the first time multiple airplanes in the sky at the same time. Five out of the then six aircraft of the Royal Airforce based at Dum Dum airport conducted a demonstration flight over Calcutta. Two of the aircraft dropped 3,000 military notifications, but a large number were 'torn to pieces during their descent by the crows and hawks that came out in their hundreds to carry their work of destruction thoroughly'.[18]

Innovation in engine design and construction by the 1920s had progressed to allow aircraft to fly long-haul routes crossing seas, oceans and continents. Initially, a series of tentative and exploratory short hops explored routes between Europe, Middle East and Asia; they were pioneered by Imperial Airways to help administer the growing empire.[19] These routes were later used for scheduled passenger flights, commercial cargo and military transport, all of which would eventually become commonplace in many countries. By the turn of the decade, Imperial Airways had established the first regular airmail service between Karachi and London.[20]

2.3 Letter from the King George V to Stephen H. Smith Commemorating the first airmail flight between Britain and India. Credit Trevor Copestake

The Indian Airmail Society held regular airmail exhibitions to stimulate interest in the then new airmail service. The first exhibition was held on 17th December 1930 on the premises of Sir David and

Lady Ezra in their house at 3 Kydd St. The exhibition was supported by 39 entrants with nearly 10,000 exhibits, which included menu cards from the Graf Zeppelin on its Mediterranean flight, ribbons issued at the International Balloon meeting in 1908 and letters carried by Sir Alan Cobham on the pioneering flight from England to India in 1924-25.

Despite the exhibits attracting a substantial number of visitors, there was some overlap between those who had donated the prizes, the entrants and the judges. Of the total of 13 prizes awarded through assessment by four judges that included Stephen Smith, Smith won three.[21] The exhibition was held again in 1932 when, the exhibition extended to 73 entrants with almost 25,000 exhibits. Pigeon mail and balloon mail were prominent exhibits as well as Smith's Vatican airmail collection.

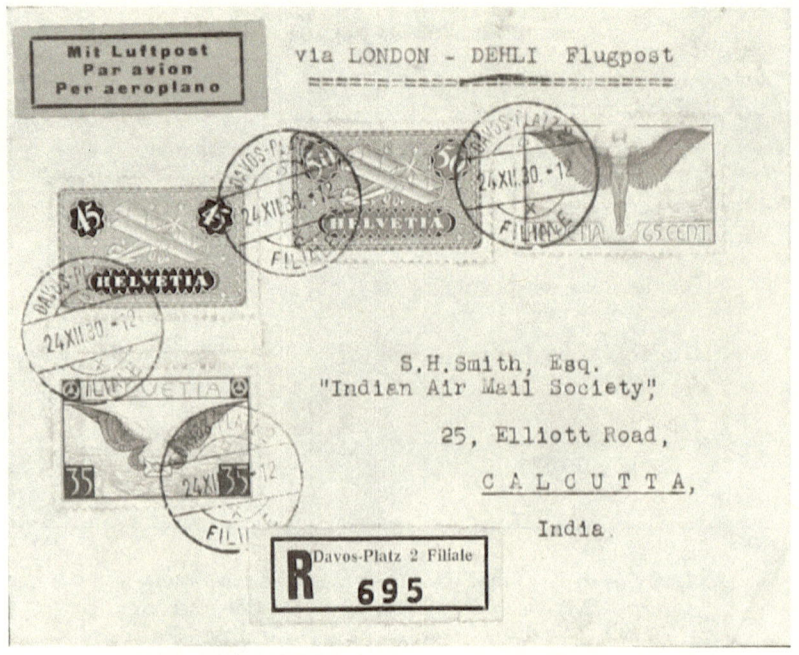

2.4 Stephen Smith received airmail from around the world. Credit Sparks Auctions

From September 1941 to December 1942, the Society initiated a victory campaign to support the war effort. Fourteen airmail flights carried specially printed envelopes printed with a large red or black letter V. The flights took off from Calcutta's Dum Dum airport to other cities in the Empire.[22] Stephen Smith, a regular visitor to Dum Dum, was actively involved in the delivery of the envelopes to the pilots. Later, he used the same V symbol on his rocket mails, too.

In 1941, the Empire of India Philatelic Society was established in Bombay, headed by perhaps the leading Indian philatelist at the time, Jal Cooper. He acquired an existing publication called *India Stamp Journal* from Carl Neukom, a Swiss national who moved from Iran to India in 1936 to establish a philately business.[23] Jal Cooper travelled to England to present a philatelic collection centred on George V's son, the Prince of Wales. Writing in an Indian newspaper, Cooper refers to himself as 'one of India's foremost philatelists'.[24]

As a leading light of Indian philately, Cooper had established an international following and his endorsement for Smith's work was significant.[25] Over time, the mutual admiration between Cooper and Smith developed into a deep and sincere friendship. Smith provided 'authentic records' of his experiments to Cooper, so that Cooper could chronicle in detail Smith's early rocket experiments in India.[26] Cooper acquired a substantial part of Smith's collection when Smith died in 1951.

The disruption and displacement resulting from World War II marked the decline of the Indian Airmail Society. By December 1946, only two of the Calcutta members had returned. In late 1946, Smith states that 'we are in a very depleted state' with a membership of just 11.[27] Many Europeans left India following Indian independence in 1947 and large proportions of the Jewish community left for the newly founded state of Israel.

3

MAIL TRANSPORT

Pigeon Mail

In 1931, Stephen Smith marked the 20th anniversary of the world's first airmail with a Pigeonogramme. A total of 42 pigeons, each with a distinctive name, carried 100 covers from Asansol, where he had been educated, to Calcutta, where he lived. Although pigeons had been used to carry messages in India for a long time, this was the first time that the Indian Post Office was formally involved. The stamps were cancelled at the Park Street Post Office in Calcutta.

Some of the earliest documented examples of mail carried by pigeons come from ancient Rome. The first-century Roman historian Pliny writes, 'winged messengers' carried plans to overcome the siege of Modena. Mail from homing pigeons also played a part in the Siege of Leiden in Holland by Spain in 1574 and the Siege of Paris by Germany in 1870/71.

In the Middle East, Sultan Nur ad-Din (1118–1174) built a network of pigeon lofts in places including Jerusalem, Cairo, Baghdad and Aswan. The tradition persisted and in 1288, there were 2,000 carrier pigeons used for mail transport in Cairo. In 1870, during the Siege of Paris, in addition to pigeons the then new technology of photography and hot air ballooning were also deployed. Paris was surrounded by Prussian forces, and balloons were the only way of getting pigeons out of the city. The messages they carried weighed about one gram and were photographically reduced to facilitate longer messages.Europe

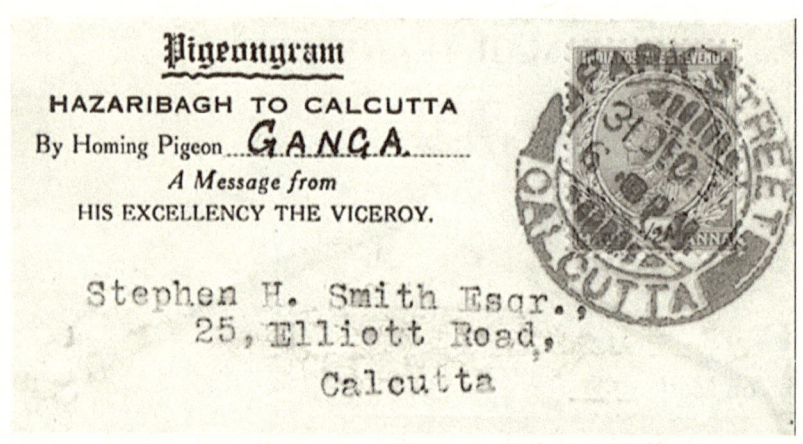

3.1 Viceroy Homing Pigeonogramme Hazaribagh to Calcutta 1931. Credit Stamp Auction Network

During World War I, Britain deployed 22,000 carrier pigeons to transmit sensitive military information, especially across enemy lines. During World War II, when technologically sophisticated methods of communication were deployed for the first time, simple and inconspicuous homing pigeons were still being employed for military communication. Pigeon mail was one of the means used by the Channel Islands, the only UK territory to be occupied by Germany during World War II[1], to communicate with the outside world.

Also during World War II, the code breakers in Bletchley Park, England, used over a quarter of a million military pigeons 'dropped behind enemy lines from bombers. Resistance fighters picked them up, before releasing them homeward bound with top secret messages'.[2]

Stephen Smith's association with pigeon mail was limited to what interested collectors. On 29th December 1931, 70 pigeons from the Calcutta Homing Pigeon Club carried 311 messages from Hazaribagh to Calcutta, a distance of 215 miles (325 km).[3] One carried the message 'I wish the Indian Airmail Society all prosperity in 1933' from Major Freeman-Thomas, First Marquess of Willingdon, who was the viceroy of India at the time. Smith sent some copies of these 'pigeongrammes' to his contacts abroad. In one letter, he indicated his role in this venture, stating: 'I may mention that it was at our request that his excellency kindly forwarded his message to us'.[4]

> GOVERNMENT HOUSE,
> Bombay, 27th March, 1941.
>
> To
> Vice-Admiral Herbert Fitzherbert, C.B., C.M.G.,
> Flag Officer Commanding, Royal Indian Navy.
>
> I am very glad to hear of your novel idea of "Pigeon Flight" in order to swell the War Funds.
>
> It is really an excellent scheme, and I take this opportunity to express the hope that the public of Bombay, which has shown its loyalty and generosity in more ways than can be enumerated here, will not be wanting in its support to the efforts of the feathered friends of our cause.
>
> I therefore appeal to the public to buy the Souvenirs carried by the pigeons and thus help the Naval War Purposes Fund.
>
> Sd. Roger Lumley,
> GOVERNOR OF BOMBAY.

3.2 The Royal Indian Navy's First Pigeons flight performed on 6th April 1941.
Credit Jeevan Jyoti

On 11th January 1933, a further flight of 26 homing pigeons from the same Calcutta Homing Pigeon Club carried 265 missives officially sanctioned by the Post Office.[5] On 6th April 1941, 250 pigeons were released in Kalyan by the British Government in India to help the war effort. They flew 30 miles (approximately 50 km) back home to Bombay. Each pigeon carried 30 messages from Sir Roger Lumley, G.C.I.E., T.D., Governor of Bombay to Vice-Admiral Fitz-Herbert, C.B., C.M.G., Third Flag Officer Commanding, Royal Indian Navy. One of the messages read in part 'I therefore appeal to the public to buy Souvenirs carried by the pigeons and thus help the naval war funds'.[6]

Balloon Mail

A century before the Wright brothers' invention of the airplane in 1903, another pair, the Montgolfier brothers, had enabled humans to become airborne for the first time with their new invention of the hot air balloon. On 7th January 1785, a hydrogen balloon flight across the channel from Dover in England to Felmores Forest in France carried the first international balloon airmail, although it was not officially sanctioned by postal authorities of either country.[7] The first flight with humans took place in Paris on 15th October 1783 and was repeated without a tether on 21st November the same year. The Montgolfier brothers had designed and built the balloon but were not the first passengers. They gave that honour and the risk to a friend, Jean-François Pilâtre de Rozier. The news spread quickly, and this feat was replicated in other countries around the world, with Vincent Lunardi making the first ascent from England in 1784.

3.3 Cover was flown on a manned balloon called 'Le Bayard' during the Siege Of Paris to London. Credit David Hudson

According to Stephen Smith, the first balloon flight in India was conducted in 1785, just two years after the Montgolfier brothers' historic flight in France. General Claude Martin, initially a member of the French East India Company but later of the British East India Company, was probably the first to give public balloon exhibitions in India. On 16th March 1836, Frenchman Dimitri Robertson, whose parents were professional balloonists, was probably the first casualty of ballooning in India.[8] He died on 23rd December the same year and is buried in South Park Burial Grounds in Calcutta.[9]

In 1870–71, during the Siege of Paris, trapped Parisians communicated with the rest of their countrymen by using hot air and hydrogen balloons. Most balloons carried homing pigeons to allow mail to come back in. As the only means of communicating from a city under siege, 67 hydrogen balloons carried 2.5 million mail items. Not all of them reached the intended destinations. Some balloons carried people not just mail or homing pigeons. Claims that hot air balloons were used for evacuating 160 wounded French soldiers were later proved to be unfounded.[10]

The technological developments of the twentieth century made larger balloons possible that were capable of reaching higher altitudes. On 18th August 1932, physics professor Auguste Piccard, accompanied by Max Cosyns, ascended to an altitude of 16,250 metres in a pressurised aluminium gondola attached to a helium balloon. This flight in Switzerland exceeded his own altitude record, set in the previous year. Piccard was the first to see the earth's curvature and to explore the stratosphere with scientific instruments. He carried 50 covers on board this record-breaking balloon flight.

On 10th June 1928, Friedrich Schmiedl in Austria launched his first stratospheric mail on a balloon. It reached an altitude of 59,000 feet (18,000 km), a remarkable achievement but one that was not a new record. Through this test, Schmiedl hoped to demonstrate the existence of east-west winds in the stratosphere. He had observed the east-west motion in the fleeting residue of a falling meteor. In this instance, the balloon landed south-west of the launch sites, so it was not considered a completely successful test.[11]

Schmiedl also used balloons as a rocket launch platform to attain higher altitudes. He configured a rocket to launch from a balloon once it attained a specific altitude. In a letter to Robert Paganini in 1933, Schmiedl wrote that he, and not Piccard, was the first to demonstrate rocket mail from the stratosphere. On 10th July 1928, Schmiedl had launched a balloon from Graz in Austria to an altitude of 16,000m. At this height, a tiny rocket ignited and launched automatically from the balloon, carrying 200 specially prepared covers. Schmiedl called this rocket FS1.[12]

3.4 Flight cover flown on stratospheric balloon to an altitude of 16250m Prof Auguste Piccard on 18 August 1932. Credit Beatrice Bachmann

Smith acquired letters and descriptions of balloon ascents from more than 150 years earlier, intending to include them in his book. The first balloon flight carrying a human took place in the 1783, a century and a half before Smith embarked on his research in rocket mail. Stephen Smith was curious about the role that balloons had played in aerial transport in India. During his lifetime, he had seen rapid progress in the development of airplanes. Even though he did not engage in experimenting with balloons, in October 1930 he completed his first draft of a book about balloon flights in India, following an extended period of research. It was called *Balloon Ascents in India,* but it was never published.[13] The book was to have ten chapters:

1. General Claude Martin - 1785
2. Mr A Wintle - 1785
3. M. D Robertson - 1836–1837
4. Mde D'Lasanta - 1850
5. Several Chapters of Mr Knight 1850–1853
6. Monsieur Maigre - 1849
7. Mr Ram Chunder Chaterjee - 1889
8. Mr PC Laha - 1890
9. Miss Van Tassel - 1892
10. Mr Spencer - 1889

Apart from the absence of living witnesses to these events, his research was hindered by one specific event in Indian history: the Indian Mutiny. The Indian Mutiny (1857–1858) was an unsuccessful attempt by Indians to take back the control of India from the British East India Company by force. Today, many in India consider it India's first war of independence.[14]

The early balloon flights in India mostly happened a couple of decades prior to the mutiny. In a letter to Robert Paganini, Smith complains that 'no one I have met shows any interest in my research, before the Indian Mutiny, and therefore will not extend me a helping hand in any way'.[15] Almost 70 years after the mutiny, his research became a casualty of the prevailing norms to suppress the knowledge of Indian history.

During his research, Smith collected covers from balloon flights from around the world, not just from India. One of the covers came from the very first balloon mail flight from the northern England city of Manchester[16]. The balloon, flown by Dr Francis Alexandra Barton, took off at 17:00 on Saturday 20th September 1902. During the two hour flight it reached an altitude of 6,000 feet (1.8 km) and landed in the Wensleydale area of Yorkshire. Barton carried 4,000 covers which were dropped overboard in small parcels to help raise money for the Lifeboat Saturday Fund. The finders of the parcels were encouraged to take the parcel to the nearest post office for onward delivery.

India's fascination with balloons continues today. The record altitude of 21,027 metres by hot air balloon is held by Vijaypat Singhania for his flight from Mumbai on 26th November 2005.[17] The Balloon Facility in Hyderabad has an international reputation for building and conducting high-quality research using high-altitude balloons. It made the balloon used on 24th October 2014 to set the world record for a human parachute jump from an altitude of over 42 km (26 miles).[18] With wind and weather determining when balloons can be launched, the direction they fly, and the time taken to arrive at the intended destination, balloon mail did not establish itself as a serious long-term method of mail transport.

Tin Can Mail

On Sunday 30th September 1934, Stephen Smith attempted to demonstrate the swift delivery of mail from a ship to the shore using a rocket. Although he was the first to use rockets for this purpose in India, it had been tried decades earlier on the other side of the world. At around the turn of the twentieth century, the use of mail canisters attached to Congreve rockets was attempted on the Niuafo'ou Island as an alternative solution to the then current system of using swimmers.[19] Although the island was well within the 2-mile range of Congreve rockets, they lacked the precision to be a reliable solution.

Niuafo'ou Island is a tiny volcanic doughnut-shaped island in the South Pacific located between Fiji and Samoa and is the northern-most island in the Kingdom of Tonga. The island had no shallow water where ships could anchor, and no natural harbour. In 1882, a plantation manager on the island, William Travers, came up with the idea of swimming out to the passing ships and exchanging mail wrapped in oilcloth and sealed in biscuit tins. Passing ships would toss tin cans overboard for swimmers to collect and deliver to the island.[20]

As a result of this aspect of its philatelic history, Niuafo'ou Island is also known as the Tin Can Island. Tin can mail became an integral part of Tonga's postal service in 1882. Following a shark attack in 1931, canoes replaced swimmers. In 1946, a volcanic eruption forced an evacuation until the population returned in 1958. This unique Tongan mail system continued until 1981, when an airstrip was built on the island.

Walter George Quensell, an experienced seaman of German origin, saw the potential for philatelic interest in the Tin Can mail system. Writing in 1947, he claimed that he 'made it known to the world'.[21] He designed a rubber stamp and added a cachet 'Tin Can Mail' to every mail item that used tin cans. Over time, the cachets became more elaborate and were much sought after by collectors. Quensell claimed that during his 27 years on the island, he had sent more than 1.5 million letters to 148 nations and states.[22] Tonga still issues a Tin Can motif for philatelists.[23]

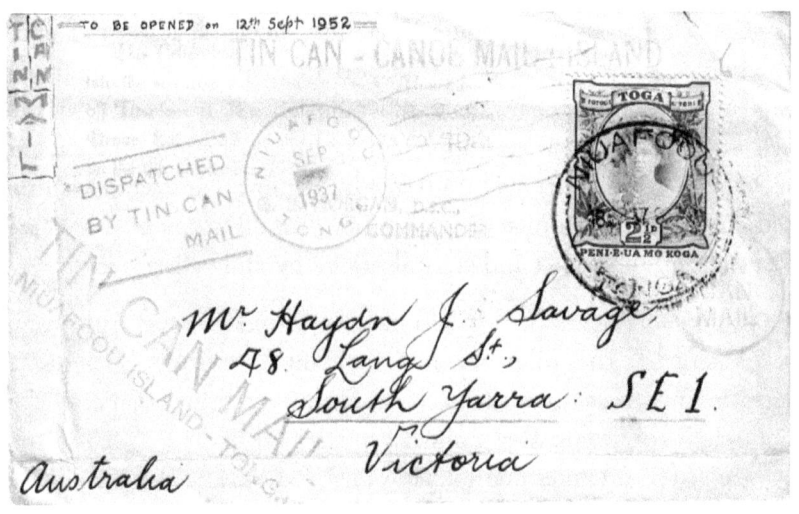

3.5 Tin Can Mail written in 1937 and opened 75 years later. Credit Angela Savage

Decades after the demise of Tin Can mail, an intriguing story was published by Angela Savage on her blog. In January 2012, she delivered a letter to her father Leslie Savage that had been written to him by his father Hyden almost 75 years earlier. The record-breaking letter had travelled by air, ship, tin can, canoe, registered mail and train before being delivered unopened to the intended recipient 75 years after it was written in Melbourne, Australia.[24]

Catapult Mail

A runway provides an aircraft with the space to achieve the required air speed to get airborne. A catapult offers a similar but compact solution for large and heavy aircraft where a runway is not available. Smith's testing did not advance to rockets large or heavy enough to require this kind of assistance at take-off. Had rocket mail matured to some level of commercial operations, a catapult would have been developed to launch the large load carrying rockets.

In the 1930s, aircraft did not have the capacity to fly long distances, for example across the Atlantic Ocean. Huge airships and ocean-crossing liners were the only solution. Limitations in aircraft frame, avionics, engine power, engine reliability, load capacity and speed prevented routine transatlantic transport of mail. In the absence of a long runway, a catapult mechanism would launch an aircraft from the deck of a ship when it was approaching its destination. The catapult mechanism speeded up mail transport by at most a few day.s Mail that used rockets or catapults in its journey from Europe to New York received a special cachet and are still valued by philatelists today.

The catapult service was used within Europe and between Europe and the Americas. The pilot-operated catapult consisted of a launch platform on wheels upon the deck, accelerating a fully laden aircraft of about eight tonnes on a very small runway (approximately 10 m) to a flying speed of 60 miles per hour (96 km per hour).[25] The catapult was powered either by slow burning powder, such as cordite, melinite or compressed air.[26] The French liner Ile de France operated the catapult service between 1928–1929 and the German ships Bremen and Europa were operational until 1935. Britain, however, did not deploy the catapult mechanism on any of its ships. In late 1928, an assessment was carried out in secret by the Air Ministry, Admiralty, Post Office and Imperial Airways to determine whether the two existing White Star Liners, the Majestic and the Olympic, should be fitted with a catapult. The assessment concluded that it was not cost effective.

3.6 Catapult Mail 21 September 1930. Credit invaluable.com

The catapult mechanism would add about 30 tons (including the aircraft) to the total weight and take about six months to install on an existing liner at a cost of £20,000.[27]

Data from France's Ile de France and Germany's Europa and Bremen ships indicated that the number of people willing to pay the extra for the slightly earlier postal service did not warrant the expense of installing the catapult facilities. It was largely considered to be a 'marketing stunt' and there was 'little value' for the transport of mail.[28]

Britain concluded that it was not economically effective to either retrofit a catapult facility on existing ships or incorporate one on ships about to be built. If the programme had gone ahead, ships arriving in Calcutta would have launched their aircraft using their catapults as the entered the River Hooghly. Not far from where Smith had conducted his first rocket mail experiments.

4

AIRMAIL

Airships

In the pursuit of philately and rocket mail experimentation, Stephen Smith was original, dedicated, industrious and persistent. He was also an opportunist. Whenever there was a potential for mail to make history, he wanted to be part of it. He was eager to have mail items in every event of interest to philatelists. He had mail items on the first aircraft to fly from India to England in 1925, the first regular airmail from India to England in 1929, the first flight from England to Australia in 1931 (which passed through Calcutta), and also on board the first airplanes to fly over Everest in 1933.

Although aircraft were relatively new, airships had been travelling the globe for several years. The mail service was an integral part of the airship industry from the outset. Smith did not have a substantial airship mail collection but anticipated a change coming.[1]

Airship development started long before the Wright brothers' 1903 historic milestone. Commercial transatlantic airship flights were available in the 1930s about two decades before aircraft. Between 1930 and 1937, the primary means of transport between Germany and

South America was an airship. With the exception of the winter months, the Graf Zeppelin flew weekly, carrying cargo, passengers and mail to Rio de Janeiro. The Hindenburg could carry 20 tonnes over a distance of 9000 km at a speed of about 60 knots. At the time, airplanes could not match that. The accelerated investment during World War I introduced improvements in aircraft development so that by the late 1930s, airships were already in decline. World War II further accelerated aircraft design. Innovation in engines, aerodynamics and materials allowed aircraft to surpass airships as a means of aerial transport. The cargo aircraft, C1-30 Hercules, entered service in the mid 1950s, initially offering a payload capacity of 12 tonnes over 400 km and was able to cruise at more than 300 knots.[2]

4.1 *Graf Zeppelin airmail cover from Max Kronstein to Stephen Smith in 1938.*
Credit Lady Ezra Collection

The catastrophic end of the R101 marked not only the death of the designers, engineers and key the politicians leading the programme but also the end of the airship programme itself in Britain.

Had the airship arrived as planned in India, it is unthinkable that Smith would have missed the opportunity to have his covers flown on board on its return from India to England. From the outset, airships carried mail as well as cargo and passengers. Airmail was carried in 1908 by the LZ4 (Luftschiff Zeppelin) built by the German airship pioneer Ferdinand von Zeppelin.[3] Airships were the premier form of air travel for most of the first half of the twentieth century. The lavish Hindenburg had 5,000 square feet (464 sq m) of carpeted passenger space, a restaurant, bar, library and a promenade with large windows to watch the landscape gently drifting by below.

Germany had pioneered the design and building of airships during the closing years of the 19th century. After the first two decades of the twentieth century, they demonstrated commercial and military success, which fostered an uptake in the building of airships across Europe and the USA. Britain had acquired two German airships following the Armistice, but they were dismantled once the Air Ministry deemed them unsuitable. In a haste to catch up, in 1924 Britain committed to building seven airships (R.33, R.36, R.37, R.38, R.80, R100 and R101) which would eventually be part of a large fleet linking London to the widely dispersed countries of the British Empire including Egypt, India, Canada and Australia. Despite having spent £1.8 million, five of the seven were never built.

The Labour government deployed a unique political approach in designing and building the R100 and the R101.[4] The 'R' prefix referred to the rigid airframe structure around which the ship was built. A private company would build the 'capitalist' R100 and a public-owned company would build the 'socialist' R101. The R100 flew to Canada on the 29th July 1930 and arrived after a journey of 78 hours. After a short passenger-carrying flight within Canada, it departed for England on 13th August, arriving 57 hours later. Following its successful return flight to Canada, the R100 was placed in a hanger and it never flew again.

The success of the R100 had hastened the launch of the R101 on its journey to Karachi via Cairo on the evening of 4th October 1930. Less than 12 hours after departure, whilst in the French countryside near the town of Allonne, it went into an uncontrolled dive, crashed and burst into flames killing 48 of the 54 people onboard. It never made it to India.

4.2 LZ 127 Graf Zeppelin. *The first commercial passenger transatlantic flight service in the world. Cover signed by passengers during a flight in September 1929. Credit Museum of Communication, Bern, Switzerland*

Although more were killed on the R101 (48 of the 54 onboard) than the 36 on the Hindenburg in 1937, the harrowing images and agonising narration of the newsreel coverage of the Hindenburg have left a more permanent scar in the public conscience. The passengers who perished on the R101 flight included the Secretary of State for Air, Lord Thomson, and the Director of Civil Aviation, Sir Sefton Brancker. Many of the British engineers that had built and flown the R100 were the same team that worked on the R101.

Neither the R100 nor the R101 carried any authorised mail. However, one cover appears to have travelled from Canada to London on the R100.[5] The cover, with a post mark of 13th August 1930 in Canada and another five days later in London, appears to have arrived in Britain via the R100 flight. It is most likely that this cover was carried unofficially by a member of the crew at the request of a dealer.

4.5 Airship hanger and mast in the background in Karachi. The office building in the bottom left is an indication of the huge scale of the size of the hanger. Credit Airship Heritage Trust

In preparation for its arrival in Karachi, an airship mast, hydrogen plant and hanger were built 13 miles from the centre. At the time this was the largest building in the British Empire and cost of £93,000 in 1928.[6] The R101 never made it to India and none of these facilities were ever used.

Since that crew member was also on the R101, he is likely to have perished on 5th October 1930. The cover is addressed to A. C. Roessler, a well-known New Jersey-based dealer at the time. This kind of 'private' delivery was not unusual. It was the kind of arrangement that Stephen Smith frequently engaged in, with pilots flying through Dum Dum airport in Calcutta.[7]

In the 1930s, Germany persisted and cultivated what became probably the most successful decade for global airship travel in history. During their short reign, airships chalked up an impressive safety record. The 13 fatalities on the Hindenburg were the only passenger lives lost on passenger-carrying commercial operations. But the spectacular and catastrophic airship failures, including the R101, left a permanent scar on the public psyche that helped to crystallise the global permanent demise of airships.

4.3 R101 Crashed 5 Oct 1930. Credit Museum of Communication, Bern Switzerland

The spectacle and the romance of a huge airship flying gently and quietly over villages and farmland now lives only in the pages of history books and the memories of a tiny and decreasing population. Innovations in industrial processes and new materials in the second half of the nineteenth century had enabled the huge structure of an airship to be built. They included processes to manufacture aluminium, hydrogen and small powerful combustion engines.

Prior to 1914, Zeppelins had carried 37,250 passengers over 90,000 miles across established routes with a one hundred percent safety record. In the lead up to World War II, it was clear that large slow airships could not compete with swift and nimble aircraft. German expertise and experience in designing, building and operating airships was internationally recognised as world-leading.

In the December 1931 edition of the Indian Air Society's monthly bulletin, Stephen Smith carried a report describing the fate of the R101. Despite its unblemished record and an accumulated cost of £1 million, it was sold for scrap. A month before its catastrophic end, Friedrich Schmiedl in Austria had demonstrated the concept of rocket mail.

It is possible that Smith saw this as an end of one mode of aerial transport and the future possibility of another. Smith himself did not conduct his first rocket mail experiment until 1934. The events in the autumn of 1931 could have inspired him with an interest in rocket mail for which he is now remembered worldwide.

First Airplanes in India

Having founded the Aerophilatelic Club of India in 1924, Smith immersed himself in the evolving aviation industry. The first of his three volumes, *Indian Airways*, was published in 1926. He lived close to Dum Dum airport in Calcutta and visited it frequently, not only to conduct research for the book but also to make personal contact with the pilots from around the world.

It was through this close contact that he kept up with the latest developments in aviation. It was also an opportunity to pass on in person letters and covers to international pilots, who would post them when they returned to their home countries. This allowed him to expand his personal collection of airmail and sell some to other collectors. The benefits of air travel were more obvious and necessary for the vast and challenging Indian terrain than smaller countries like England.

Aviation has deep roots in Indian mythology. One Indian tale talks about an Indian ivory carver who travels to ancient Greece. The craftsmen of Alexandria were highly proficient in the construction of complex mechanisms such as Automatic Theatres (Automatopoetike), Hero's steam turbine (aeolipile) and the Antikythera mechanism around the first century BCE. It was this technical accomplishment that convinced the Indian poets that the first aircraft could also have been a product of Greek civilisation.[8] Ancient Indian texts talk about two distinct flying machines: the Garuda airship, constructed in India on the principle of bird-flight and the Yavana airship from Greece, the design and construction of which was a closely guarded secret. Despite the absence of any evidence, theories of ancient Indian aircraft or 'vimanas' persist in India today.

The flight in July 1909 by Louis Blériot across the English channel inspired Giacomo D'Angelis to make the first powered flight of an aircraft in India. He had arrived in India from Italy in 1880 and eventually established a hotel business in Madras. Using a aircraft he designed and built he conducted the first flight of a powered aircraft in India on 26 March 1910 in the town of Pallavaram which today is close to the site of Chennai's international airport.[9]

In 1910 aircraft were brought in to India for the first time by two independent groups. The Maharajah of Patiala sent his British Engineer C W Bowles to bring planes from Europe. In the autumn of 1910, he returned to Patiala in the Northwest of India with a Farman biplane made in England and a Gnome-Bleriot monoplane made in France.[10] Before either of these got airborne, the English pilot Edward Keith Davies made his first flight on 10 December 1910 in Allahabad in north East India. On the following day at the same venue, the

French pilot Henri Pequet, flew his biplane. Davis and Piquet were part of Captain Walter George Windham's group that had arrived from England in the summer of 1910.

Captain Windham was one of earliest to learn to fly in England in the first decade of aviation. As a pilot, he had participated in several aerial exhibitions including in Blackpool, Doncaster and Bournemouth. Aerial exhibitions were common around the world in the early years of aviation. For many, it was the first opportunity to see at close quarters the revolutionary machines that would allow a people to fly. Windham had been invited to the industrial and agricultural exhibition in Allahabad along with his aeroplane.

With only 30 horsepower, the monoplanes had the weaker engine and could not climb to a substantial height. The biplanes with a 50 horsepower engine offered better performance; three days after Davies' flight the French pilot Piquet successfully flew the biplane for ten minutes. Both planes were made in Coventry by the Humber Company, which had started out making automobiles.

Windham ensured he made the most of the commercial opportunities. The airplanes were put on public view at one rupee per ticket, but if wealthy members of Calcutta society wanted to purchase one, the monoplane was available for £500 and the biplane for £1000.

In the early 1920s, India saw the introduction of aerial transport of cargo, regular airmail and scheduled passenger flights. Smith took an interest in tracking and recording developments in airmail. In the early days aerial exhibitions were extremely popular. On January 6th, 1911, during Smith's final year at school, more than 100,000 people gathered at the Calcutta racecourse to witness the magic of man-made flying machines.[11]

In practice, it was the British government's recognition of the potential of aviation to help administer the large parts of its Empire that fostered its development. By 1930, there were six flying clubs in India (Bombay, Calcutta, Lahore, Delhi, Madras and Karachi) with 1,596 members. In 1930, they successfully completed their training and qualified as pilots, two of them were women.[12] Supported by a subsidy from London, aviation clubs saw a growth across the Empire (Australia, New Zealand, Canada South Africa and India). By 1930 there were 72 clubs, 15,641 members and 1,061 qualified pilots. This growth was inevitable, given the advantages over existing modes of transport, but also essential in managing an Empire that stretched over vast distances across challenging terrain.

4.5 Ville_de_Paris 1906. Credit eBay seller nf_stamps

In the preface to Stephen Smith's three-volume book *Indian Airways*, H A Outhwaite, president of the Aero Philatelic Club of India, captured the life-changing potential of the airplane. He wrote 'there is no reason why the Calcutta man should not in the near future be able to run home every year for a month or six weeks at an outlay of £50 to £60'. He estimated the journey would take about three or four days.[13]

Outhwaite and Smith knew each other through their mutual interest in philately. Both must have been aware of the rapid progress in aviation. In the preface, Outhwaite summarises the technical advances that were already in place or in production, including all-metal (not wooden) airframes, 1,000 horsepower noiseless engines and multi-engine triplanes with capacity to carry 100 passengers. With remarkable prescience, he envisaged that with 'wireless directional rays, airplanes can be guided safely to aerodromes through the thickest fog or at night'.[14]

In 1929, at about the same time as Smith published the third volume of his book *Indian Airways*, Jehangir Ratanji Dadabhoy Tata (1904–1993) became the first Indian national to acquire a pilot's licence in India. His flight, delivering mail in a de Havilland DH.80A Puss Moth on 15th October 1932 from Karachi to Bombay, marked the beginning of commercial aviation in India. He founded Tata Air Services, India's first commercial airline in 1932. In 1946 it became Air India and continues to serve as the national airline today.

About two months after his first flight in India, Piquet, still in Allahabad was set to make history and fly the first official airmail flight.

Airmail in India

Stephen Smith was 12 years old when the Wright brothers conducted their pioneering flight. Just eight years later, an airplane made postal history in India. The first time an aircraft was used in the delivery of mail was in Allahabad on 18th February 1911, just 600 km from Asansol where he was at school. This milestone emerged from Captain W Windham and his team of aviators who arrived in India in the autumn of 1910.

The idea for the airmail was borne out of a request to Captain W Windham to raise funds from the Chaplain of Holy Trinity Church in Allahabad, who was also the warden for a hostel. Windham was participating at the Allahabad exhibition demonstrating mankind's latest invention, the airplane. The Reverend Holland approached Windham with the idea and Windham grasped it, seeing the potential to boost the cause for aviation and to advance his own financial interests.

These seminal events in aviation came at the right time and place for a bright young man looking to make his way in the world. It would have filled Stephen Smith with excitement and wonder, just as the railways had done for a generation earlier or drones and space launches are doing for today's generation.

The pilot for that first mail flight was a 23-year-old Frenchman, Henri Piquet, who had been in India for only a few months. With an official sanction from the Indian Postal Service, at 17:30 on 18th February 1911, Piquet flew his Humber-Sommer biplane carrying the world's first official airmail.[15] The flight, carrying 6,500 letters and cards, covered 10 km from the Allahabad polo field to the nearby town Naini Junction over the River Yumana and back again in just 13 minutes. Interestingly, the first official airmail in England took place on 11th September 1911, to mark the coronation of King George V.[16]

Piquet's interest in aviation started early. In 1905 he was flying balloons; he moved to airplanes in 1909. He obtained his pilot's licence #88 on 10th June 1910. Apart from flying in India, he had flown airplanes in Germany, South America, Russia and his home country France.[17] Piquet initially started flying balloons, airships and then steerable airship (dirigible), 'Ville de Paris'. He turned to airplanes and acquired his licence (number 88) on 10th June 1909.[18] In addition to his historic airmail flight in India, he flew in Germany, South America and Russia.[19]

Saint Patrick's school in the city of Asansol lies two hundred kilometres north east of Calcutta. In 1911, Smith was completing his final year at St Patrick's and it is highly likely that he was aware of the historic flight; indeed, he may even have been present at it. At the age of 20, it must have been a formative experience, triggering or consolidating his interest in transport technology and flying machines. Perhaps it was this single experience that inspired his preoccupations, first with aviation and then with rockets, which stayed with him for the rest of his life.

Smith lived in a Calcutta which had started out as the British Empire's centre in India for trade and commerce. Initially it was access to the sea via the Hooghly River that made it a hub for the European navies of Britain, France, Portugal and Spain. With growing trade, Calcutta flourished as the home of the wealthy and the location for the growth of an influential elite, mostly Europeans. The city acquired further enhancement and a new strategic significance once the Dum Dum airport opened in 1928, becoming a critical waypoint between London, South East Asia and Australia.

Stephen Smith regularly visited Dum Dum between the late 1920s and the start of World War II. He met many of the pilots flying through India and gave them covers to post when they returned to their home countries, which included Germany, Burma, Singapore and Australia.[20] He used these contacts to collect first-hand information for his three-volume book, *Indian Airways*. It also allowed him to be first off the block in sending mail on special flights. Between 1925 and 1934 he sent at least four separate mails which received responses from King George V at Buckingham Palace.[21] They included the first airmail from Karachi to London, the first airmail stamps produced in India, and the first flight from Delhi to Croydon, all in 1929.

Although Smith is known for his rocket mail experiments, he is not known for his contribution to astronautics, the study of travel beyond the atmosphere.[22] He is better known for his accomplishments with the philatelic community. It is in that community of collectors and dealers that most of his work has been preserved and perpetuated. Indeed, in some instances had the philatelic community not preserved details of his rocket experiments, they would have been lost completely.

Flight over Everest

Two decades before Tenzing Norgay and Edmund Hillary reached its summit on foot, aircraft had flown over the summit of Everest. As they carried some mail, Stephen Smith ensured that he and the Indian Airmail Society were involved. Twice in April 1933, the Houston Everest Expedition flew over the summit of Everest in two biplanes, each with two men onboard. The expedition was named after its sponsor, philanthropist Lady Houston. The expedition to fly over the almost 9 km high summit of the world's tallest mountain was led by RAF squadron Leader Douglas Douglas-Hamilton, also known as Lord Clydesdale.

4.6 Houston Expedition to fly over the summit of Everest. April 1933. Credit Jeremy Argyll Etkin

Stephen Smith travelled to the expedition headquarters in Purnea, Bihar, about 500 km north of Calcutta. Following a meeting with

Colonel Blacker, Smith passed over 87 covers to be carried over the summit of Everest. The expedition had received many similar requests. To help prioritise these requests and to raise funds for the expedition, a charge of one guinea per cover was agreed.

The high price reflected the uniqueness of the flight and the risks taken by the pilots. By this time, Smith's primary income probably came from collecting and dealing in philatelic items and he would have correctly assessed the financial risk on his part. On 21st February 1934, Smith wrote to his friend in Switzerland, saying that the covers were being advertised for sale at £12 each.[23]

The Everest expedition involved two Westland PV-3 aircraft with supercharged Pegasus 8.3 engines.[24] One aircraft was christened Houston and the other was named Wallace. The Houston was piloted by Lord Clydesdale with Colonel Blacker as observer, and Wallace was flown by Flight Lieutenant McIntyre with S. R. Bonnett as the observer.

The first of the two flights took place on the 3rd April and the second on the 19th April. Both aircraft were equipped with multiple high-resolution cameras. One camera looked straight down through a hatch in the floor, to capture high-quality survey images suitable for use by climbers to plot a climbing route.

The quality of these survey images on the first flight was marred by low level mist obscuring the detail in the landscape below, but this was not the case for the second flight.

The expedition used a small airfield in a hamlet called Lalbalu in Purnea. Each flight involved a take-off at around 8am, returning about four hours later with about a fifteen-minute flight at 30 metres above the summit.

The aircraft flew through the 'plume of Everest' that can be seen on the leeward side of the summit. Once there, they discovered it was not the gentle benign phenomenon that it appeared to be. Blacker described the experience of being in it as 'something quite different to what we had conceived. Here was no drifting cloud wisp, but a prodigious jet of rushing winds flinging a veritable barrage of ice fragments for several miles to leeward of the peak'. In fact, the rear cockpit celastroid window of the Houston was cracked by the impact from one fragment of ice.[25]

A year earlier, between 7th and 12th January 1932, two American pilots, Haliburton and Stephens, flew their Stearman C-3B NR882N Biplane 'The Flying Carpet' to the 'area of Everest'. They had flown from Calcutta to Bagdogra in Sikkim and eventually returned via the same route. The flight carried 50 covers and unsuccessfully attempted to climb to the summit. Another Himalaya flight the German Nanga Parbet Expedition was flown in 1938 but no covers were carried. Although this was a German aircraft and a German expedition, one of the pilots in the crew of three was an RAF pilot.[26] A feat that would not have been possible a year later.

Smith wrote a piece about this trip to Purnea and the meeting with the expedition leader in the US publication, *Air Post Air Journal* on 9th June 1933.[27] In this piece, Smith says that he arrived in Purnea on the 6th June. On the 7th, he met the expedition leader, handed over the covers to be flown and returned to collect the flown covers on the following day. These dates are not consistent with the official dates for the Everest summit flight on 3rd and 19th April. The letters that had been carried over the mountain bore a special cancelling stamp and were dispatched to His Majesty the King, the Prince of Wales and Lady Houston.

Piggyback plane

As a dedicated philatelist, Stephen Smith was interested in unique and unusual modes of air transport. Handwritten letters in the postal system still represented the most popular mode of communication for the global population. To extend their capabilities, aircraft were carried and launched by ships, airships, other planes and even submarines. The mail they carried was of particular interest to collectors, including Stephen Smith.

During World War I, Britain and Germany built airships that carried small aircraft, mainly the Sopwith Camel for launching planes from the air. But it was after the war that significant developments took place. Between 1931 and 1935, the U.S. Navy developed and operated two airships, the Akron and Macon, each with a capability to launch and recover a number of light biplane fighters, the Curtiss F9C Sparrowhawk. The aircraft were lowered for deployment from a trapeze-type mechanism in a hanger within the airship. After the mission, the same mechanism would capture and return the aircraft to the hanger for servicing and refuelling.

In the 1930s, the USSR's Zveno project used a Tupolev TB-3 heavy bomber which carried up to five fighters close to a target, launched the fighters and once the mission was complete could return to base on its own power. There was also a limited capability for the fighter to return to the bomber for 'inflight redocking'.

4.7 Maya-Mercury Composite Aircraft. Credit Museum of Communication, Bern, Switzerland

The earliest submarine to carry an aircraft was the German SM U-12. On 15th January 1915, it carried an FF-22 sea plane on its deck. The submarine would travel out to sea to a point where it would submerge, leaving the seaplane on the surface from where it would make a normal take-off. In 1927, the British submarine HMS M2 became operational. It was built with a small waterproof hanger that could deliver aircraft to a predefined place, then surface to launch the sea planes using a ramp and a hydraulic catapult. Returning aircraft would land on the water and be recovered using a derrick.

Perhaps the most intriguing solution was an aircraft that carried an aircraft. Known as the Maia-Mercury composite, it consisted of two sea planes: the larger Maia below carrying the smaller Mercury aircraft above it. Maia would take off, and on reaching a predefined altitude, Mercury would detach and fly free on its own engines. It was designed by The Short Brothers, a company that had been building aircraft for Imperial Airways to serve countries in the British Empire. It was designed to carry 450 kg of mail over a distance of 6200 km.

The Maia-Mercury composite did not have a long life, but prior to its demise it set two world records. In July 1938, once separated from Maia, Mercury was the first commercial non-stop east-west flight across the Atlantic to Montreal in Canada. It carried mail, newspapers and newsreel.

On 8th October 1938, with modifications, Mercury acquired a world record by making the longest seaplane flight of 9,726 km from Dundee in Scotland to Cape Town in South Africa.[28] Maia was destroyed whilst in Poole harbour in southern England in May 1941 and Mercury was retired a few months later.

The Maia-Mercury was not the only composite aircraft. Other composite designs have carried smaller experimental aircraft to extremely high altitudes; for example, NASA used a modified Boeing 747 to deliver the space shuttle from one part of the US to another. In 2017, a new private space company Virgin Orbit, part of the Virgin Group, was established to develop a modified 747 as the first stage of a rocket launch system designed to place satellites into low Earth orbit from southern England.

5

ROCKET MAIL

Rockets in Europe

In addition to their use as a weapon and a means of transport, rockets were also used for propaganda. The delivery of propaganda (transport of leaflets designed to undermine the morale of the enemy) as employed by Stephen Smith's propaganda rockets in Calcutta during World War II, was one that had been contemplated and patented more than half a century earlier. In 1810, Heinrich von Kleist, playwright and editor of a German newspaper, was the first to suggest the idea of using artillery shells to carry mail instead of explosives. The shell would be fired once, recovered and fired again multiple times to reach the next town. A lengthy and cumbersome process but significantly faster than traditional mail.[1]

Paris came under siege for the final six months of the Franco-Prussian War (19th September 1870 to 28th January 1871). One of the innovations to breach the siege was the use balloons for communication. The other was to use rocket mail, for which J D Schneiter submitted a patent on 31st December 1870. He hoped that it would 'open[ing] the eyes of the invading soldiers' by means of a journal transported by a rocket with a container made from sheet iron or zinc.[2]

Schneiter's patent was granted after the siege and the war were over. There is no evidence that either Kleist's or Schneiter's ideas were ever implemented in their lifetimes. Schneiter's idea for rockets were a product of a military conflict. It would take two further military conflicts in the first half of the twentieth century to realise fully the military and research potential of rockets. It was the collective effort of many individuals working mostly alone and unfunded for many years to make the incremental breakthroughs. While Stephen Smith was the only one experimenting with rocket mail in India, significant progress was made by several individuals in Europe, USSR and the USA.

Reinhold Tiling

Stephen Smith corresponded with rocket experimenters, philatelist and writers in Austria, Switzerland and England. There is no evidence of Smith corresponding with Reinhold Tiling in Germany. Had Tiling not died prematurely in 1934, they most likely would have done.

One report asserts that, 'Smith was inundated with letters from abroad. The most significant of these were the letters that came to him from America and Germany. The latter country's interest in Smith (sic) efforts was very evident as considerable correspondence was exchanged between him and German scientists'.[3]

Reinhold Tiling was born in southern Germany in 1893 and became a flight controller at Osnabruck airport in 1926, a role that was not available to previous generations. In 1928 he joined the emerging Luftwaffe and became a skilled pilot. Later, he worked as an aerobatics pilot and as an engineer, but during the depression of the late 1920s he turned his skills to rockets. Once his success with launching rockets was officially recognised, he was given access to the island of Wangerooge by the state of Oldenburg. This is one of the chain of the Frisian Islands in the North Sea where he tested one of his rocket planes to an altitude of 8 km.[4]

Tiling was probably inspired to work on rockets by the rocketry pioneer Hermann Oberth and his ground-breaking PhD thesis 'Rakete zu den Planetenräumen' (The Rocket into Planetary Space), published in 1923. He conducted rocket mail tests using solid fuel. His innovation was to combine the airplane with the rocket. This was an idea that had occurred to others, but it was Tiling who designed, patented and built such a rocket plane. In a test on 13th March 1931, a solid fuel-propelled rocket flew to a height of 1,800 metres. A film of his launch on 13th November 1932 shows a smooth launch. Once the fuel was exhausted and the rocket started its descent, the wings popped out and it glided back to Earth.[5] On 15th April he conducted another test flight with a rocket 12 feet and 8 inches (3.9 meters) long, carrying 188 postcards. This was Germany's first official rocket post.

Less than three decades since the pioneering work of the Wright brothers, this was still the very early days of flying machines. One of the factors clearly understood was the need to develop more powerful engines. Tiling promoted the idea of using rocket engines as a source for this power. In one of his patents, he proposed an airplane with 'oscillating wings'. The modern term is 'variable geometry', whereby a rocket had wings which were swept back during the high-speed launch and could then be swung forward at the end of the powered phase of flight, allowing the craft to glide at a slower speed.[6] This approach not only did away with a need for parachutes, something that Schmiedl had concluded was a tough technical challenge and which Smith had tried and rejected, but it also introduced the concept of reusability. He submitted a patent in 1933, which in part reads:

'A flying rocket, comprising in combination a rocket body, supporting planes shiftable on said body adapted during the ascending to lie behind the centre of gravity of the rocket and in passing over into gliding to move towards the front portion of said body so that their centre of pressure is in line with the centre of gravity of the rocket.'

On 10th October 1933, Tiling and his assistants Angela Buddenböhmer and Friedrich Kuhr were all severely injured in an explosion within his workshop. They died on the following day.[7] Tiling is considered to be one of the earliest victims of rocketry.

Following Reinhold Tiling's sudden demise, his work was continued by his brother Richard. Richard's first focus was on improving the safety of the solid fuel propellent. On 17th April 1934, at the Navy and the Army Ordnance Department range in Meppen, he successfully demonstrated his modified rockets which reached an altitude of 12 km.[8]

5.1 *Tilling's Rocket April 1931. Credit Bundes Archiv*

Max Valier, another Austrian rocket pioneer, had probably been the first casualty of rocketry when he was killed when testing a liquid-fuelled rocket engine for a car in May 1931. Valier was an enthusiastic member of the VfR. Initially, he worked as a freelance science writer, but later engaged with Fritz von Opel to build and test rocket-powered cars and briefly aircraft, including gliders.

Despite the initial success of testing cars on the road and rail, the VfR considered Valier's contribution to be counter-productive in two ways: 'he side-tracked public attention to rocket-powered land vehicles, which could never utilise rocket power to its fullest potentialities and he directed attention to powder rockets instead of towards liquid fuel rockets'.[9]

Smith understood the magnitude of the risks associated with testing rockets, especially in the handling of solid fuel rockets in the dry heat of India. In 1934, the year he commenced his rocket testing, he suffered minor burns to his face and hand.[10] It is unlikely that Smith learnt immediately of the deaths of Tiling and Valier. All three, Tilling, Valier and Smith are now better known in the international philatelic community than they were at the time.

Until the late 1940s, aircraft engines were inefficient, heavy, and limited the range and cargo they could carry. Tiling's idea of using rockets to power aircraft was pursued by many others including Karel Roberti, Willy Ley and Sergei Korolev. Eventually, the idea of rocket planes was superseded by innovation in combustion engines and the advent of the jet engine. On 25th April 1945, Smith launched an all metal rocket (number 162)about 2 meters long called 'Miss Fortune'. It was not as sophisticated as Tiling's rocket planes but Smith also used the term Rocket Plane to describe it.

Friedrich Schmiedl

Friedrich Schmiedl was probably the most highly trained and technically competent rocket mail experimenter working in Europe during the 1920s and 1930s. He was in contact with the key individual in the international rocket mail community, including Stephen Smith. Schmiedl had studied Chemistry and Natural Sciences at the Technical University in Graz, Austria. Between 1928 and 1935 he conducted at least 44 rocket launches, with hundreds of experiments testing rocket engines and developing instruments to record meteorological data: the spectroscope, a movie camera and a still camera to take aerial photographs.[11]

Schmiedl investigated the impact of radiation on plant growth by launching plant buds to high altitudes in his rockets. In 1931, he was the first person to transport live animals (beetles and butterflies) using rocket power, not Stephen Smith in 1935 as is widely believed. Smith used larger species including a small hen, chick, mouse and a snake, but unlike Schmiedl, Smith frequently wrote about it. In 1938, in a letter to Robert Paganini from Smith says: 'your remarks about our mutual friend Mr Schmiedl have surprised me. He should NOT STOP his valuable work'.[12]

5.2 *Friedrich Schmiedl with rocket and launcher. Credit Museum of Communication, Bern, Switzerland*

Stephen Smith lacked the technical equipment available to Schmiedl as well as the knowledge and training to use it. He would have learnt about Schmiedl's work through their shared memberships of international philately and rocketry groups, as well as through personal correspondence. Amongst the many individuals around the globe working alone on developing rocketry, Schmiedl was undoubtably the leader not only in his ambitions but also in his accomplishments.

In mid-1937, Schmiedl responded to the British philatelist Francis J Field, asserting that his rocket R1 had covered a distance of 2,700 meters but he would no longer share details of distances covered. This was in response to claims by Gerhard Zucker that his rockets covered a distance of four to nine kilometres, which Schmiedl considered 'cannot be right'. He also expressed his frustration: 'I have written to Calcutta and Berlin and asked them to tell me which distances had been covered, but I have received no replies'.[13]

From the very outset, Schmiedl had set space as the ultimate goal of his experiments. In his memoir, he says 'In the 1920s I started some preliminary rocketry experiments towards spaceflight'.[14] Schmiedl built and tested several rockets between 1928 and 1931, the V1-V8 (V for 'Versuchen' meaning experimental), demonstrating the utility of rockets for the transport of mail, bio experiments using living creatures and scientific instruments to investigate the earth's upper atmosphere. Above all, he honed the technical capability of his rockets to fly precise trajectories over a longer range, coupled with safe recovery and reuse. His earliest attempts with V1 and V2 in 1928 carried covers which announced his intentions: 'The final aim of my experiments are postal rockets and space flight'.[15]

Schmiedl learnt from each launch attempt and by 1931 he gained the trust of the Austrian post office to carry registered letters in his V7, which was launched on 2nd February 1931. This rocket flight is recognised as the first authorised rocket mail flight in history. His V7 transported 102 letters from the Schoeckel mountain near Graz to St Rudegund, five kilometres away. The rocket was stabilised with a gyroscope and equipped with short-wave remote control. It landed safely using a parachute.

5.3 Friedrich Schmiedl in Austria 1931. Credit Museum of Communication, Bern, Switzerland

For its time, the V7 was remarkable for its advanced technology, especially given that it was the work of one man. In the subsequent years, his success encouraged rocket mail testing in countries around the world including Australia, Austria, Belgium, Cuba, Denmark, France, Germany, Holland, Italy, Yugoslavia, Luxembourg, Spain, Switzerland, India and the US.

In April 1931, Schmiedl launched three rockets with home-made instruments, including a spectrograph, to investigate the upper atmosphere and record the performance of his rockets. One rocket he referred to as 'Registering Rocket', was a two-stage rocket where each stage returned to Earth using its own parachute. The first stage carried mail and the second stage carried instruments to measure and record pressure and ultraviolet radiation, a chart recorder for acceleration, and a camera for aerial photographs.

On 9th September 1931, his 1.5 metre-long postal rocket R-1 successfully carried 333 mail items and another 33 'special delivery letters' from Hochtrötsch and then landing by parachute in Semriach 7 km away. In the first of its kind, this rocket contained, what he called "a bio experiment". In addition to the mail, the rocket carried beetles and butterflies in a specially constructed capsule lined with grass and leaves. The condition of the butterflies was unclear, but the beetles were still healthy on landing.[16]

Date	Rocket	Flight	Letters Total	Letters Registered
02/02/1931	V7	Schoeckel to Rudegund	101	0
21/04/1931		'Kalte Rinne'	79	0
09/09/1931	R1	Hochtrötsch to Semriach	333	36
25/10/1931	V8	Grazer Feld	84	(Night test)
28/05/1932	V9	Schoeckel to Rudegund	228	125
28/05/1932	V10	Schoeckel to Rudegund	192	113
11/06/1932	V11	Grazer Feld	28	(Storm test)
23/06/1932	V12	Schoeckel to Kumberg	231	187
23/06/1932	V13	Schoeckel to Kumberg	200	100
16/03/1933	V14	Garrach to Arzberg	283	0

Summary of Schmiedl's launches by 1933. Credit Friedrich Schmiedl

Apart from his innate capabilities, Schmiedl benefited from a high-quality education and brought scientific rigour to his rocket testing. One of his professors was the Nobel Laureate Victor Hess (1883–1964), who had detected radiation coming from space in the stratosphere using high-altitude balloons. Inspired by Hess, Schmiedl used the 1,500m-high mountain Schöckl about 15 km north of Graz as a base for his high-altitude experiments.

Unlike Hess, Schmiedl did not fly in the balloons but used them as rocket launch platforms, which in the 1920s he called Strato-balloons. On 28th May 1928, he launched a hydrogen-filled balloon carrying a 15cm rocket. The rocket was automatically ignited from the balloon at

16,000m. In the tenuous upper atmosphere, the rocket reached an altitude of over 18 km, but it was never recovered. However, the balloon and gondola containing 200 tissue paper envelopes were returned to him after they landed in neighbouring Hungary.

5.4 Friedrich Schmiedl's parachute 1931. Credit Museum of Communication, Bern, Switzerland

Schmiedl[17] was the first to develop and use what he called a Stufenrakete rocket. Launched on 27th December 1933, V-17 and V-18 were known as 'step-rockets' or 'multiple stage rockets'. Two days later, he conducted an experiment to see how mail transport by ship could be enhanced by rockets. At this time the range of a rocket was limited to a few kilometres, so it could not replace the role of a ship delivering mail from one end of the Atlantic to the other. However, once a ship was almost at its destination, a rocket launched from the ship and landing on the shore a few minutes later could potentially save a day or two in the mail delivery process. Schmiedl's launch of two rockets from a ship on Lake Stausee included an experimental catapult. The rocket was placed in a catapult that was released at ignition. The range of the rocket could thus be extended. Schmiedl referred to these flights as Katapultflug - K-1 and K-2.

During his time at the K-1 and K-2 launches on Lake Stausee, Schmiedl experimented with launching a rocket underwater. His design involved a using a two-part ignition system. Initially using a specially designed slow- burning underwater propellent, once above the surface a normal propellent would continue the flight. The attempt was largely unsuccessful, but the 100 numbered covers carried the 'Mit Raketenpost-Katapultflug' (catapult rocket post flight) and a hand written inscription 'Unterwasserstart-Misslungen-Schmiedl' (unsuccessful underwater launch Schmiedl) was added.

Stephen Smith's motivation to experiment with rocket mail in India came not from Schmiedl's 1931 success with the R-7, but from Gerhard Zucker's more limited work in England in early 1934. This work had attracted substantial international press coverage. In his report describing his first rocket experiments, Smith says 'When the first Rocket Dispatches of Austria were being experimented upon in 1931, the general public, including the writer, viewed these early endeavours as short-lived stunts being of little or no practical value. It was not till the first British Rocket firings in June this year that any serious consideration was given to this new method of transporting mails in India by rocket'.[18]

Interestingly, despite Schmiedl's demonstrable success with parachutes, Smith was opposed to their use. In a letter dated 11th October 1937, he stated 'I do not believe in parachutes, never HAVE, a rocket must be independent of atmospherics as far as possible'.[19] He had tried but found it useless, since once the parachute was opened, 'it is at the mercy of the atmosphere and may be carried miles from the spot intended for landing'.[20] Instead, Smith used his time and effort on developing wings, fins and control surfaces to help guide the rocket to a safe landing at a designated point. It was this research that led him to his Boomerang rocket.[21]

Most of Schmiedl's work has been well documented with at least one exception, Schmiedl pursuit of smokeless fuels. Apparently he experimented secretly for some time. This work culminated in two rocket mail experiment conducted on his behalf in Yugoslavia in August 1935. One rocket mail flight, called Jug1 was conducted on 19 August 1935 in the town of Maribor and Jug2 on the following day in the town of Hoce. The 227 covers on the, Jug1 received a pink rocket cachet and a green one on the 282 covers of Jug2.[22]

The timeline of Smith's rocket experiments (including the use of camera, parachute, smokeless fuel and multiple rocket stages) indicates that he was following in Schmiedl's footsteps, as were so many others.

Although he Schmiedl experimented with rockets as early as 1918 and to a limited extent after 1950, his most productive periods were the 7 seven years between 1928 and 1935.[23]. He abandoned all space research after the end of World War II.[24] Writing at the end of World War Two, he expressed his frustration at being sidelined by the Austrian authorities, asserting that his contemporaries '"now hold university professorships. I haven't become anybody"'. He destroyed all his '"scientific instruments and special apparatus to prevent them from being misused for military purposes"'.[25]

William S Sykora

William S Sykora conducted the USA's first rocket mail flight near New York on 22nd September 1935. This was about a year after Stephen Smith conducted his first rocket experiments from a ship on the Hooghly River to Saugor (today known as Sagar) Island. Like Smith, Sykora met only only limited success.

Sykora undertook two flights; the first took place at 16:35 and the second almost an hour later. During both flights the rocket exploded, but the second was a little more successful than the first. In the first flight, the steel rocket had exploded immediately on launch; the second, constructed from aluminium, exploded later in the flight when much of the fuel had been consumed, so the explosion was less intense. Despite the spectators watching from almost 100 metres away, two people were hurt. One, Mr Edward Vozab, was seriously injured and both were taken to hospital.[26]

Each rocket carried 250 covers. Only 28 covers (severely damaged) were recovered from the first flight, but 236 survived from the second. Despite the outcome, in terms of design and construction, Sykora's rockets were technically well ahead of what Stephen Smith was using in India. Smith's rockets, especially at this early stage in 1935, were pretty much rockets supplied to him by commercial firework manufacturers, whereas Sykora had designed, built and repeatedly tested these rockets prior to the launch attempts.

In common with so many early rocket experimenters, Sykora had an interest in science fiction. He was a subscriber to science fiction magazines such as *Amazing Stories* and *Science Wonder Stories*. He was also a member of the International Science Association and for a time was its president.

Gerhard Zucker

Stephen Smith records that his interest in rocket mail was inspired and motivated by Gerhard Zucker.[27] Whereas Friedrich Schmiedl brought scientific and technical rigour to his research in rocketry, his contemporary Gerhard Zucker (1908–1985) from Germany 'was little more than a non-technical business entrepreneur with a slight touch of the visionary'.[28]

Zucker conducted his first rocket experiment on 9th April 1933 at Cruxhaven on Germany's North Sea coast. The rocket belly-flopped and was the first of many failures. During the first half of 1934, he conducted several rocket mail experiments in the Hartz Mountain region of northern Germany, in support of the Winterhilfe (winter social assistance work). He conducted several more day and night experiments in Blankenburg and Halberstadt before departing Germany for England.

The German Air Force, the Luftwaffe, had been disbanded following the First World War and was prevented from developing aircraft for military use. Rockets had not been deployed during World War I and so were not explicitly excluded in the Treaty of Versailles. Thus, Germany was not prevented from developing rockets for military use.

Zucker offered to develop rockets for Germany's military. Unaware of Hitler's secret plan to develop liquid fuel rockets, he asked for 10,000

DM to develop his idea. Zucker's blatant showman attributes and spectacular failures persuaded the authorities to decline the offer.[29]

In the summer of 1934, the Air Post Exhibition (APEX) in London invited him to attend and conduct a rocket launch. At the exhibition he met with stamp dealer C H Dombrowski and together they formed the 'British Rocket Syndicate' with the intention of establishing a regular rocket mail service between Britain and France.[30] Dombrowski claimed that they had raised £50,000 for future flights and planned to recoup the investment through the sale of rocket mail covers. Zucker displayed his aluminium rocket and launching rack at the APEX in May 1934. At the exhibition he met Lord Londonderry and Postmaster General Sir Kingsley Wood.

5.5 *Gerhard Zucker (on the right marked by the letter X) Duhnen, Germany 1933.*
Credit Lore Krame

On Wednesday 6th June 1934, he used the same rocket to conduct two flights in the Brighton and Hove area in southern England.[31] The first flight, carrying 1,400 letters, rose to about 800 metres and covered a distance of 1,500 metres between Rottingdean and Telscombe in Sussex. Once the rocket was recovered, it was recharged and fired again with 1,464 letters. Each letter carried one or more of the Apex Souvenir Exhibition labels, over printed with 'ROCKET POST FIRST BRITISH FLIGHT'.

Apart from Zucker himself, the only other witnesses were C H Dombrowsky, Zucker's representative in Britain; Robert Hartman, press agent; S Sherman, photographer; Raymond Moore from the London Daily Express and Albert Harris from a philatelic magazine. No one else saw the rocket launches. Mail from both flight, which included six covers for King George V were taken to a post in Brighton and delivered using the normal postal service. Neither of the two flights covered the intended distances. Nevertheless, he attracted sufficient interest for the possibility of 'postal rockets' to be raised in the British parliament.[32]

Once he had demonstrated that a rocket could transport mail from one town to another, Zucker planned to use it to send mail between two islands in the Scottish Hebrides. His highly publicised launch on 28th July turned out to be a spectacular failure. Zucker's plan was to demonstrate high-speed communication between isolated Scottish island communities by sending a rocket with mail from the Island of Scarp to the Island of Harris, which were separated by half a mile of sea.

The 14 kg one metre-long solid fuel rocket exploded during the launch attempt, littering the beach with scorched letters and fragments from the rocket.[33] An account in the local paper stated that once the smoke had cleared, 'We could see a tangle of wood and iron: a beach strewn with letters, some of them smouldering, with people running around stamping on the little fires and salvaging the mail; a disconsolate Herr Zucker with his head in his hands'.[34] He repeated the attempt three days later from Harris to Scarp and that attempt also ended in a similar dismal failure.

Zucker's third and final launch attempt in England was planned for 17th December 1934, but the Home Office permit had not arrived. 'I am bitterly disappointed. The rocket I intended to launch today cost me £45', he said to a reporter. Two days later the permit did arrive, and he launched his rocket. He wanted his rocket to be launched from the mainland to land on the Isle of Wight but permission was refused. His rocket had to land in the water of the Solent. He reduced the quantity of propellent to reduce weight and ensure buoyancy.[35] However, a strong wind pushed the rocket back over the mainland rather than south to the Isle of Wight. The letters were removed from the damaged rocket and posted at the Lymington Post Office.[36]

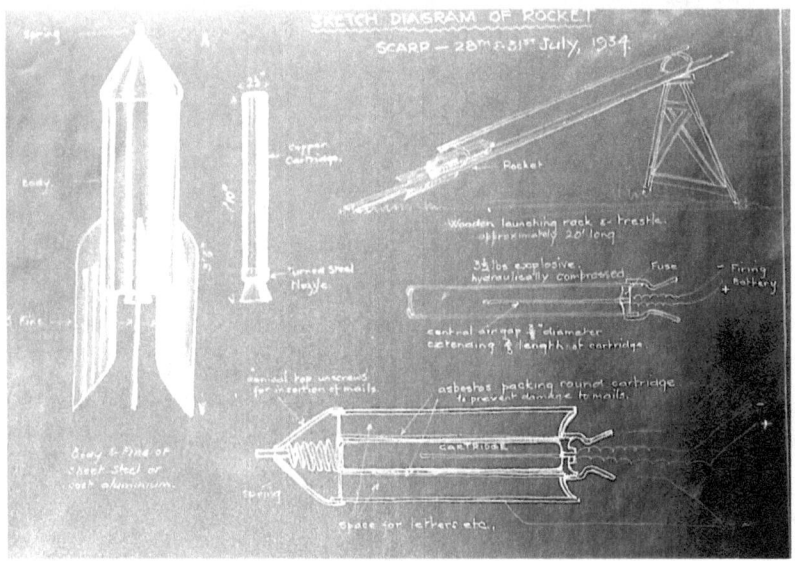

5.6 Sketch of rocket and launch rack designed by Gerhard Zucker. Credit Postal History Museum London

As someone who was actually building and testing rockets, Zucker also attracted interest from the authorities and rocket societies. Whilst in England, he met with Phil Cleator and Professor A P Low from the British Interplanetary Society. Since most of his experiments were failures, his efforts were not highly regarded by serious rocket experimenters.[37] Phil Cleator's records indicate that following his unsuccessful and unauthorised rocket mail experiment in England, Zucker ended up in prison.[38]

In practice, none of Zucker's efforts advanced the science of rocketry significantly, but through his highly publicised exploits, he raised the profile of rockets and rocket mail amongst the general public. He was criticised within the philatelic community for his lack of rigour and for causing reputational harm to the nascent field of rocket mail. During World War II he worked for the German Luftwaffe and after the war ended he became a furniture dealer in West Germany. Later, he returned to testing rockets again and again experienced failure. One tragic demonstration in May 1964 resulted in three fatalities, which led the West German authorities to ban all civilian rocket research.

Zucker was one of rocket mail's more colourful characters. National security was looming large in Europe during the pre-war period of Zucker's visit to Britain. His motivations for coming to Scotland were unclear.[39] He was regarded with suspicion by the British authorities whilst in Scotland and also by the German authorities when he eventually returned to Germany. The spectacular failure in Scotland did not diminish his enthusiasm. His maverick antics are still remembered in Scottish culture, with both plays and films about his activities.[40] Whilst in England, he was arrested after he left a quantity of gunpowder at a railway station cloakroom. He was imprisoned at least twice in Germany, first after he returned from England under suspicion that he had shared military secrets, and secondly when he attempted to return to experimenting with rockets in 1964. His rocket exploded and killed two schoolboys.[41]

Zucker's mostly unsuccessful rocket mail attempts in England during the summer of 1934 were the trigger for Stephen Smith's first experiment in India in September of the same year. In the minds of the authorities, Zucker's spectacular public failures undermined the credibility of such a transport mechanism. This in turn resulted in Smith being unable to attract government support (in England or India) for his own experiments.[42]

Karel Roberti

In the autumn of 1934, Stephen Smith conducted his first rocket experiment in India. At about the same time, Karel Roberti conducted the first rocket mail in the Netherlands. He is documented as being both Dutch and Belgian and flew his rockets in the Netherlands, Luxemburg, Belgium and France. Record of his work indicate that his was a more scientific and quantitative approach than that of Smith's.

Roberti had been working on his ideas of rocket propulsion since 1931, but his first rocket launch took place in December 1934 on the shores of Katwijk-aan-Zee in the Netherlands. He went on to conduct many more tests in, around Europe with mixed results.[43] Like Smith, he had no special training and was initially using commercially available rockets manufactured by A J Kat in Leiden, a company which produced fireworks.

Roberti experimented with rockets, rocket airplanes, recovery by parachute and liquid fuel (carbon dioxide).[44] This is unusual fuel for the time and probably recorded incorrectly. The author notes that there were no witnesses to this launch. His rockets and rocket airplanes were substantial and some had covered a distance of up to 3 km. A rocket he named 'Barbara' was 1.75 metres long with a total weight of 5 kg.

Smith was aware of Roberti's work. A piece appeared in the December 1936 Quarterly Bulletin of the Indian Airmail Society which had originally been published in Belgium. It described Roberti's work and included technical details on speed, exhaust gases, momentum and the scope of his ambitions which included developing interplanetary capability.[45]

Whilst Smith operated under the auspices of the Indian Airmail Society with an established track record in philately, Roberti operated under what appeared to have been a hastily established company, ' Nederlandse Rakettenbouw (NRB - Dutch Rocket Construction Inc). Whilst some of his rockets met with success, his numerous failures attracted public criticism. The Dutch stamp magazine 'Maanblad voor de Philatelie' concluded that he had no scientific background and was just a 'conman'.[46] This was probably one motivation to conduct further rocket experiments abroad. In pursuit of larger publicity and commercial benefit, he sought permission to demonstrate the transport of mail by rocket between Dover in

England and Calais in France. He successfully gained the consent of the authorities in Dover but not from Calais, so he was unable to proceed.[47]

The Nederlandse Rakettenbouw was owned by stamp dealer Gerard Thoolen. His primary motive was 'to peddle the covers at high prices'.[48] Gerhard Zucker's spectacular failure in Scotland had attracted headlines such as 'Rocket Rackets' which gave rocket mail a poor public image.

Following Roberti's tests and the public criticism that followed, Francis Field, a well-known philatelist and publisher in the UK, commented in September 1935 that 'there are "rackets" in every popular philatelic speciality'. He went on to explain that there are 'serious exponents in rocketry' who conduct experiments patiently for years before engaging in public demonstrations. He also notes that the rocket's future is 'assured, not just postally but for other commercial and military purposes'.[49]

Roberti and Smith each came to rocket mail testing from similar but not identical perspectives. Both had limited technical skills, limited resources and used the media of the day to promote their work, while funding it through the sale of rocket mail covers. Smith was an established international philatelist when he embarked on rocket mail testing in 1934. Roberti's approach was more overtly commercial and had no roots in philately.

Willy Ley

One of the key event that validated the faith that Stephen Smith and others had in rocket mail took place on the cold mid-winter morning of 23rd February in 1936. It was a joint venture between the Rocket Airplane Corporation of America and the German rocketry societies, and the first rocket-powered airplane was flown in the USA. The five metre-long aircraft 'Gloria', which had a four metre wingspan, was brought on toboggans to the then-frozen Greenwood Lake about 100 km north of New York. The public audience numbered about 500, many of whom had purchased small stamps and affixed them to postcards or letters. Prior to the flight, the postal items were housed in an asbestos bag and placed in the nose cone of the aircraft.[50]

The plane had been built by the German Rocket Society and designed by its president Willy Ley, a fugitive from Hitler's Third Reich who left Germany in 1935 to make the US his home.[51]

The plane was brought on to the thick ice of the frozen lake, in a launch rack inclined at 20 degrees. On 23rd February 1936, dressed in a protective asbestos suit, Ley lit the fuse to launch the aircraft. This first launch was not a success. With the aid of the rocket motor and the catapult it achieved an altitude of about 15 metres before falling back to Earth. The German team was prepared for this eventuality and had brought a second plane with them. Once the postal cargo was recovered and placed in the second plane, christened 'Gloria II', its launch was more successful. The second flight achieved a slighter higher elevation and including multiple touchdowns as it skidded to a halt about 700 metres from the launch site.

5.7 First rocket mail in USA 23 February 1936. Credit Art Lizotte

The postal cargo consisted of more than 6,000 postcards and letters carried with privately printed commemorative labels. They sold for 50 or 75 cents, which helped to fund the experiment. The envelopes also carried a purple stamp 'Via rocket airplane Gloria' but dated 9th February, which had been the original target date for the launch. Greenwood Lake is long and narrow, running north (New York) to south (New Jersey). In addition to being the first rocket airplane flight in the USA, it was also the first flight to carry mail across state boundaries.

Willy Ley signed many of the flown covers on the day of the flight. He was one of the many individuals who had been inspired into rocketry by Hermann Oberth's book *Die Rakete zu den Planetenräumen* (The Rocket into Interplanetary Space). He was one of the first members of Germany's amateur rocket group, the Verein für Raumschiffahrt (VfR – Society for Spaceflight), established in 1927. Ley wrote many popular articles in German newspapers during the late 1920s and went on to write many critical books on rocketry.

5.8 Left to Right. Heinz Haber, Wernher von Braun and Willy Ley 1954. Credit NASA

Supported by Phil Cleator, who founded the British Interplanetary Society in 1933, Willy Ley headed for the USA but made a stop-over in Britain.⁵² During his brief visit to Liverpool in February 1935, he gave a presentation to the BIS,⁵³ speaking about his plans to build a rocket-powered airplane for the delivery of mail between New York and London, and even outlined plans to reach the Moon. He settled in the USA, where he received the support of the founder of the American Rocketry Society, Edward Pendray.⁵⁴

Despite the success on Greenwood Lake, Ley later concluded that rocket mail was a 'gimmick' and that using rockets for meteorological research was a more scientifically sound proposition. He was, however, convinced of the potential of rockets for space travel and believed that he could make the necessary technological enhancements required for space travel in his lifetime, given sufficient time and financial support.⁵⁵

There are no records that show Smith corresponded directly with Ley, but both Ley and Smith were in contact with Robert Paganini. They would certainly have been aware of each other's activities, since they were both members of the British Interplanetary Society. Ley had a richer pedigree in the science of rockets, through his research and development work in rocketry during his time in the VfR in Germany. At the time, Ley was probably one of the leading rocket scientists in the world. It must have been encouraging for Smith to see someone of international repute like Ley devoting his efforts to the development of rocket mail.

6

ROCKET MAIL IN INDIA

First Indian rocket mail

The phrase 'Rocket's red glare' in the American national anthem was inspired by rockets developed in India by Tipu Sultan in the late eighteenth century. After his defeat in 1799 at the Battle of Srirangapatna (also known as Srirangapatinam), Tipu's rockets were taken to England and enhanced by William Congreve. These rockets were then used by the British in the Napoleonic Wars and the Battle of Waterloo. They were also used by the British in 1814 during the Battle of Baltimore in the American War of Independence. It is widely believed that the development of rocketry in India did not start again until the start of India's space programme in 1963. But this is not so. Three decades earlier, Stephen Smith was testing rockets in the suburbs of Calcutta.[1]

Stephen Smith had been motivated less by the success of Friedrich Schmiedl's first rocket mail demonstration in 1931 and more by that of Gerhard Zucker in southern England on 6th June 1935.[2] It was three months after Zucker's work that Smith conducted his first experiment. He chose Saugor Island (today it is spelt Sagar Island) which is 125 km from Calcutta. Typically, it took about five days to get to even in good weather and nine if the conditions were bad. The objective of his rocket experiments was to demonstrate their ability to quickly transport mail to Saugor Island from a passing ship. Using this technique, he estimated that mail could be delivered four days earlier or eight in bad weather conditions.

Smith may also have been motivated by the emergency airmail service between Jacobabad (in the Sind province of modern Pakistan) and Reti, following a period in which severe floods had washed away roads and bridges.[3] It was facilitated by the RAF between 10th August and 9th September 1930 and operated until an alternative ground infrastructure was re-established.

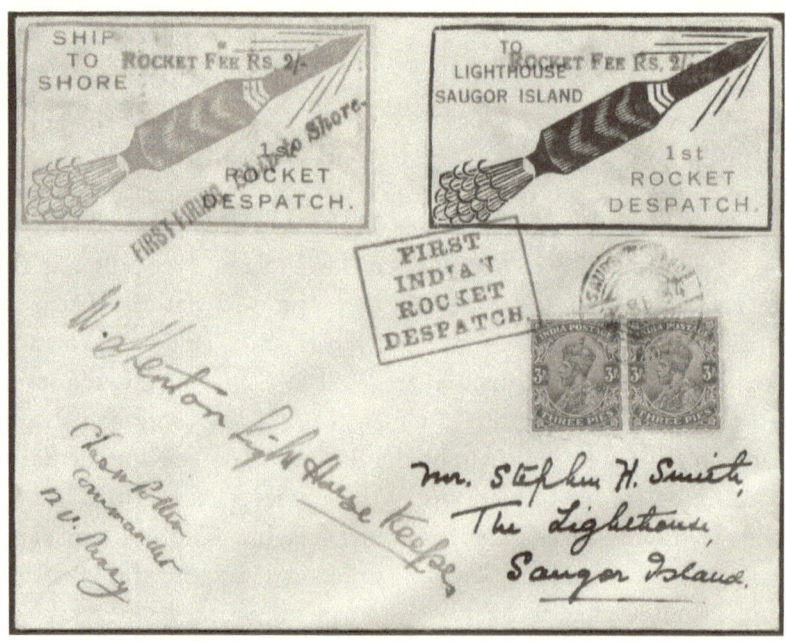

6.1 First Rocket Mail Experiment in India 30 September 1934. Credit Sparks Auctions

On Sunday 30th September 1934 at 15:30 the first experimental rocket to carry mail in India was launched from a ship called 'Dispatch Vessel Pancy' on the Hooghly River. The rocket was intended to deliver mail across the water to Saugor Island. Instead, it exploded in mid-air shortly after launch, or 'burst', as Stephen Smith described it in his diary. The 143 covers rained down into the river. This was Stephen Smith's first foray into rocket mail.

A second launch attempt also failed, not even leaving the launch rack. The third generated sparks which resulted in a minor injury to Smith. It was one of a few that he would endure over the decade of testing. Towards the end of the day, he left the ship for Saugor Island and conducted his first test on land. Even though this rocket only travelled 122 meters a third of the intended distance, he considered it a success because it did not burst.

At 10:30 on 1st October, Smith conducted a launch which also resulted in a mid-air burst. He expressed his frustration by noting in his diary that he 'got absolutely fed up'.[4] Of the two tests on 2nd October, one burst in mid-air but the other covered a distance of over 2 km and was probably his most successful launch of the whole trip.

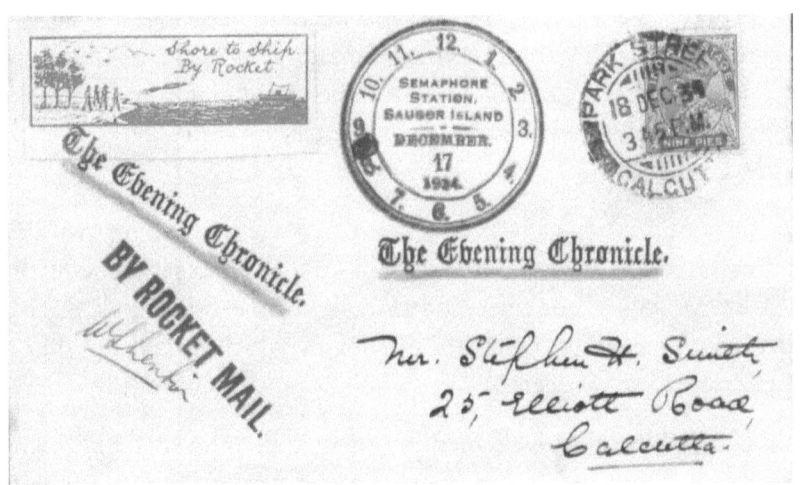

6.2 First Shore to Ship Rocket mail experiment 17 December 1934. Credit Sparks Auctions

On 3rd October he attempted two launches from shore-to-ship; one burst over the river and the other did not burst but missed its target, the RSV Guide, by over a kilometre and was thus considered a failure. The mail had been secured in a waterproof container and was recovered from the river as arranged. On 4th October, Smith attempted to launch a mail-carrying rocket from ship to shore once again, this time from Diamond Harbour on the Hooghly River, about 30 km north of Saugor Island. Once again, a mid-air burst left him 'very, very disheartened'.[5]

Despite the mixed level of success, through these early tests Smith attracted significant international recognition. His experiments were covered by the international press with headlines such as 'Ship-to-Shore Mail Delivery Success' in the Mercury newspaper in the USA[6] and 'Rocket Post Experiments' in the Sunday Times in Britain.[7] In addition to placing his work on the international stage, it attracted collectors of flown rocket mail covers from beyond India.

Smith sent four flown covers on his first rocket test to King George V, but the King was not as enthusiastic as he had hoped. The four covers were returned to him because 'His Majesty does not wish to acquire them'.[8] This was an exception. In practice, Smith was dealing with a boom in demand for rocket mail covers. In a letter to the Swiss philatelist Robert Paganini he says: 'The demand for Indian rocket mails is very, very heavy, I am getting letters from people all over the world for them'.[9]

On December 16th, 1934, he returned to Saugor Island for two days and repeated the Ship-to-Shore and Shore-to-Ship experiments with a total of 13 rocket launches. The first night-time firing took place at 20:45 during a heavy swell in the Hooghly which caused the ship to pitch from 15 to 80 degrees.

His collapsible firing rack, despite being frail, proved to be highly effective.[10] The first three firings on the 16th were from Ship-to-Shore; all made the journey to the island successfully and were retrieved from 'the jungle' by the lighthouse keeper with the aid of lanterns. Two of the rockets carried 220 miniature copies of the newspaper *The Statesman*.[11] Following the three Ship-to-Shore firings, he conducted a further three firings on Saugor Island itself that constituted his first night-time rocket tests on land. The following day he carried out a further five firings during daylight and three after dark. These tests were designed to establish rocket performances by varying the weight carried, the angle and the direction of launch relative to the wind strength and direction.

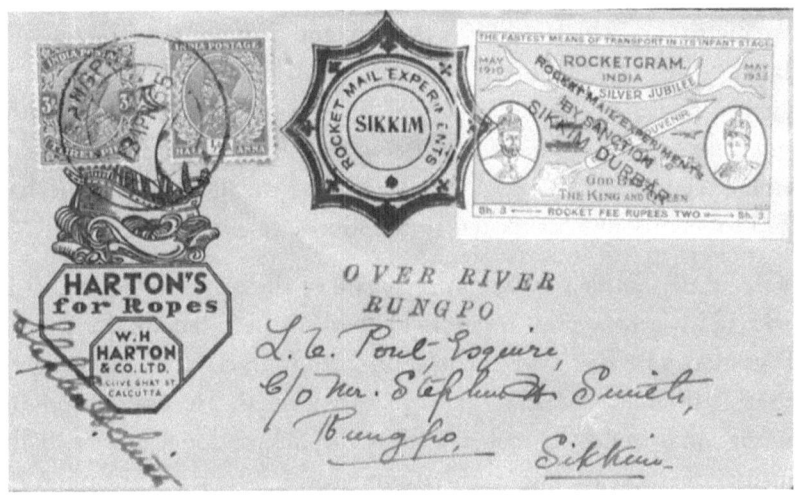

6.3 Rocket Mail in Sikkim 13 April 1935. Carrying advertising for a rope manufacturer. Credit Sparks Auctions

The first rocket test in 1935 took place on 28th February in Dakhuria, just south of Calcutta. The Calcutta press had requested this demonstration and Smith accepted, believing that it would be an opportunity to showcase his rockets to a larger audience. Unfortunately, the resulting failure was magnified by the vivid reports that resulted.

Smith had arranged to launch three rockets for the event. Two were particularly large at about 18 feet (approximately 3 m but likely to be an error), with the propellant cartridges alone weighing 7 kg[12]. The first one to be fired was relatively smaller. It left the rack but burst when in mid-air, scattering 250 covers over the ground. The second, one of the two 'gigantic' rockets, bellowed out lots of sparks and dark smoke and then slowly moved up the rack, only to fall off and lay still on the ground. The third (the other gigantic rocket) failed even to leave the rack. It bellowed out sparks and black smoke to such an extent that the rack itself melted and collapsed.

Despite this complete failure during this high profile event, Smith was not discouraged and continued his testing in 1935. He returned to Diamond Harbour on 23rd March and conducted Seven test flights, two flights in Behalla on 27th March and five in Tangara on 30th March. These flights, in the south of Calcutta were designed to establish rocket performances under varying conditions, to satisfy the 'very, very heavy' demand for flown rocket mail and to generate income to support his work. As 1935 was the Jubilee year, he had plans to incorporate his rockets in the Jubilee celebrations.

At this time, Smith was becoming aware of the early developments in rocketry in Europe and America. He had seen the remarkable growth of air transport that had emerged in his lifetime. However, progress was still slow, hazardous, expensive and limited. He understood the international trends in rocketry from the international press and the journals of international organisations of which he was a member. He was persuaded that the future of high-speed transport lay in rocketry. But first, this rocket technology had to mature and become safe, accurate and reliable, and he was convinced that he could play a part in achieving this in India.

Through his own experiences in Calcutta, he was familiar with the danger to life and property from flooding associated with the annual monsoon. Emergencies such as earthquakes and drought were also not unusual in the region of West Bengal. During his childhood in Assam, he appreciated the difficulty of transport in undulating mountainous regions. By 1934, he had already contacted the King of Sikkim asking to demonstrate how rocket transport might be used in such a Himalayan terrain.[13]

First Visit to Sikkim

Stephen Smith visited the kingdom of Sikkim twice in 1935. On the first visit between 7th and 13th April, he conducted 25 rocket tests and another 15 between 27th September and 4th October 1935. In addition to Gangtok, the capital, Smith conducted his rocket flights in Sarumsa, Ray, Singtam and Rangpo.

Smith had written to the King in January 1935 formally requesting permission to conduct his experiments in Sikkim and to print four special rocket stamps that he used on the covers flown during his visit. Whilst in Sikkim, Smith engaged the active participation of the King of Sikkim (Sir Tashi Namgyal), the General Secretary (C E Dudley), the Private Secretary (Tashi Dadul Densapa), the Sikkim Postmaster (R P Rai) and the Political Officer (F Williamson). These individuals witnessed the launches, autographed some of the covers they carried and, in some instances, ignited the rockets.

6.4 Rocket Mail in Sikkim 13 April 1935. Carrying advertising for a rope manufacturer. Credit Sparks Auctions

His visit to Sikkim was particularly successful. He was able to engage the participation of the King, and none of the experiments resulted in a mid-air burst or a failed to launch. The sixth firing, rocket number 52, at 15:35 on April 10th, established a new world record for the transport of parcel by means of a rocket. The parcel carried 12 items including a packet of tea, sugar, a spoon, handkerchief, toothbrush, cigarettes, and other items. The parcel rocket was dispatched over the River Rani Khola from Surumasa to Ray. After crossing the river, Smith opened the parcel to find the contents intact. On the missives the word 'mail' was cancelled by hand and replaced by the word 'parcel'.[14]

6.5 Postmaster loading mail in to the rocket in Gangtok. 7 April 1935 Sikkim.
Credit Museum of Communication, Bern, Switzerland

A file dated 1934 entitled 'Proposed visit of Mr Stephen Smith' is preserved in the state archive in the Sikkim capital, Gangtok. It is a testimony to the bureaucracy of the time. The file contains some of the correspondence between the King, the Sikkim Political Officer, and Smith. Smith sought the king's permission and wrote to him directly, addressing his letters to 'His Highness the Maharajah of Sikkim'.

The exchanges between Smith, the Political Officer and the King's staff recorded in the file indicate that Smith had found influential individuals who were supportive of his vision of rocket mail. Intriguingly, following his successful April 1935 visit, Smith sent the King some photos of the rocket launch but in July the king declined the offer, and the photos were returned.[15]

Smith designed the various stamps and covers that he flew on board his rockets. To raise the prestige and collectability of his flown stamps and covers, Smith successfully sought official sanction from the King for his personally designed covers. This in part would also increase their monetary value and their desirability amongst collectors, especially on the international market. Smith's activities were covered by the local Indian press and some international press.

On 11th April 1935, following a successful firing of his rocket number 54 in the presence of the King of Sikkim, a certificate was awarded to him by Mr C E Dudley from the Indian Civil Service. This was a formal high-level recognition that, 'The utility of Rockets as a means of transport during floods and landslips has been clearly demonstrated'. This was possibly the only formal acknowledgement of Smith's work with rockets and rocket mail in his lifetime.[16]

Rockets and Living Creatures

In 1783, a ground-dwelling animal was taken to an altitude of 500m and experienced being airborne. The animal was a sheep, which the Montgolfier brothers included in their tethered balloon test, along with a cockerel and duck.

The advent of balloons and especially that enabled high altitude research. What were the conditions of temperature, pressure and wind speeds in the atmosphere? Were the conditions hostile or benign for life? In January 1934 edition of Advance Daily, carried a piece entitled Germ Hunt by Airplane. The piece described an experiment conducted in Cambridge England that concluded "high altitude wind currents could carry germs and disease including foot and mouth from one country to another." The experiment also revealed that "at times the concentration of germs at higher altitudes was higher than at lower altitude."[17]

Within the international aero-philatelic community, Stephen Smith is well known for his rocket Number 65 fired on 29th June 1935. This rocket carried a chick called Adam and a hen named Eve, flying over the River Damodar, north west of Calcutta. He conducted a further three rocket flights carrying living creatures: another small bird in September 1935, a snake in September 1936 and two mice in September 1937.[18]

The rocket that carried the mice was one of Smith's larger rockets (7 ft 2 ins or 2.1 m) with four compartments; hence he called it the 'rocket train'. The rocket had large wings and an unusual cargo: mail, an apple, a small bottle of Long John whisky and two mice whom he dubbed Mr and Mrs Mousie. In a letter to Leslie Johnson on 11th October 1937, he offers to sell the bottles of flown Long John whisky to the whisky manufacturers, if Johnson was able to put him in contact with them.

The compartment in the rocket that carried the birds Adam and Eve had some holes for air and very basic padding for the very short journey. Despite the extreme acceleration and fairly hard landing without a parachute on the sandy beach, both birds survived. The rocket was fitted with gliding vanes and a tail fin which increased its range and reduced the impact speed at landing. The rocket flight of 850 metres concluded with the rocket sliding along the beach for about 15 metres on landing.[19]

According to Smith, the fact that the chick and hen survived was a down to 'Sheer Luck with a capital L. The wind and the soft sand helped me. These were in my opinion the greatest factors to the birds being alive'.[20] He notes with the prefix 'not for publication' that the rocket had three cartridges for propulsion, but one had dropped out and was used on subsequent firings. Had it not dropped out, the birds may not have survived the longer journey. Both birds were thriving 18 months later when Smith visited them at his patron Sir David Ezra's private zoo in Calcutta.[21]

The rocket carried 189 yellowish covers with a Rs. 2 stamp and a special yellow rectangular stamp reading 'Rocket Parcel Dispatch R. No 65 Livestock' along with a violet rectangular cachet reading 'By Rocket David Ezra R. No. 65 Livestock'. Stephen Smith named many of his rockets, especially those that marked some specific unique achievement. The names he chose were the names of individuals he held in high regard and included his benefactor David Ezra, the philatelist Robert Paganini in Switzerland and Marianne Kronstein, the daughter of a New York based philatelist Max Kronstein.

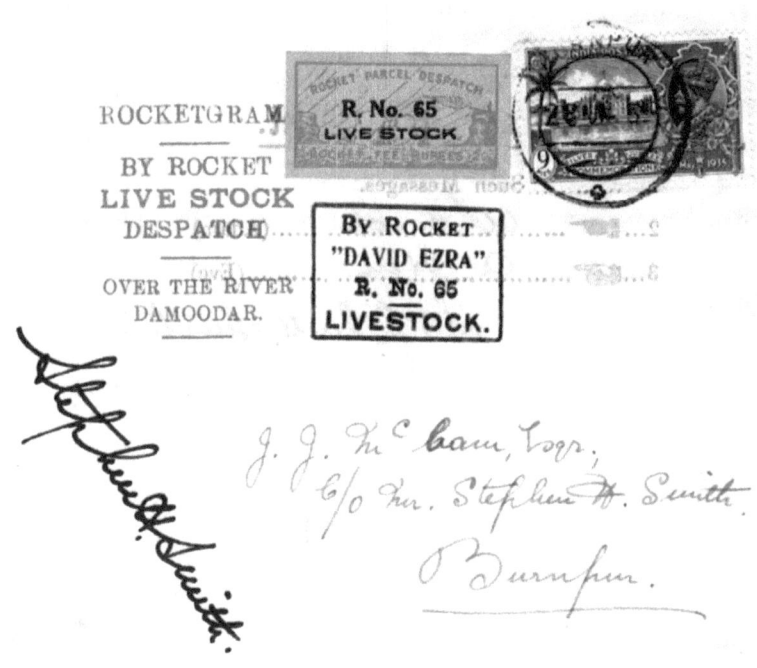

6.6 Cover carried in number 65. Livestock experiment on 29 June 1935. Credit Ramu M Srinivasa

The transport of livestock made headlines in both national and international newspapers. The 9th August 1936 edition of the San Francisco Examiner carried details of this flight under the headline 'The First Rocket Ship to carry Living Passengers'.[22] The August 1936 edition of the American Weekly concluded 'This puts India, one of the world's least inventive nations, ahead even of America which usually heads the procession'.[23]

Smith was a member of The British Interplanetary Society, one of the many rocketry societies that emerged in the early 1930s around the world. The success of rocket number 65 was reported in its publication *Journal of the British Interplanetary Society*: 'What is said to be the first transportation by rockets of animate objects is claimed for Mr S H Smith, our new Calcutta member'.[24] However, this was not true. On 9th September 1931, Friedrich Schmiedl had earlier conducted a rocket flight in which he transported beetles and butterflies. The beetles were well enough to scuttle away once his rocket R1 had returned to Earth using a parachute.[25]

Schmiedl's rocket was altogether more substantial, 1.5 m long with a diameter of 24.5 cm. At launch it weighed over 30 kg and the flight covered a distance of 7 km.[26] But it was Smith whose exploits attracted much more international public attention and he is still widely but incorrectly, considered to be the first to use rocket propulsion to transport living creatures.

6.7 Helpers at Damodar River Rocket 66. 29 June 1936. Credit Private Collection of Leslie Johnson, Liverpool, England

The experiments in transporting living creatures using only rocket propulsion by Schmiedl and Smith were pioneering achievements, but were overshadowed by what came later. During the 1950s, numerous biological experiments were conducted in the USA using captured V2 missiles from Germany. Mice, hamsters, fruit flies, cats, dogs, frogs and guinea pigs were all taken to extreme high altitudes by rockets with a power that Schmiedl and Smith could only dare to imagine. On 20th

February 1947, fruit flies were taken to an altitude of 109 km and after landing were recovered and found to be both alive and healthy. These flies were probably the first life forms to visit space.[27] During a seven-day mission to the Moon, the USSR's 'Zond 5 Mission' carried the first living creatures to the vicinity of the Moon. It was launched on 14th September 1968 and the algae, bacteria, fruit fly eggs and two tortoises survived the splashdown in the Indian ocean.[28]

Second Visit to Sikkim

Smith wrote to King of Sikkim on 14th August 1935, requesting a visit to Sikkim between 25th September and 15th October to 'carry out further rocket mail experiments'.[29] He also sought official sanction for a proposed 'rocket label and stamp' for the rocket mail he proposed to include in his rocket mail experiments. In addition, he sought the King's consent to bring his wife and son Hector with him. The King agreed.

6.8 Rocket number 87 with the Sikkim Postmaster General R P Rai 1 October 1935. Credit Piyush Khaitan

During this second visit he conducted 15 rocket launches between 27th September and 4th October 1935. By this time, his rocket design and construction had evolved; many of his rockets now had a metal construction and were fitted with gliding vanes and stabilising fins.

Following Indian independence in 1947, Sikkim first became a Protectorate of India and then following an almost peaceful plebiscite on 4th April 1975, Sikkim formally became part of India.

6.9 Rocket 84 Gangtok Sikkim 28 September 1935. Credit Private collection of Leslie Johnson, Liverpool, England

It was one of the smallest and least populated states in India and, according to the 2001 Provisional Census, had a population of 5.4 million between its four districts of Gangtok, Geyzing, Namchi and Mangan. It had been ruled by a monarch during the colonial period but in the mid-seventeenth century it became a British Protectorate. Situated in the foothills of the Himalayas, it is blessed with some of the world's most beautiful and challenging landscapes on Earth. Sikkim has a predominantly rural economy, with tourism playing a key role, and it enjoys a reasonable level of political stability. This mountainous region lying in the shadow of the Himalayas was an ideal terrain for testing transport using rocket power.

Sikkim was the first place in the world to issue official rocket mail parcel postage stamps. A total of 5,000 Rocketgram stamps were printed, 1,000 of which were used during the experiments in Sikkim. To record the unique nature, the stamps were overprinted with 'PARCEL'. Writing in 1980, one collector concluded that of the 1,000, only 11 could be accounted for.[30]

The first launch at 16:00 on 27th September was a parcel containing an eclectic mixture of items, useful in an emergency: 1. Dried sea horse; 2. Glass tube of Carter's Liver pills; 3. A tube of euthymol tooth paste; 4. A box of matches; 5. A tin of Rofein; 6. A cake of soap; 7. 190 messages[31]. The second launch at 13:00 on 28th September contained a single chick and 155 messages. Rocket number 88, launched at 09:15, carried another parcel containing quinine, Pepsodent, iodine, butter, cigarettes, matches and 166 messages. Rocket 89 was the last one to carry mail during this second Sikkim visit, and it was the first to be fired by the King's daughter, Princess Pemtsidon, who also signed some of the covers that it carried. In total, the eight rockets carried 1,274 covers.[32]

6.10 *The King of Sikkim with rocket 86 1 October 1935. Credit Piyush Khaitan*

Permission to enter Sikkim ostensibly required the King's consent, but in practice was provided by the designated Political Officer. As a British Protectorate in the 1930s, the authority of the British Empire in Sikkim was expressed through the role of the Political Officer, a role first established in the 1880s when it was held by John Claude White.[33] Formally, Smith sought permission from the King of Sikkim, but the mandatory frontier permit was authorised by the Political Officer, Frederick Williamson.[34] The 42-year-old Williamson, the son of a telephone engineer from Lancashire and member of the Indian Civil Service, was appointed two years before Smith's arrival in Sikkim. In her memoirs, Williamson's wife recalled Smith's visit, writing that a 'rather more unusual visitor was a man named Stephen Smith, who at the time was pioneering a rather far-fetched scheme for sending letters across the Himalayan valleys by rocket'.[35]

The second visit to Sikkim was equally as successful as the first. Unlike the visit in April, the formal recognition of his work was not repeated. However, in dealing with both the King of Sikkim and Frederick Williamson, Smith had connected with authority figures who shared his optimism on the potential of rocket-powered transport. Frederick Williamson died in November 1935 following a short chronic illness whilst visiting Lhasa. In addition to Sikkim, he also served as the Political Officer for Bhutan and Tibet. Had Williamson not died, Smith would probably have conducted his rocket mail experiments in Tibet and Bhutan too.[36]

Earthquake and Floods

Challenging terrain is one scenario where rapid transport by rocket is a solution. Another is at times of natural disasters which compromise roads and communication infrastructure. Within a year of Smith's first rocket experiment, a natural disaster resulting in enormous loss of life provided Smith with an opportunity to demonstrate the potential life-saving utility of rocket transport.

At around 15:00 on Friday 31st May 1935, the town of Quetta suffered an earthquake of a magnitude 7.7. It is estimated that between 30,000 and 60,000 lives were lost as a result. The 12,000 empire troops lived in a cantonment area which was built on firmer grounds and suffered fewer casualties.[37] Located more than 2,000 kilometres to the west of Calcutta in modern Pakistan, Quetta's mountainous topography was very similar to that of Sikkim.

The collapse of the transport infrastructure such as roads, bridges and railways compounded the distress and suffering by hindering the prompt delivery of aid. This was just the sort of scenario for which Smith considered rocket transport could be the solution. The scale of this particular incident was vast and would have posed a severe challenge even for a modern state equipped with twenty-first century technologies.

```
                    QUETTA  CAMP.
                    H.Q., WESTERN COMMAND.
                    Saturday, 8th June 1935.

Dear Sir David & Lady Ezra,

        As you are no doubt aware, the civil
city of Quetta has been wiped out, with about
30,000 killed.   The British casualties were
200 killed and 200 wounded.
        Thank God my wife and I escaped with
our lives, and although we have been shaken up,
we are as well as can be expected under these
trying circumstances.
```

6.11 Letter from Sargent Cohen to Lady Ezra 8 June 1935. Credit Neil Donen

Motivated by the plight of the victims of the earthquake, Stephen Smith carried out several rocket firings to demonstrate that they could provide aid in an emergency. On 6th June, Smith repeated his parcel post experiments by firing two rockets, number 60 and 61, from

Kolaghat over the River Roopnarain to Deulti. Rocket 60 carried a sample of items that stranded victims might need in the aftermath of an earthquake.

6.12 Rocket John Winterton. 21 September 1936. Credit Private collection of Leslie Johnson, Liverpool, England

The rocket was small and the quantities were limited but sufficient to illustrate the principle. They included uncooked rice, turmeric, cloves, chillies and biris (cigarettes). One hundred covers with a special Rs. 2 stamp 'Quetta Earthquake Relief Rocket' in red and blue were also carried. Each cover was impressed with a violet date cachet from the

Kolaghat Station Master and the second from Smith himself, a three line reddish cachet reading 'R. No. 60 over River Roopnarain Kolaghat'.[38]

Rocket 61 was fired immediately after Rocket 60. Addressing the need for medical supplies at times of emergency, it carried lint, iodine, Iodex, Lucasprin, Haliverol, Epsom salts, bandages and 110 yellow covers. It too made a successful journey across the river and, because it caught some tail wind, travelled further. These covers were nearly identical to those carried by Rocket 60, with the exception that the stamp had a prominent red cross in the centre. All the proceeds from the sale of the covers went to the Viceroy who had set up a relief fund for the victims of the earthquake disaster.

Rocket transport could also help with recurring crises, not just unexpected ones. The monsoon season in north east India starts around May or June and recedes from northern India in early October. During an actual flood on 9th June 1936, Smith launched rocket number 126 in central Calcutta. He deployed what he called a 'telescopic rocket', a rocket design that allowed its size to vary in order to accommodate variable loads. The small quantities of dahl, rice and chillies it carried once again demonstrated the ability to transport food to areas that have become isolated. It also carried 80 covers with black on yellow labels bound by a black double line cachet: 'Telescopic Rocket 126'.

Just before the monsoons ended, Smith completed the second flood firing on 21st September 1936 from Chringripotat to Malikpur. Rocket number 127, with large wings, had an unusual cargo of mail, including a snake and an apple.[39] The rocket was recovered and the snake, which he named 'Miss Creepy' was healthy and escaped into the bushes close to the recovery site. Each of the 160 mail covers bore a dark red label and a cachet summarising the details of the rocket posts and the items it carried.

The monsoon in the following year was just as traumatic. In August 1937, Smith was building another he called the 'rocket train'. Writing to Leslie Johnson in Liverpool, he confesses 'I am at times sixes &

sevens at the moment building my rocket train, my nerves are on edge. I try and cool myself down by gardening and playing with my dog. I shall have no rest until I complete my experiment'.[40] The design involved multiple compartments so that it could carry segregated multiple types of cargo in the same vehicle. August is the middle of the rainy season, which in some years can be very intense.

Smith considered he had shown the way to mitigating the effects of the monsoon for ordinary Indians. In the midst of the monsoon in 1938 he shared his frustration in a letter to Leslie Johnson, saying: 'although I have demonstrated the utility of the rocket during the monsoons, the government, or the people in power will not introduce anything NEW'.[41]

7

SPECIAL EVENT ROCKET MAIL

Silver Jubilee 1935

In 1977, Queen Elizabeth II celebrated her Silver Jubilee. It was a huge international event involving the countries of the Commonwealth. Royal events attracted huge public attention in the past, as they do today. In 1935 King George V (Queen Elizabeth II's grandfather) marked his silver jubilee. Smith was always seeking an opportunity to demonstrate rocket mail publicly and acquire support for his experiments. For Smith this jubilee was timely.

In 1901 Queen Victoria died and ended one of history's longest and eventful reigns. She was followed by her son Edward VII, who took over a vast empire encompassing almost a quarter of the earth's land surface and a fifth of its population. His reign was brief; on 6th May 1910, he died and his son, Victoria's grandson, took the throne as George V of the United Kingdom and the British Dominions, and Emperor of India. He reigned through the tumult and carnage of WWI and celebrated his Silver Jubilee in 1935.

The intervening 25 years had been a testing and turbulent time for people all over the world. The Ottoman and Austria-Hungarian empire had ended. Millions had died in World War I, and millions more through the Spanish flu epidemic of 1918–1919. Those who had survived then had to endure the financial chaos and privations of the great depression of 1929. However, there was cause for optimism too: women had won the right to vote, telephones, radio and television transformed communication, and high-speed rail travel, personal automobiles and regular scheduled flights connected people around the globe as never before. The atom was understood in detail for the first time and Albert Einstein became the first global poster boy for science.

7.1 Silver Jubilee. Cover addressed to L. V. Pont. A former member of the Indian Air Mail Society. Credit Sparks Auctions

On 30th July 1934, the British Parliament formally established that the King's 25th year would be celebrated as a Silver Jubilee. The date, 6th May 1935, was declared as a public holiday across the United Kingdom and the Empire in celebration. Sixty countries around the world produced new postage stamps, including India, which issued five stamps to mark the occasion.

A Silver Jubilee Fund was established to receive all the proceeds at an informal meeting at the Viceroy's house in New Delhi on 22nd November 1934. Four charities were selected to receive the funds: the Red Cross India, St John's Ambulance Association, the Countess of Dufferin's Fund and the Indian Army Benevolent Association. All funds raised were collected by local organising committees and passed on to the central organising committee. In the end, more than £100 million was raised.[1]

For a philatelist and the only one experimenting with rockets in India, Smith would have been aware of the potential value of launching his rockets as part of the Jubilee celebrations. It would let him connect with the higher echelons of society, stock up on his flown covers to sell and raise his public profile.

On 23rd March 1935, Smith returned to Diamond Harbour and conducted four Ship-to-Shore launches to commemorate the Jubilee. Two of these rockets carried 100 commemorative Jubilee covers each. A special blue and yellow stamp to the value of Rs. 2 was created for this occasion and bound to the cover with a diamond shaped violet cachet reading 'Royal Silver Jubilee 1935'. At the very centre of the cachet was the word "ROCKETGRAM" with one crown above and another below. All of the covers were signed by Smith, but a few were also signed by D D King, the Customs Officer at Diamond Harbour.

It was not just Smith in India who was marking the Jubilee with rocket mail. Alan H Young conducted two firings in Australia, with rockets called Zodiac and Orion. The Zodiac was fired at 07:00 on 28th October 1935. It did not go entirely to plan; the 400 letters and 100 postcards subsequently had to be fished out of the Moggill River. The second flight was postponed to February 1936 but it met a similar fate, and the mail items had to be recovered from the river once again.[2]

Coronation Rockets

A year after celebrating his Silver Jubilee, George V was dead, precipitating a very rare occurrence: in 1936, Britain had three Kings, George V, Edward VIII and George VI. George V died on 20th January 1935 and Edward VIII came to the throne on the same day. Just 326 days later, he abdicated. George VI stepped in immediately, agreeing to be crowned on 12th May 1937, the date originally chosen for Edward VII's enthronement.

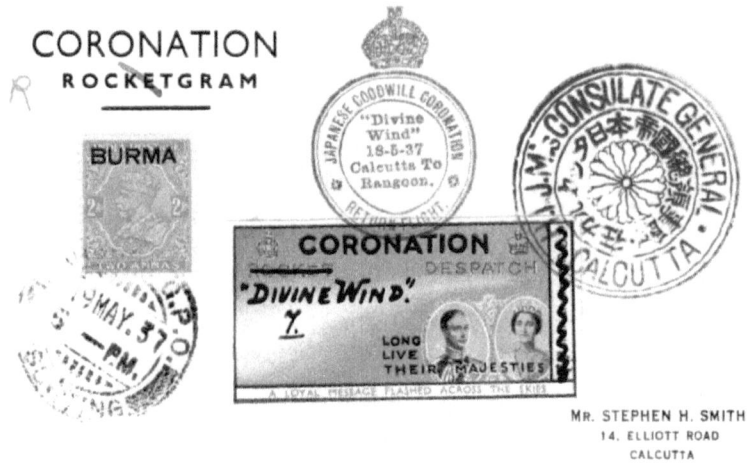

7.2 Coronation Rocket with a special vignette tied with cachets of the Japanese consulate. Credit Ramu M Srinivasa

Stephen Smith marked this coronation with the launch of two rockets, a small pilot rocket Number 141 followed by the Coronation Rocket which had the same number, 141. Both were launched early in the morning from Alipore in the presence of the public, including children and representatives of the press. The small pilot rocket, designed to detect the wind speed and direction at altitude, carried 200 'Loyalty Cards' and was immediately followed by the much larger rocket. That was over 2 meters long, painted red, white and blue and carried 300 Loyalty Cards. Following the firing of the smaller rocket, the angle of the firing rocket was reduced to avoid high-speed winds at higher altitudes.

Both rockets were recovered about a mile from the launch site. Covers for each flight were marked in the top left with 'Coronation Rocketgram' and had a specially designed Rs. 1 stamp with a picture of the new king and queen. The rockets were distinguished by the second cachet which read 'By Coronation Pilot Rocket No P IX' or 'By Coronation Rocket No. 141'. Both rockets were meant to be fired by the Postmaster General but he was not available on the day, so the editor of the *Star of India* Mr L P Atkinson was invited to initiate both rockets. The covers were addressed to leading government officials, scientific bodies, governors of provinces in India and overseas addressees including King George and Queen Elizabeth.[3] On the same day, the recovered covers were taken to the Park Street post office and posted to the various recipients around the globe. Smith received an acknowledgement from the Queen and Princess Margaret Rose for their covers.[4]

Smith commemorated the British coronation internationally. On 19th May 1937, he visited the Japanese consulate and acquired a special cachet for 54 cards numbered 1 to 54.[5] Smith himself did not visit Japan. The only country he visited outside India during his adult life was Sikkim (which until 1975 was independent of India). He intended to visit Bhutan and Tibet but his primary contact, Frederick Williamson, the Political Officer representing those two states died prematurely.

Boy Scouts and Girl Guides

Smith's first deployment of propaganda rockets was in peacetime. It was a large and spectacular occasion in the presence of high-ranking officials. Smith could have suffered a major setback, but in the end it was a remarkable success. Smith had been invited on 26th Jan 1937 by the Secretary of the Boy Scouts Association, to provide a 'demonstration of Rocket Mails and propaganda by rocket'. The

Association offered to pay his passage, food and stay at the camp where the total did not exceed Rs. 20.[6]

The first 'All-India Boy Scout Jamboree' was held in Delhi between 1st and 3rd February 1937. Smith carried out 11 rocket flights, 6 propaganda and 5 mail experiments, all of which were successful. Between them they carried 6,358 items (810 mail covers, 35 copies of the newspaper *Jamboree Daily* and 5,513 leaflets).

The Scouting movement had been founded in 1907 by Robert Baden-Powell, designed for young people to develop their understanding of the outdoors and survival skills. The 'World Scout Movement' spread initially through the British Empire and then globally. For the first time, the All-India Jamboree was held in India, with multiple Scouting events across India. It had several sponsors including the East India Railway. During the first three days of February 1937, Stephen Smith had launched 11 rockets carrying propaganda leaflets and mail.[7]

7.3 All India Boy Scouts rocket number 134 called Dr. R. Paganini 2 February 1937. Credit Ramu M Srinivasa

Smith was in the presence of some high-profile dignitaries including the Scout Movement founder Lord Robert Baden-Powell and his wife

Lady Baden-Powell, the Marquess of Linlithgow, the Viceroy and his executive council, and 10,000 other spectators.[8] As designed, the first propaganda rocket burst at an altitude of 1,500 metres as the Chief Commissioner was addressing the scouts, showering them with the messages of loyalty: 'The Indian Scouts offer their homage and Loyal Affection to their Imperial majesties'.[9]

A month later, Smith repeated this spectacle during a gathering of the Girl Guides of Bengal. With two launches on 2nd March in Calcutta, the audience was showered by over 2,000 covers and messages reading 'I am so glad to be here with you all today, I am sure that you will carry away happy memories to help you to be the best of Guides, and Happy, and Healthy, and Helpful'.

7.4 Propaganda rocket number 8. Girl Guides Rally 2 March 1937. Credit Stamp Circuit

Between them, the two rockets launched that day carried 2,000 leaflets and 65 covers. The covers used the special stamp produced for the All-India Jamboree tied to the cover with a circular violet cachet reading 'Girl Guides Rally Bengal'. One of the two rockets was launched by Lady Baden-Powell and carried messages signed by her.[10]

War Rockets

In September 1939, the *Star of India* published a small piece listing Smith's accomplishments in rocketry. The piece was written on the day that war was declared and suggested that Smith's work could be of value to the authorities. The title of the piece was 'War Rockets'.[11] Despite Smith giving several of his rockets this name, they were never used against a military target or for military objectives. Instead, through a series of rocket firings between September 1939 and October 1944, he conducted many tests carrying patriotic slogans under the heading of 'War Rockets'. The rockets carried slogans on the covers such as 'Au Revoir', 'Liar', 'Victory' and 'Just a Sting for Nazi Goalbirds'.

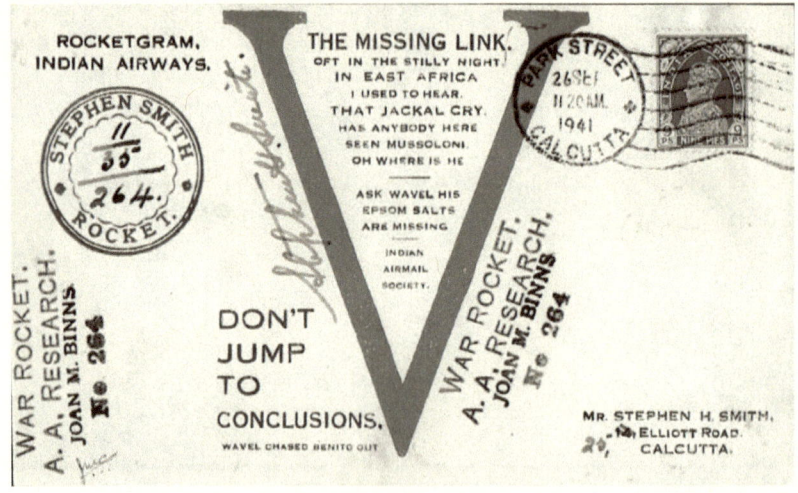

7.5 *War rocket launched on 21 November 1941. Credit Walter Hopferweiser*

Once war broke out, India was directly impacted. Thousands of Indians travelled to Europe and took an active part in the defence of the British Empire. Despite the distance, India experienced the privations of war including travel restrictions, limited availability of goods and services and the price hikes.

In the mid 1930s, Smith had travelled widely between Sikkim, Delhi and Asansol. But with the uncertainty and danger of wartime, he did not want to be too far from his wife and son, so he chose not to travel. All of his War Rocket launches between 1939 and 1944 therefore took place within the suburbs of Calcutta. During this time his record-keeping became sparse, the witnesses to these launches were limited and the number of covers his flights carried was markedly reduced.

Prior to the outbreak of World War II, Smith had placed hundreds of covers in his rockets, but once the war started, each launch carried less than 100 and occasionally less than 10. There may have been launches that carried no covers and thus have left no record. He designated about a dozen launches between 1939 and 1944 as War Rockets. In total between them they carried around 437 covers.

The war interfered with the reliable delivery of airmail and thus Smith's ability to communicate with the outside world. One communication did get through. In a piece published in England in April 1943, the recipient writes: 'I have obtained information from Mr Stephen Smith, who fired certain War Rockets during 1940-41'.[12] The details he had received:

War Rocket	Number	Date	Missive Carried
3	228	25/6/1940	53
3a	230	17/7/1940	1
3b	231	17/7/1940	1
4	252	17/5/1941	4
5	253	17/5/1941	4
5a	255	1/7/1941	10
5b	256	1/7/1941	10
6	258	7/7/1941	7
7	259	10/7/1941	8
8	260	3/8/1941	2
9	263	26/9/1941	8
10	264	26/9/1941	35

The first two war rockets (number 207 and 208) were launched on 19th September 1939. The first carried 91 covers with two cachets – 'Au revoir' and 'Carried by War Rocket the Liar No. 207'. The second carried 81 covers with two Cachets – 'Au revoir' and 'Carried by War Rocket Grog-Nee-Gin No. 208'. Four days later, he writes to his friend Robert Paganini in Switzerland saying: 'No press representatives or photographers were invited to view the firings and were conducted in secret somewhere in the suburbs of Calcutta'.[13] The uncertainty of war that had now descended across the Empire led him to consider that these might be his final rocket experiments. That was the motivation for the choice of the cachet 'Au Revoir'.[14]

The two war rockets of 1st July 1941 (numbers 255 and 256) called 'Parachute War Rockets' did not deploy any parachutes within the rockets, but the covers they carried had a white label depicting a descending parachute. Why he called them Parachute War Rockets is unclear. After all, in 1937, he had written to Leslie Johnson in Liverpool saying: 'I do not believe in parachutes and never have'.[15] In this launch, he was depicting a typical military symbolism? Perhaps he was motivated by his daughter-in-law's brother Stanley Surin. Stanley was a fluent Burmese speaker, a parachutist in the American army who was dropped in Burma during the war.[16]

Throughout 1941, Smith fired several other War Rockets in and around Calcutta. As the war continued, he introduced new propellants: compressed air and gas. Until then he had been using commercially acquired solid fuel. Compressed air and gas were the two new propellents. This was probably his most technically advanced innovation that he experimented with. In 1944, he tested new forms of propulsion which had inherent advantages for use by the military. The compressed air left no trace of smoke in the atmosphere and was invisible, especially at night.

Smith was aware of the propaganda value of rockets. That merit had been established in Europe at the time Smith was conducting his experiments. During the Spanish Civil War in 1936, General Franco's rocket squadron deployed rockets containing thousands of printed sheets of propaganda, delivering messages written in Spanish and

Arabic to his enemies in Madrid, the legionnaires and Moors. The rockets exploded over their targets, distributing the leaflets directly to the soldiers below with messages such as 'to prolong resistance is the sacrifice of life needlessly'.[17] The leaflets were hastily prepared in makeshift printing facilities on the front lines. They were delivered by rockets across no-man's-land and exploded above the trenches, scattering the leaflets over the surrounding area.

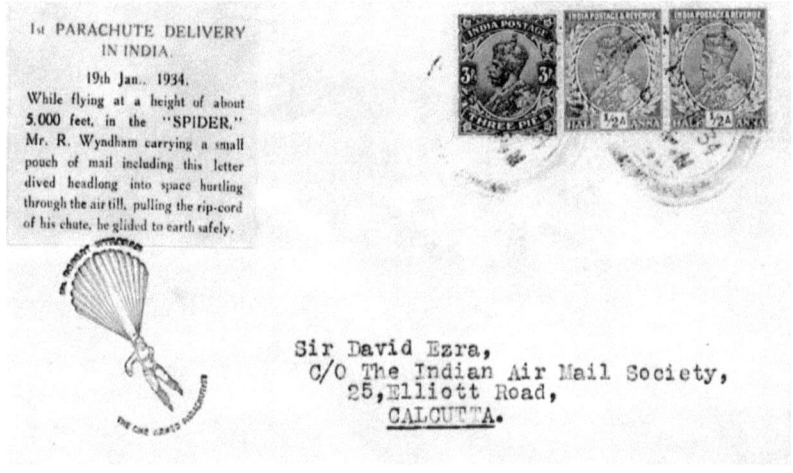

7.6 First parachute mail in support of Bihar Earthquake 19 January 1934. Credit Romano House of Stamp

The largest deployment of wartime propaganda rockets occurred in August 1944. Leaflets initially carried by the V1 from Germany into occupied parts of Europe and south east England. Once the war had finished, another started, the Cold War. Propaganda leaflets were then delivered mostly by the allies' aircraft across the Iron Curtain.

The destructive power of rockets was epitomised for the first time by the V1 and V2 flying bombs that were launched from Germany and dropped from the sky over Belgium, The Netherlands and southern England during World War II.[18] Prior to that, rockets had been used to deliver propaganda to undermine the morale of the enemy, especially of soldiers on the front line. It is likely that Smith only learnt about the V1 and V2 after he had stopped his own experiments.

7.7 Stephen Smith (sitting on the left) Calcutta 28 July 1938. Credit Ramu M Srinivasa

The Space Age was ushered in by the launch of Sputnik in 1957, ultimately leading to humanity's greatest technological achievement of two dozen men walking on the surface of the Moon. It was the Space Race, powered by rockets, that kept the Cold War cold. These same rockets, with their ability to transport atomic weapons thousands of miles, have dominated geopolitics ever since.

8

GLOBAL CONNECTIONS

Global Contacts

How individuals in a society live, travel, work and interact is determined largely by the available means of communication and transport. High-speed, undersea fibre optic telecommunication links and geostationary communication satellites of the twenty-first century allow us to communicate with anyone on Earth instantly at incredibly low cost, using technology available to most households. In Smith's lifetime the concept of email, Skype and WhatsApp would have been tantamount to magic. For him and his generation, airmail and rocket mail were just as revolutionary and magical.

Smith's life coincided with the advent of aviation and to a lesser degree rocket technology. Born in 1891, he was 12 years old when humanity first took to the air in 1903 and 20 years old at the advent of airmail in Allahabad. Being close to Calcutta, he probably read about it in the local Indian press and it must have made a lasting impression.

It was largely through airmail that he developed and sustained links with individuals around the world who shared his interest. By the early 1930s, regular routes and schedules for cargo and passenger flights were established around the world. At about the same time, small self-funded rocketry groups began to experiment with a form of transport that one day would supersede aircraft. Many of the pioneers were Smith's contemporaries, including Hermann Oberth, Wernher von Braun and Robert Goddard are now considered as the fathers of modern rocketry.

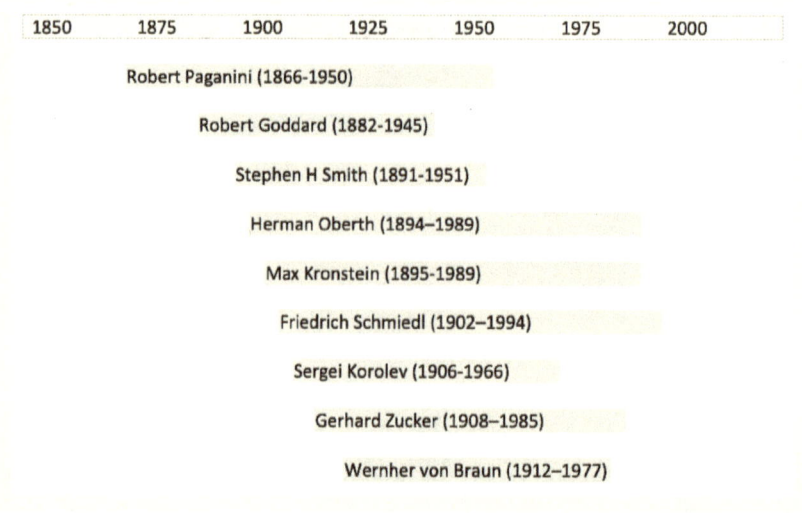

8.1 Stephen Smith's Contemporaries. Credit Author

Whilst the Wright Brothers' pioneering flight took place on the other side of the world, the world's first airmail flight on 18th February 1911 had taken off from Allahabad, a mere 600 km from Asansol where Smith was studying. Although born in Assam, Calcutta was his home. Not only was Calcutta the capital of British India, but it was also strategically situated halfway between Britain and South East Asia and Australia. As the first long-haul aerial routes evolved, they all made Calcutta a pivotal staging point. Smith would frequently make visits to Calcutta airport, then known as Dum Dum airport, to meet aviators personally, probably passing on signed covers for them to post when they returned to their home countries.

During his lifetime, first through airmail and then rocket mail, Smith fostered his connections, friends and eventually his professional standing amongst philatelists around the world. He connected with people in places like Bern, Liverpool and New York to Calcutta. During the 1920s, he founded the Aero Philatelic Club of India (which on 19th January 1930 changed its name to the Indian Airmail Society). In 1935, Smith had joined the British Interplanetary Society (BIS), which had been founded in Liverpool in England two years earlier. In April 1928 he exchanged letters with King George V and on 11th April 1935 the King of Sikkim awarded him a certificate recognising the 'utility of the rocket as a means of transport during floods and landslips'.

Long after his death, he became an honorary member of the American Air Mail Society and in 1989 he was inducted into the AAMS Hall of fame.[1] In 1992, a year after the centenary of his birth, the Indian government celebrated Smith's achievements by issuing a stamp and a first day cover dedicated to him and his work.

Although his work and achievements were celebrated largely after his death, during his lifetime he made a formidable contribution to Indian philately on the international stage. He did this with many of his international contacts, some of whom later became his friends. They included Walter Bruggmann in the Philippines, Leslie Johnson and Francis Fields in England, Friedrich Schmiedl in Austria, Sir David and Lady Ezra in Calcutta and Max Kronstein in the USA.[2] The primary contact through whom most of these contacts were initially established and later sustained was Robert Paganini in Switzerland.

Robert Paganini

The first official airmail stamp to be issued in Switzerland was on 9th March 1913 for an experimental airmail run in Basel[3]. The task of recording and preserving the details of this historic event was undertaken by Robert Paganini (23rd April 1866–6th December 1950). He had been recording the progress of airmail from around the world and therefore recognised the historic significance of the new mode of transport when it started in Switzerland. Although he never met

Smith, Paganini corresponded with him for over 25 years and was the most influential of all of his international contacts.

Convinced that airplanes and airmail would transform communication, Paganini added data and documents associated with the Basel experiment to his growing airmail collection. It consisted of official publications, reports, advertisements, published books and articles and his personal correspondence with collectors and dealers around the globe. To accommodate the anticipated growth in airmail, in 1913 he compiled his 'Grand Archive', dedicated it to the state of Switzerland and submitted it to the Postal Museum in Bern.[4]

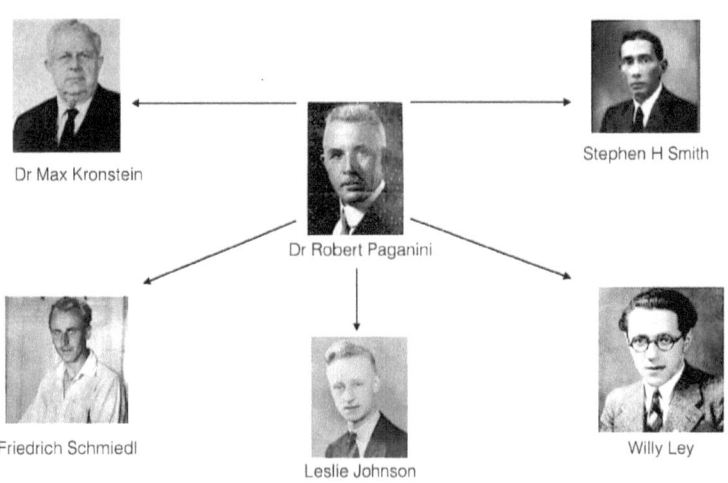

8.2 Stephen Smith's International Contacts. Credit Author

He also had a clear vision that this new technological development would have global consequences, and he set out to collect information, documents and photos of similar events around the world. The contributions in his collection from India came almost entirely from Stephen Smith. By 1928, Paganini was an internationally renowned authority on airmail and a member of at least 14 international philatelic organisations in France, Britain, USA and India.[5] It was through this desire to track the global evolution of airmail that he came into contact with Stephen Smith in India.

Paganini was considered to be 'one of the most outstanding aerophilatelists on the globe'. His wife Martha, played an active role and was sometimes referred to as the 'First Lady of Aerophilately'.[6] Post from around the world, including from Elliot Road in Calcutta, found its way to their Swiss 'Huesli' close to the slopes of the 'Wild Strubel', one of Switzerland's highest mountains.[7] In 1920, he compiled the information he had gathered for almost a decade in *Geschickte der Luftpost, Historischer Katalog Samtlicher Luftpost* (Airmail history, Historical catalogue of all airmail). This became the world's first airmail catalogue.[8]

During the first two decades of aviation, Paganini's systematic collection had grown to 1,250 items. As the collection became too large for his house, he donated more of it to the postal museum in Bern whilst still continuing to collect. At that time, his was the 'world's largest and most complete library collection of material related to aviation and air posts'.[9]

Paganini was not only a curator of aero-philately but also a champion of it in all its forms, including rocket mail. A resolution during the Congress of Philatelique in Luxembourg in 1936 concluded that the 'envelopes transported by rockets are unanimously considered as covers without philatelic value'. Paganini was disappointed by this conclusion and wrote a forceful piece defending rocket mail in the December 1936 issue of the *Air Post Journal*. He protested 'I cannot understand why philately takes such an unfriendly attitude towards the efforts and special branches of aero-philately' and predicted that 'the time will come and one will laugh with pity at the resolution taken during the congress in Luxemburg'.[10]

In a preface to a 64-page catalogue of his collection, Paganini states: 'My work should give an accurate picture of a very important cultural phenomenon. It would be impossible to view the material except chronologically. It would be desirable for the whole thing to be funded along scientific, commercial and philatelic lines. This would, however, need a great deal of further work which I cannot carry out. I am, however, completely confident that younger forces will come forward to undertake the historical research to produce reports and dissertations, over individual parts if not of the entire range'.[11]

Whereas the initial airmail flight in 1911 in India had an experimental and perhaps even a fund-raising motivation, it also demonstrated the tangible benefits of aerial transport at high speed over difficult terrain. It was this vision of the future that Paganini saw long before others and he chose to dedicate most of his adult life to his collection. During the 1920s, airmail had established a firm footing and mail was beginning to be delivered within Europe and between Europe, India, south east Asia and Australia.

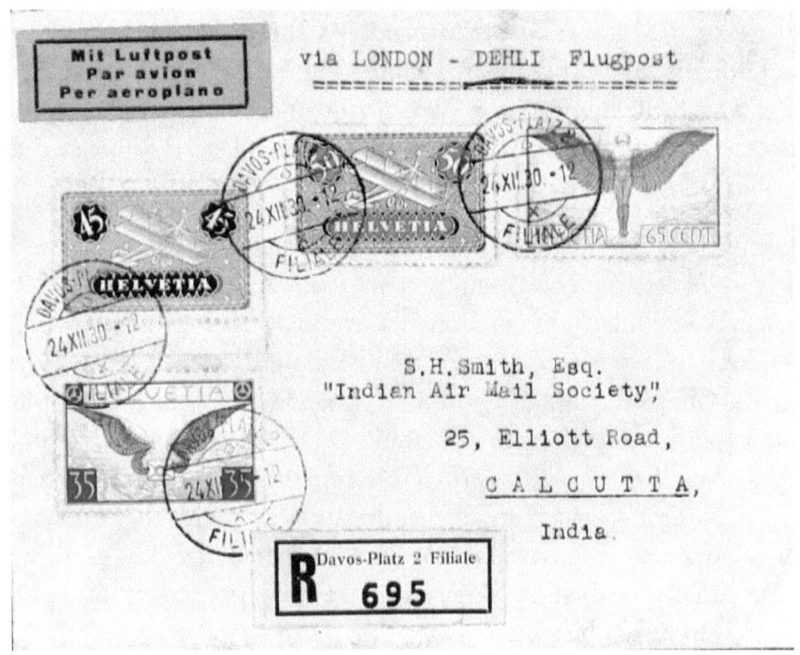

8.3 Mail from Davos in Switzerland so most likely from Robert Paganini to Stephen Smith 24 July 1931. Credit Sparks Auctions

Throughout his lifetime, Paganini promoted, fostered and supported airmail and rocket mail. In defending rocket mail, he was shielding the work of rocket mail experimenters around the world, including Stephen Smith. During the first half of the twentieth century, Paganini, Switzerland's first aero-philatelist, went on to become one of Philately's leading figures. He was highly regarded and is considered by many as the founder of aero-philately in Europe. Despite Paganini's efforts and expectations, rocket mail never developed beyond the experimental phase.

Paganini had numerous contacts around the world throughout his life, but the most enduring, unexpected and poignant relationship was with Smith. He was the only contact for air and rocket mail in India. It was philately that had brought them together in 1925 but it was living through some of the darkest events of the twentieth century that brought them closer. During World War II, Paganini lived in the relative peace of a neutral Switzerland, while in India, Smith toiled through the civil unrest of Indian independence, World War II, famine and partition. In his letters, in addition to the exchange of philatelic material, Smith conveys to Paganini his first-hand experiences of living through these dramatic events in Calcutta.

Paganini died in his sleep on 6th December 1950 at his nursing home in St Gallen, Switzerland, where he had lived since the death of his wife Martha, in 1946. It was only then that his will revealed the closeness of his relationship with Stephen Smith, to whom he left a quarter of his estate. Sadly, Smith himself died two months later.

Max Kronstein

Max Kronstein first came across the work of Stephen Smith through his contact with Dr Robert Paganini. He recalled that 'the doctor told me about Stephen Smith and showed me some of their correspondence from the 1920s and up to the second world war'.[12] Kronstein was probably the first person outside India to know that Smith was preparing to conduct the first rocket mail experiment there. Kronstein brought Smith's work on rocket mail in India to a wider international audience through his prolific writing as the Director of Foreign Relations for the American Air Mail Society.

Despite the vast distance that separated them, they developed a friendship through private correspondence which started in the 1920s and ran through to World War II when regular mail services were interrupted.

Kronstein recalls a story of Stephen Smith approaching American soldiers who had landed in Calcutta asking them if they were from New York. When they responded affirmatively, Smith invited them to his house on Elliot Road for dinner. He proudly pointed to a picture on the wall of Kronstein and his daughter, declaring that in New York 'these are my friends'. Kronstein and Smith never actually met, but a contact of Kronstein who met Smith described him as a 'small slender Indian with great enthusiasm'.[13]

Kronstein was born in Basel in Switzerland in 1895 and whilst still a child the family moved to Karlsruhe in Germany. He acquired his interest in chemistry and philately from his father. During World War I, he was wounded at the battle of the Somme and spent two years in England as a prisoner of war. Following a prisoner exchange, he ended up in Holland where he was allowed to resume his education in Leiden before eventually returning to Germany.

In 1939, as a widower accompanied by his teenage daughter, Kronstein arrived in New York, where he lived and worked for the rest of his life. Professionally he was a research chemist and a teacher at New York University College of Engineering. He registered at least 20 patents during his lifetime and as a research chemist he also published books on surface coatings and the absorption characteristics of camouflage paints.

He joined the American Air Mail Society (AAMS) which had been founded in 1923; it continues to publish a monthly Journal, *The Air Post Journal*.[14] His experience of WWI and subsequent exposure to European countries and languages prepared him well for his role with the AAMS as Director of Foreign Relations and later as an Associate Editor for the AAMS. He contributed numerous articles to the monthly journal throughout his life. As World War II approached its conclusion, he wrote a piece entitled 'Air Mail and World War II' in

January 1945 for the *Air Post Journal*. He highlighted the impact of the war on postal services:

- In 1944 the German post office carried airmail postcards from US prisoners of war to Lisbon at an extra air fee of 40 pfennigs in stamps.
- In the USA a special airmail letter cards had been used since May 1944 for correspondence to prisoners in Europe at a fee of 6 cents.
- The main air route between Russia and the USA was operated by way of Siberia, 540 miles across the Bering Sea to Nome and Fairbanks, Alaska. About 5,000 American-built planes had been flown over that route since the autumn of 1941 (2,200 of them in the first four months of 1944). The route was also open for mail from the USA to US prisoners in Japan. The mail was handed over to Japan at Vladivostok, Siberia.
- During World War II an airmail exhibition took place in Paris, between 1st and 17th October 1943. On that occasion aero-philately was called the 'Third Philately'. A post-war project called for about 400 airfields, around one per 50,000 inhabitants, to facilitate the expected demand in airmail.[15]

Initially, Smith and Kronstein corresponded on the emerging scene of aero-philately, but a decade later the subject turned towards rocket mail. It was at the 1932 International Air Post Exhibition in Danzig that Kronstein first came across rocket mail, with contributions from Schmiedl, Tiling and Zucker. Perhaps it was through this personal correspondence with Kronstein that Smith learned of rocket mail for the first time in the early 1930s.

In addition to his long association with, and regular contributions to, the journal of the AAMS, Kronstein wrote several books, including:

- 1945: *Stamps: A Weekly Magazine of Philately*
- 1978: *Pioneer Air-post Flights of the world 1830-1935*
- 1987: *Rocket Mail: Flights of the World June 1, 1987*

During the period of WWII, he used his extensive international connections and language skills to communicate the impact of both mail on the war and war on the mail. To commemorate his substantial contribution to philately in the USA, the March 1963 issue of *The Air Post Journal* carried his portrait on the cover and was dedicated to him. On 22nd November 1992, at the age of 97, Max Kronstein died peacefully in his sleep in New York following a brief illness.[16]

Three years after Smith died and with the consent of his widow, Kronstein collaborated with another author to revise Smith's *Rocket Mail Catalogue*, which has become an established resource within the philatelic community on Smith's work.[17] To mark what would have been Smith's seventieth birthday, Kronstein wrote a piece entitled 'In Memoriam', in which he described Smith as carrying out 'the greatest one man campaign for rocketry'.[18]

Walter Bruggmann

In 1939 the American Airmail Society established a new award for aero-philatelic works, not just for those published in America but for anywhere in the world in any language. It was called The Walter Bruggmann Award and the winner was selected by a panel of twelve philatelists of international repute in the field of philately, based around the world including USA, England, Australia, Cuba and India. The panel member from India was Stephen Smith.[19]

Walter Bruggmann was born in Switzerland in 1877 and served in the Swiss army before going on to study in Switzerland, England and Italy. Unfortunately, he suffered for much of his adult life from an illness that he had originally contracted in 1919. He met and married a girl from Manila then moved to live permanently in the Philippines. As a result of acquiring several plantations, he subsequently became wealthy, allowing him time for his primary interest of aero-philately. Initially he was a collector but later became a dealer too. Modern-day philatelists interested in philatelic matters from the Philippines from the period between the wars will be familiar with his name.

The award submissions would be assessed by the panel based on the importance of the article or work for aerophilately, human interest, relation to aviation and its layout. Other members of the panel included George Angers (USA), Brigadier General R Ridgeway (England) and Robert Paganini (Switzerland). These were individuals that Smith knew well and frequently corresponded with. The award winner would receive a gold medal to the value of 50 US dollars inscribed with the year and name of the winner. It was not an annual award but was offered from time to time.

When not collecting or dealing directly in airmail items, Bruggmann was writing about them. He was the managing editor of the *Airmail Digest* and frequently contributed pieces to it. He is regarded as the father of philately in the Philippines. He also became one of the principal founders and stockholders of the first commercial airline established in the Philippines, The Philippine Airways Company. His reputation and high esteem within the community attracted the attention of the Japanese army during the war. He was detained and placed under arrest in isolation[20] in Manila, where he died on 24th October 1943.[21]

Sir David Ezra

Stephen Smith's work as the Honorary Secretary of the Indian Air Mail Society brought him in contact not only with people of similar interests but also with people of influence. Mostly they were from the wealthy elite in high society and business. Predominantly they were British or Europeans rather than Indians. His success in philately and rocket mail, limited as it was, was mainly the result of his dedication and persistence, but he also benefited from the support he received from his network of contacts. Two of the most significant individuals in Calcutta were Sir David and Lady Ezra.

The Ezras were a successful Jewish family who had built their wealth, reputation and a place in Calcutta high society as a result of their business interests which included real estate and investments. Both had an interest in philately. Lady Ezra in particular became an active collector and they provided prizes for regular philatelic exhibitions which were hosted on their premises on Kyd Street in Calcutta.

As an Anglo-Indian, Smith saw himself as something of an outsider. Within the cosmopolitan community of Calcutta of the early twentieth century, he probably felt comfortable in the company of those from other countries who had chosen to make India their home. The Jewish community in India can be traced back to the earliest Jewish communities in Cochin about 2,000 years ago. But the Ezras belonged to a subsequent wave of immigrants known as the Baghdadi Jews.

8.4 David and Lady Ezra in Calcutta. May 1928. Credit Jeremy Argyll Etkin

According to evidence from 1798,[22] a Jewish jewel trader from Syria called Shalom Cohen became the first Jew to settle in Calcutta. Over time many more came from the Middle East and a large number from Baghdad established the community that came to be known as the Baghdadi Jews.[23] They were traders, actively exploiting the commercial opportunities opened up by the British Empire. Gradually, the community grew and thrived in the opium, indigo and silk trades as well as in real estate.

In the 1930s and 1940s, India experienced further Jewish immigration of European Jews fleeing persecution by German Nazis. The Jewish community from Burma also relocated to Calcutta as the Japanese army invaded Burma. Albert Einstein was offered the post of Vice Chancellor of Travancore University in Kerala, but he declined and went instead to Princeton in the USA.[24]

The Jewish community in Calcutta was around 3,500 strong for most of the twentieth century. It had grown quickly to around 5,000 during World War II, but afterwards many of the European Jews were keen to return to their former homes. Many went to the new State of Israel once it was founded in 1948, and the numbers therefore dropped even more dramatically than they had risen. In the 1991 census there were around 5,000 Jews in the whole of India.

Stephen Smith served as the Indian Airmail Society's secretary for many years, during which time he recorded the development of airmail in India in the society's monthly bulletins. These bulletins highlight his regular interactions with the Ezra family.

David Ezra had come from a prominent Iraqi Jewish family; he married Rachel Sassoon, the daughter of another successful Jewish family. Ezra was both a successful businessman and a real estate tycoon.[25] He is remembered for his philanthropy and served as a Director of the Reserve Bank of India, the Sheriff of Calcutta and the President of the Asiatic Society in 1938. He established a private zoo at his home in Calcutta. His name is associated with many of Calcutta's buildings, such as Esplanade Mansions and Chowringhee Mansions, and he has a street named after him.

It was Lady Ezra who played a more active part in philately and the newly developing aero-philately. She joined Smith's Indian Airmail

Society and became a philatelic collector. In addition to material support, this connection elevated Smith's work, bringing it to the attention of the higher echelons of Indian society and providing Smith with some level of international recognition.

In the summer of 1938, Sir David and Lady Ezra spent six months in London, in part to avoid the excessive heat of the summer in Calcutta. In advance of this visit, Stephen Smith had contacted Leslie Johnson, Secretary of the British Interplanetary Society in Liverpool.[26] He asked Johnson to 'call on them' during this time, with the intention to forge new and stronger relationships between the BIS and the Ezra family. In Calcutta the Ezras had shown some limited support to the Indian Airmail Society. The potential for larger-scale support for his rocket mail experiments or the nascent BIS, which had just moved to London from Liverpool, did not materialise.

Through his contact with Lady Ezra, in September 1936 Smith wrote to her cousin, Sir Philip Sassoon, a Member of Parliament in London, seeking financial assistance for his rocket mail experiments. He stated: 'we can congratulate ourselves on our success so far' and went on to say that 'these experiments entail a certain amount of expense' and 'I invite your help'.[27] Unfortunately, Gerhard Zucker's spectacular rocket mail failures in the previous year had influenced the British government's views on rocket mail and no support was forthcoming.

9
PRELUDE TO SPACE

Rocket Propellent

In 1944, as he neared the end of his rocket mail experiments, Smith used two new propellants for his rockets, compressed air and gas. Before this, for the decade over which he tested rockets he had used common gunpowder, also known as black powder. Gunpowder was an established explosive used in firearms, artillery and fireworks. It is a mixture of 75% potassium nitrate (also known as saltpetre), 15% charcoal and 10% sulphur. Variations on these ratios and tiny amounts of other ingredients can change the propulsive or explosive attributes to suit the many uses to which it is put, such as mining, road building, quarrying and rocket propulsion.

For rockets, the powder was pre-packed in cylindrical cartridges which would then form the lower part of the rocket, with mail or other items being carried in the section above. It was the quality of the formulation and the physical construction of the cartridge that would determine whether or not the rocket would explode. How high and far it travelled depended on the size of the cartridge, the angle of the launch, the mass of the payload, the aerodynamic shape of the rocket and the physical attributes of the atmosphere at the time of the launch.

At the outset and for most of his rocket mail testing, Smith used rockets commercially produced by two companies, The Orient Fireworks Company and James Pain and Sons. Gerhard Zucker in Germany also used a German-based commercial supplier of cartridges. Based on his rocket failures there, the German authorities prevented further attempts. When in England, Zucker was prevented from acquiring the cartridges from Germany and so was instead forced to turn to a British supplier, Brocks Fireworks.[1] When Zucker's rocket failed, he attributed the failure to the cartridge. He claimed that the 'powder had not been properly packed and air pockets caused the explosion'.[2] Karel Roberti in the Netherlands used a well-known firework supplier called A J Kat based in Leiden.

REGULATION
SIGNAL ROCKETS AND LIGHTS
AS ORDERED BY
THE BOARD OF TRADE.

THE CHEAPEST AND BEST IN THE TRADE.
MAGAZINES, containing the requirements of the Board of Trade, viz :—
24 Regulation Rockets. | 24 Regulation Friction Tubes.
24   ,,   Flannel Cartridges. | 24   ,,   Blue Lights.
In fitted Zinc and Copper Magazines.

Magazines taken off from vessels on arriving in River Thames, stored, refilled, and reshipped when required.
Board of Trade Regulation Guns, Carronades, and Mortars supplied with all equipments.

PRIVATE SIGNAL LIGHTS
Made to order, any colour or colours (except blue), from 12s. per dozen.
Manufactured by JAMES PAIN, MITCHAM, SURREY.
LONDON OFFICE :—
15 HEYGATE STREET, WALWORTH ROAD, S.E. (pro tem.)
GRAVESEND OFFICE :—16 HARMER STREET.

9.1 James Pain and Sons. Lloyd's List September 1874. Credit British Library, London

Both the Orient Fireworks Company and James Pain & Sons were producers of munitions, mortars and rockets for the British Navy as well as fireworks for public consumption. This was a dangerous industry; both companies had suffered from explosions in their factories, resulting in public scrutiny.[3] The Oriental Fireworks Company supplied Smith with 16 rockets between 23rd March 1935 and 29th June 1935. Some rockets were supplied at reduced cost or perhaps free.[4] It would have been in their commercial interest if Smith was successful in his goal for establishing rocket mail. The increase in demand for rockets is something from which these companies would benefit commercially.

Virtually all those experimenters using powder cartridges experienced explosions and loss of their mail covers. Some of Smith's contemporaries such as Willy Ley, Friedrich Schmiedl and Reinhold Tiling experimented with the efficiency of propellants. They conducted static tests and Schmiedl conducted tests within a vacuum chamber to measure efficiency at varying altitudes. There is no record of Smith conducting such quantitative experiments on the ground.

Smith's rockets consisted typically of a tube constructed from cardboard, wood, leather or metal. The lower section would hold the powder cartridge or cartridges (from the commercial providers) and the upper section contained the payload of livestock, food, medicine or mail. He experimented with what he called 'Telescopic Rockets' where he could vary the length of the sections and 'Rocket Train' where the rocket had multiple sections. Occasionally he would launch a small rocket prior to the larger main rocket carrying the primary payload. The trajectory of the small rocket would indicate the strength and direction of wind at the higher altitudes. This allowed Smith to adjust the angle and direction for the launch of the main rocket. On 3rd April 1935, just prior to leaving for Sikkim, he acquired a box of signal rockets from a railway engineer in Calcutta.[5]

In principle, the lowest section of each rocket housed the gunpowder cartridge and was separated from the next section by a strong fireproof barrier. On ignition, the powder cartridge burned gradually, generating propulsion. If the mixture was uneven, or the construction was below standard, instead of a slow propulsive burn, the cartridge would explode. This is what happened to the first rocket that Smith fired on 30th September 1934. The rocket burst and all 143 messages ended up in the River Hooghly. The frequency of bursts declined as he gained experience of launching rockets and he started to advise the manufactures on how to enhance their quality control.

Today, rockets use solid, liquid and cryogenic propellants to reach space. Cryogenic propellants (liquid hydrogen and liquid oxygen) are the most efficient and also the most difficult to produce, store, transport, handle and use. During the 1920s and 1930s, groups and individual in Germany, USA and the USSR successfully experimented with liquid propellants for the first time.

Smith's tests in 1944 with compressed air and gas are shrouded in mystery. He conducted these tests in wartime and did not have any press covering the launches. There is no documented technical details about the type of gas he used or where he acquired the compressed air. Conditions in Calcutta were difficult because of the war and they would get worse through independence and partition that followed. Smith's compressed air and gas rocket experiments were the last he conducted.

Beyond the Atmosphere

In 1942, Jal Cooper had asserted that mail transport by rockets was 'fast becoming a fact' and acknowledged the progress made by Stephen Smith in India as well as others across the globe.[6] He placed Smith's work alongside that of Robert Goddard & George Pendray in the USA, Robert Esnault-Pelterie in France, Willy Ley in Germany and Friedrich Schmiedl in Austria.[7] In retrospect, Cooper's assessment of Smith's technical contribution was generous.

Cooper was optimistic, insisting that just as the television and submarine had only recently moved from science fiction to science fact, transport of mail by rocket would make a similar journey in the not too distant future. At the beginning of the twentieth century, mail by ship from India to England took around 100 days. At the time Cooper was writing, airmail had already reduced that to 100 hours.

Rockets opened the theoretical possibility of shrinking this journey time to just an hour or two.[8]

The impact of Smith's successful livestock rocket experiment in June 1935 was dramatic and global. His continued success with rocket mail along with that of others raised the profile and credibility of rocket mail around the world. The Philadelphia Enquirer of 29th November 1936 captured the prevailing enthusiasm for rocket mail, saying: 'It may only be a few years when someone will point upward to a silver projectile streaking across the skies and say in a matter-of-fact voice: "There goes the six o'clock mail to San Francisco". That night he'll drop a letter marked 'Via Rocket Post' in his corner mail-box, confident that it will reach its destination within a few hours'.[9] Rocket mail was not a fad. The same report recorded that there were 17 rocket launches planned somewhere in the world in the next 24 hours.

Aeronautics, the study of the science and principles of flight-capable machines, allowed the Wright brothers to make their breakthrough in 1903. Two decades later, interest grew in flight beyond the earth's atmosphere, and the term Astronautics (the study of spaceflight) entered the lexicon.[10]

One of the seminal theoretical works in spaceflight was conducted in 1897 by a Russian mathematician Konstantin Tsiolkovskii who formulated the 'Rocket Equation'. In it, he calculated the horizontal speed – 8 km per second (or 5 miles per second) – that would enable a rocket to attain Earth orbit. Tsiolkovskii had already conceived an idea about cryogenic liquid propellants, rocket stages and weightlessness. Goddard built and tested the first rocket engine to use liquid oxygen, and Friedrich Schmiedl had demonstrated staging through his Step Rocket, in which one rocket stage falls away as its fuel is exhausted and the next is ignited whilst in the air.[11] The same rocket equation and principle of staging took Yuri Gagarin to Earth orbit on 12th April 1961.

Several amateur groups and societies were established in the late 1920s and early 1930s in Germany, Austria, Russia, America and Britain. They were mostly small grass-roots initiatives without backing from large organisations or government. Many of those involved had parallel interests in science fiction, philately, aviation and engineering. The Great Depression of 1929 resulted in many talented engineers finding themselves without work and consequently with time on their hands. Some of them joined these groups and provided their services free.

Philatelists also joined these groups. For example, Robert Paganini was a member of the Cleveland, American and British Rocketry Societies. Willy Ley and Stephen Smith were both members of the British Interplanetary Society.[12] Robert Goddard, Willy Ley, Friedrich Schmiedl all actively, albeit temporarily, participated in rocket mail.[13] In 1936, Willy Ley had successfully demonstrated rocket plane using liquid propellant on Greenwood Lake in the USA, carrying 5,000 postcards.

Gerhard Zucker's largely unsuccessful rocket mail tests in England and Scotland had portrayed the whole rocket mail community in a poor light. It was Zucker's multiple and spectacular failures that led Ley to rethink the value of rocket mail, but it had a more tangible impact on Stephen Smith's rocket mail testing in India. The refusal of Philip Sassoon MP to respond positively to Smith's request for financial assistance in 1936 was one such consequence'.[14]

The Postmaster General, who had been closely following Zucker's work, concluded that rocket mail attempts in this country 'have come to an inglorious end' and 'have shown a marked tendency to convey the letters to anywhere but their proper destination'. It was on this experience that he concluded, 'I think that Sir Philip would be very well advised to ignore the request for financial assistance'.[15]

The launch of Sputnik in 1957 is considered to be the start of the space age, but the threshold of space had been breached long before that. The internationally recognised boundary between the earth's atmosphere and space is agreed to be 100 km (62 miles). The first object made by humans to breach that boundary was the A4 Rocket (also known as the V2). The two-tonne liquid fuel rocket was launched on 3rd October 1942 from Peenemunde off Germany's Baltic Coast, rising to an altitude of 190 km (118 miles).

Other than the reference to the work of Gerhard Zucker in Britain in the summer of 1934, there is nothing to indicate what inspired Smith to rocketry. Through his membership of organisations such as the British Interplanetary Society, he was aware of the international interest in space and his achievements, as minimal as they were, were brought to the attention of the American Rocketry Society and probably Robert Goddard in the USA.[16]

In his writings or correspondence, Smith never addresses the theme of space directly. In the 1960s, Smith's work was reassessed by some writers (including one for NASA) in the light of the advances made in space exploration.[17] Writing in 1960, John Britt entitled his piece 'Stephen H Smith Rockets and Space Missiles'. He considered Smith's work as 'forerunner of the many types of rocket missiles now in use by military services of the great powers of the world'.

Against the backdrop of international events, Stephen Smith had cut a lonely figure in India, working unfunded and in isolation on a goal beyond his reach.[18] Existing evidence indicates that Smith's direct contribution to the technology of spaceflight was negligible. The realm of spaceflight was at the cusp of realisation when he died in 1951. In terms of raising awareness within the authorities and the general public in India and beyond, his contribution can be assessed to have been significant.

Soon after the start of the Space Age (the launch of Sputnik in October 1957), a journalist compared Smith's work with sending the dog Laika into space by Sputnik-2 in November 1957 by the Soviet Union. Unlike Laika, Smith's rocket passengers returned to Earth safely. The journalist asserted that Sputnik was not the first but the 'third example of a successful use of rockets for such transport'. Based on his membership of the British Interplanetary Society, the same journalist writes 'his ambitions included ventures into space'. The piece concludes with a question 'whether the efforts of the Calcutta inventor had any part in America's Explorer that now circles the earth'.[19] This was written just a month after the USA sent its first satellite Explorer into orbit.

Missile Mail

Despite Smith's efforts to engage the military, none of the armed forces conducted any rocket tests in India until long after Smith's lifetime. In 1980, India successfully tested its first indigenous rocket launcher called the SLV-3 (Satellite Launch Vehicle). Based on this technology, India established its Integrated Guided Missile Development Programme in the following year. Smith's idea of using rockets to transport mail was never realised in India. But it was considered and demonstrated elsewhere.

9.2 First International Rocket Mail Stamp 1936. Credit National Air and Space Museum, Washington, DC

The earliest international rocket mail can be traced to the American Legion in McAllen, Texas. The rocket mail demonstration was organised by several individuals in the American Legion including W J Burris, Post Adjutant.[20] One thousand sheets of four stamps were printed for the USA–Mexico journey and the same again for the

Mexico–USA return flight. A red stamp was affixed for the flight from the USA to Mexico with a cachet reading 'First International Rocket Flight from The Garden of Golden Grapefruit over the Silvery Rio Grande to Scenic and Historic Mexico'. A complementary cachet in green was used for the return journey.

At 16:00 on 2nd July 1936, two rockets containing mail were fired from the USA to Mexico. The first one exploded in mid-air before leaving the USA. The recovered mail were packed in the second rocket and launched successfully. After a flight of about 700 metres, the rocket arrived over the border but landed on a cantina in the town of Reynosa. No one was hurt but the Mexican authorities initially confiscated the rocket and its contents. On the following day, 922 covers which included 51 damaged covers from the first attempt were delivered back over the border to Texas by another rocket.[21]

9.3 Missile mail cover. Credit Smithsonian National Postal Museum, Washington, DC

In 1959, the American Postmaster General, Arthur E Summerfield (1899–1972) had expressed enthusiasm in the future of missile mail. Many others before him, including Friedrich Schmiedl, Gerhard

Zucker, Jal Cooper and (at least initially) Willy Ley shared this sentiment. As early as 1935, G E Pendray, President of the American Rocket Society and Edward L Hanna, founder of the Cleveland Rocket Society, were 'anxious that the USA should be the first country to establish a regular rocket mail service'.[22] Although successfully demonstrated, it never came to pass.

On 1st May 1959, A Regulus I Missile carrying 150 envelopes was launched from and returned to land at a Pacific Missile test range at Point Mugu in California. It travelled at a speed of Mach 0.85, at a maximum altitude of 37,000 ft (approximately 12 km) and completed the journey in 25 minutes. The Los Angeles postmaster witnessing the event was convinced that this was the USA's first missile mail. However, since Navy-issued envelopes were used, the post office department declined to recognise this attempt as missile mail. An attempt a month later on the East coast holds that record.[23]

The Postmaster General also made an announcement on the significance of this unofficial mail event on the Pacific coast, saying 'The United States today began experimental exploration of a major new technique of communication that is of historic significance to the peoples of the world'.[24]

In what is probably the most technically advanced demonstration of rocket mail, a Regulus I guided missile was launched from the deck of a submarine, USS Barbaro SSG-317, on 8th June 1959. The missile carried 3,000 postal items; after a flight of 20 minutes at almost the speed of sound, it landed on the runway at the Naval Auxiliary Air Station in Mayport, Florida.

To facilitate this demonstration, the US Post Office Department officially established a Branch Post Office on the USS Barbero. The mail items were entirely commemorative postal covers addressed to officials including President Eisenhower. The mail was cancelled 'USS Barbero 8 June 9:30 am 1959' prior to being loaded on the submarine. Following its arrival in Florida, this mail was forwarded to the Jacksonville Post Office.

This was the first and only time that a missile was used for mail transport. The official press release claimed that the 'great progress being made in guided missilry will be utilised in every practical way in the delivery of United States mail'.²⁵ Despite the optimism, it did not turn out that way.

Immediately after this successful experiment, the US Postmaster General Arthur Summerfield declared that 'Before man reaches the moon, mail will be delivered within hours from New York to California, to Britain, to India, or Australia by guided missiles. We stand on the threshold of rocket mail'.²⁶ This was in 1959 and the space race was already on, although Kennedy's declaration to go to the Moon was still two years away. The Postmaster's vision was overtaken by innovations in aircraft speed, reliability and capacity and the fact that people as well as mail could be carried on the same flight. These developments triggered the end of the road for regular commercial rocket mail.

9.4 Noble Upperman delivers the first missile mail to President Eisenhower with the Postmaster General Arthur Summerfield at the Whitehouse on 9 June 1959. Credit Museum of Communication, Bern, Switzerland

Smith's attempt to engage the Indian government in the 1930s was premature. Despite the success of the Indian Air Mail Society and the wide international recognition that Smith had brought to it, neither he nor his society possessed the gravitas to attract interest from the authorities.

Had he been able to attract individuals with technical experience and established a rocketry group rather than a mail society, perhaps he could have made the technical advances that would have attracted serious attention and commitment. Just at the time Smith was trying to do this, the authorities in India were preoccupied addressing the needs of a World War and Indian independence.

Space Mail - Astrophilatley

Stephen Smith's contribution to developing spaceflight is minimal. When spaceflight arrived, philately made its presence in space. Cosmonaut Georgie Grechko opened the first post office in earth orbit on board the USSR space station Salyut-6 when the crew of Soyuz 28 arrived on 8th March 1978. In 1984, Indian astronaut Rakesh Sharma cancelled several envelopes during his spaceflight on Salyut-7 in April 1984.[27] Apollo 15 commander David Scott cancelled two envelopes using a rubber stamp provided by the US postal service whilst on the surface of the Moon.

The Apollo 11 astronauts, the first to land on the Moon on 20 July 1969 were scheduled to cancel a single envelope using a rubber stamp and an ink pad they carried to the lunar surface. Instead the envelop was cancelled by all three astronauts on board the command module on their journey back to earth. Michale Collins recalls the event in his book *"Carrying the Fire"* as "Never mind that it is July 22, this is the first chance we have had to get to it. We try the cancellation out first, inking it and printing it in our flight plan three times until we get the hang of it, and then we apply it gingerly to the one and only envelope, which we understand the postmaster general will put on tour".[28]

Mail was sent into space long before the space age started in 1957. At the end of World War II, British, American and Russian teams sought out advanced German technology, especially in weapons, aviation, rocketry and the people who had built it to take back to their home countries.[29] The US forces acquired about 100 V2 rockets and a large proportion of the team that had built them and then set up a facility in New Mexico to continue the development. The first few covers to go into space were on board a captured V2 launched on 10th October 1946 from the White Sands Proving Ground in New Mexico. The covers were attached on the outside, so did not survive the re-entry from an altitude of 174 km.

9.5 First mail from Earth Orbit 15 November 1960. Credit Walter Hopferweiser

On 1st April 1947, another captured V2 was launched from New Mexico to an altitude of 129 km.[30] This time, the covers on board were damaged during the landing but survived. On the following day, two of these covers, the first ever space mail, were sent by the Administrative Assistant at White Sands, M D Silkiner, to the philatelist Robert Schoendorf.[31]

Most of the rocket mail pioneers anticipated the high speed of rockets would eventually allow mail to be transported from any place on Earth to another place within about an hour.[32] Stephen Smith made some progress over twelve years of working on rockets, a much longer period than any other individual. But his success was limited by the resources available to him. He worked alone and unsupported to the end.

Through his membership of international organisations such as the British Interplanetary Society, he would have followed the progress in rocket technology towards spaceflight. He joined the BIS in 1935 and used this membership as a form of public validation of his rocket mail experiments, using the BIS member communication letterhead when writing to influential contacts both within and outside India. Many of the newspaper reports of his work included a reference to his BIS membership to support his credentials.[33]

On 8th August 1957, the USA successfully tested its Jupiter C RS-40 missile to an altitude of 460 km. The Jupiter C missile was an Intermediate Range Ballistic Missile developed by the US and based on the V2. The nose cone of the Jupiter C RS-40 was the first object designed to withstand the heat of re-entry; it was fully recovered after a journey into space. It contained a letter from Wernher von Braun to the Commander of the Army Ballistic Missile Agency, Major General Bruce Medaris.[34]

The visions of the early rocket mail experimenters to deliver mail from one place on Earth to any other in less than an hour was finally realised by a missile originally developed for the purpose of war. The 20-minute flight of the Jupiter C RS-40 was the culmination of the vision of experimenters such as Stephen Smith, Gerhard Zucker and especially Friedrich Schmiedl, who had first demonstrated rocket mail in on 9th September 1931.

The first space mail to be recovered following an orbit of Earth included 28 covers launched on the spy satellite Discoverer-17 on 12th November 1960. The Discover series of spacecraft were part of the USA's first space-based photo reconnaissance programme called Corona. Designed to take images of 'denied areas' in the USSR, China and Asia, it ran from the late 1950s until 1978.

```
                    DEPARTMENT OF THE AIR FORCE
                     OFFICE OF THE CHIEF OF STAFF
                      UNITED STATES AIR FORCE
                         WASHINGTON, D. C.
```

General L. L. Lemnitzer
Chief of Staff
United States Army

Dear General Lemnitzer

In order to reach you, this letter will have flown a distance of almost one-half million miles both within and without the earth's atmosphere, travelling over 17 times around the world at speeds greater than 18,000 miles per hour. Contained in the DISCOVERER satellite, it will have been launched by the United States Air Force into an orbit about the earth from Vandenberg Air Force Base, California, and recovered in the mid-Pacific.

This is the first time that letters have been sent by a satellite and is in the tradition of airmen who less than thirty years ago pioneered in the first use of airmail.

This remarkable achievement could not have been accomplished without the dedication of a great many people from Congress, from science, from industry, from the Services, and from the National Aeronautics and Space Administration. We are grateful to all who have had a part in bringing this Nation one step nearer to man's transcendence over the limits of the earth.

Sincerely

THOMAS D. WHITE
Chief of Staff

9.6 Letter carried on Discoverer-17 on 15 November 1960. Credit Walter Hopferweiser

The satellites carried a 960-metre spool of 70mm film. A film container almost a meter in diameter was returned to earth inside a re-entry module was ejected by the satellite after two days of observations from an elliptical orbit of 190 km by 984 km. Whilst descending through the earth's atmosphere on a parachute, the container was recovered by a US air force aircraft over the Pacific Ocean.[35] All 28 letters from Discoverer-17 were posted to personnel holding high-ranking posts in the military and politics.

Just as airmail and rocket mail had inaugurated a new category within philately, the new realm of space eventually gave rise to Astrophilatley, although the term Space Mail is still widely used.[36] It deals with covers and cards that record space exploration-related events including launches, landings, docking and space walks. Astrophilatley arrived a few years after Smith's death. It is not something that he openly engaged in or directly contributed to.

No mail covers were flown on the first four space-vehicle types that took men into space, the US's Mercury and Gemini and USSR's Vostok and Voskhod.[37] The ultimate example of rocket mail was the mail that went to the Moon during the Apollo programme. Between 1968 and 1972, twenty-four men went to the Moon on nine crewed missions of the American Apollo programme, with half of the astronauts walking on the lunar surface.

Philately was an integral part of the story of the USA's Apollo programme. The astronauts did not receive much more than the military salary that their rank entitled them to. Each astronaut was permitted to take a limited quantity of personal items (2.5 kg aboard the command module and 0.25 kg in the lunar module). These kits included signed covers, which could then be sold to collectors once the Apollo missions were over. Not all covers were flown; some remained with family members on Earth as a form of insurance in the event the mission failed. In November 2018, one such cover flown on Apollo 11 from the private collection of Neil Armstrong sold for $156,250.[38]

A US Postal Service promotional idea was approved by NASA: Apollo 15 carried a kit 9.5 x 6 x 4 inches (24 x 15 x 10 cm))under the lunar rover. On 2nd August 1971, Dave Scott used the ink pad and rubber stamp in the kit to cancel two envelopes whilst on the lunar surface.[39] In a gesture connecting aviation and spaceflight, Al Worden, Apollo 15 Command module pilot (who was in lunar orbit while astronauts Scott and Irwin were on the lunar surface) carried a cover belonging to

Mr Forrest E Cook of Michigan signed by Orville Wright for the 25th anniversary of his first flight.

9.7 Apollo 15 lunar mail cover. Cancelled on the Moon by David Scott during the Apollo 15 mission. Credit National Postal Museum, Washington, DC

Although each Apollo mission carried souvenirs, it was the Apollo 15 mission in the summer of 1971 that attracted unwanted media attention. A few months after the return of Apollo 15, some of its flown covers came onto the market, contrary to the agreed arrangements. It had been agreed that the covers were to be sold only after the Apollo programme ended. Writing in 1972, Dr Leo Fishbein characterised the astronauts as having caught 'the contagion "GREED" and thought they would capitalise on their talents'.[40]

NASA attracted correspondence from philatelists, collectors and dealers seeking verification of covers carried by the astronauts. In one such response, dated 22nd June 1972, Alan Shepard stated on behalf of NASA that 'NASA is not in a position to pass on the validity of these covers'.[41]

The time of the rocket mail passed as instantly as it had come. The dangers associated with extreme acceleration and absence of reliable precision guidance rendered rocket transport unsafe at the very time when aircraft were becoming more reliable and safer. As airlines developed long-haul routes that could carry mail and other cargo as well as people, the potential for rocket mail diminished even further.

Nevertheless, the work of the rocket mail experimenters including Stephen Smith, was not in vain. Collectively they made a critical contribution to the technology of the twentieth-century space age. An age that eventually enabled instant global telecommunication, life-saving weather forecasts and precision navigation on the sea, land and air at anytime and anywhere on Earth. The collective efforts devoted to rocketry during the inter-war years were a prelude to the large-scale rockets that delivered space-based assets and enabled the information-rich, digital economies that shape the lives of most of the people on the planet today.

9.8 Blue Origin founder, Jeff Bezos cancelling a card on the side of the space capsule immediately after it landed in Texas 11 December 2019. Credit Blue Origin

On 11th December 2019, a new generation was introduced to space mail. The commercial spaceflight operator Blue Origin, sponsoring and working with Club For the Future, launched thousands of postcards to space and back on its New Shepard reusable space capsule. Following the sub-orbital space flight, all the cards were cancelled with a Blue Origin 'Flown to Space' stamp and returned to the students via standard post.

Proceeds from the sale of flown mail for worthy causes continues in the modern era. In June 1986, Indian astronaut Rakesh Sharma sold about half a dozen envelopes that had been signed during his spaceflight. All the proceeds were destined for a school called Asha Niketan in Ojhar, India, which serves children with learning difficulties and disabilities'. Sharma had spent almost eight days in space aboard the USSR space station Soyuz-7 between 3rd and 11th April 1984. The envelopes were signed by him and all his crew mates including Oleg Atkov, Leonid Kizim, Yuri Malishev, Vladimir Soloyov and Gennady Strekalov.[42]

The clear distinction between the early rocket mail experimenters and the modern space engineers is not as clear cut as it may appear. For example, Robert Paganini in Switzerland once received a Christmas card from the School of Aerodynamics based in CalTech.[43] One member of that organisation was Theodore von Karman, who would give his name to the threshold of space at 100 km altitude, the Karman line. The crucial contributions of Robert Goddard, Herman Oberth and Sergei Korolev are all rightly acknowledged in history. So is the work of early pioneers such as Willy Ley, Reinhold Tiling and Friedrich Schmiedl is also recognised beyond the philatelic community.[44] By contrast, the lifelong accomplishments in rocketry made by Stephen Smith are largely unknown.

British Interplanetary Society

The British Interplanetary Society was founded on 13th October 1933 in an office block in the centre of Liverpool, and Stephen Smith joined in late 1934, probably its first member from India. Stephen Smith's first rocket mail experiment in September 1934 was reported in the BIS bulletin in November 1934.[45] Whilst the BIS report recorded his work, it did not record his name.

A report of Smith's rocket flight carrying a chick and a hen across the

Damodar River was published in the October 1935 issue of the BIS journal. The report stated 'What is said to be the first transportation by rockets of animate objects is claimed for Mr S H Smith, our new Calcutta member. On June 29th last, Mr Smith successfully shot a rocket across the Damodar River containing two live birds and nearly two hundred letters'.[46]

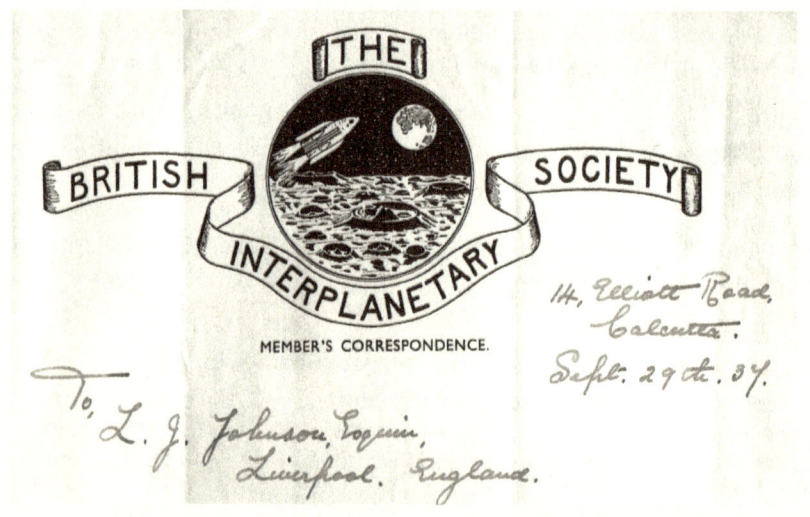

9.9 BIS Members' Correspondence. Credit Private collection of Leslie Johnson, Liverpool, England

Smith corresponded regularly with Leslie Johnson, the Liverpool-based secretary of the BIS, sending him reports and photographs of his experiments. On the day in October 1937 that he conducted his successful Boomerang rocket test, Smith wrote to Leslie Johnson in Liverpool, convinced that he had made a significant breakthrough. He claimed that '"a rocket must be independent of atmospherics as far as possible."'.[47]

Perhaps encouraged by Smith's success and optimism, Johnson wrote an article with the title 'Transatlantic Rocket Mail' highlighting the work of stamp collectors and especially Smith's work.[48] In addition to using the BIS as a communication platform to communicate his work in India, Smith also used his BIS membership to assert his international status. He used BIS member stationery when writing to the press, local officials or international contacts[49].

The BIS founder Phil Cleator had strong personal connections with the American Interplanetary Society and Germany's VfR. Edward Pendray, Friedrich Schmiedl, Willy Ley and Robert Paganini were also early BIS members. Through Smith's membership of the BIS, details of his work were brought to the notice of the people working in that field globally. Despite the name, the BIS has always been an international organisation. In a letter dated 3rd April 1936, from Cleator (BIS founder) to Pendray (AIS founder), he says 'glad the details of the East Indian (referring to Smith's experiments in Calcutta) experiments reached you. I shall be very glad to receive the report of Dr Goddard's work'.[50]

The Great Depression of 1929 was initiated by an American financial crisis that resulted in a widespread economic slowdown felt by most of the developing and developed countries around the globe. It was from within this environment that amateur rocketry groups emerged in the USSR, USA and Europe.

They included: the Scientific Society for High Altitude Research in Austria (1926–1930); the Society for Space Ship Travel (Verein fur Raumschiffahrt or VfR 1928–1934) in Germany; the American Interplanetary Society (AIS) founded in 1930 which changed its name to the American Rocketry Society (ARS) in 1934 and was subsequently involved in a merger between the American Rocketry Society and the American Institute of Aeronautics and Astronautics (AIAA) in 1963; The Paisley Rocket Society (founded in Scotland in 1935); the Group for the Study of Reactive Motion (GIRD group) founded in Moscow in 1931, which later merged with the Gas Dynamics Laboratory to form the Reaction-Engine Scientific Research Institute in 1933; and the Cleveland Rocketry Society founded in January 1933 but ceased to exist by 1938 due to a lack of funds.

Prior to the founding of the BIS in Liverpool in October 1933, the BIS founder, Phil Cleator, had been in contact with the VfR and the American Interplanetary Society. He first made contact and sought to join the AIS on 10th August 1931 when he was the Director of Research at the Scientific Research Syndicate in Liverpool.[51] Four years after it was established, the BIS moved from Liverpool to London and Cleator stood down from the Society's Council but continued to serve as one of the vice presidents.

Within a few years of the founding of the BIS in Liverpool, similar groups were established in Manchester, Leeds, Scotland and Surrey. Stephen Smith would send flown covers and stamps to the society requesting: 'when the society has its Rocket Experiments, I should like a few flown souvenirs of the experiment'. But the BIS did not build and fly rockets, mainly because the 1875 Explosives Act in Britain prohibited the manufacture of rocket propellant. Societies in Manchester and Scotland engaged with the Home Office to challenge this restriction but without success. Cleator contacted the Home Office but also without success.[52] The BIS suspended activities during World War II but by consolidating the membership of several smaller rocketry societies across England, it became active once more by the end of 1945.[53]

One of the BIS's earliest publication of the BIS Lunar Spaceship in 1939 that attracted widespread attention.[54] It was a conceptual design of a vessel that would carry a crew of three to the Moon and return to them safely to Earth two weeks later. The 1,000-tonne initial mass would be needed to deliver one tonne to the lunar surface. The 1939, lunar Spaceship included the concept of a 'step' rocket(today is referred to as staging) and multi-legged lunar lander that descends to the lunar surface using propulsive landing. These concepts were employed by the NASA Apollo programme that completed six crewed lunar landing missions.

During three weeks in the summer of 1947, Arthur C Clarke, who was one of the BIS's first members and served as treasurer, editor and president, wrote a novel based on the BIS Lunar Spaceship, called *Prelude to Space*. In his novel, the mission to the Moon was called Prometheus and was powered by nuclear engines. Many of the techniques in the BIS Lunar Spaceship and Clarke's novel were deployed by the USA's Apollo programme, which took 24 men to the Moon between 1968 and 1972.[55]

The BIS was an international organisation from the outset. In addition to being a founder member of the International Astronautical Federation in 1950, the BIS had a significant political influence in shaping Britain's space policy during the 1960s and 1970s. In 1967, as a leading think tank on space, the BIS made recommendations to the British government including devoting 5% per annum (£25 million) of the R&D budget on space research, and a proposal that the UK should actively support a European space programme and develop new forms of propulsion including nuclear.[56] Had Smith been able to establish a BIS equivalent group in India, perhaps India's space programme could have started earlier than it did.

Most of those involved in the early history of rocketry had a deep interest in reading or writing popular science or science fiction. They included Willy Ley, Arthur C Clarke, Wernher von Braun, Max Valier and Leslie Johnson. Almost all publicly declared the influence of science fiction during their formative years. Robert Goddard and Wernher von Braun cited H G Wells and Jules Verne. In 1932, Goddard wrote to H G Wells of the 'deep impression' that his novel War of the Worlds had made when he had first read it in 1899. It directly led him to 'take up the search for spaceflight'.[57] In a letter to H G Wells dated 19th July 1939, Arthur C Clarke stated that 'we have built and designed a rocket ship which we honestly believe could reach the Moon and return'.[58]

Stephen Smith was a skilled writer and authored several books. He did not write any science fiction but was the inspiration of the 1938 short story called '*Satellites of Death*'. In the summer of 1938, Leslie Johnson in Liverpool wrote to Smith explaining that 'you may be interested to learn that I'll have a story of rocketry experiment in the next issue of the new English science fiction magazine Tales of Wonder, out in a month's time. I'll certainly send you a copy when it is published'.[59] The plot incorporates the idea of using a rocket to transport and conceal the body of a murder victim in earth orbit.

. . .

International Collaboration

During the 1920s and early 1930s, several rocketry, astronautic or interplanetary societies were founded in Germany, UK, Australia, Austria, USSR and the USA. The contribution from Stephen Smith, operating alone and independently, was the nearest India came to having something similar. There was no formal cooperation between them. In the absence of a common platform, sharing of information took place through journals, personal letters and reports in the press.

By the 1950s, the total number of members between the American, Argentinian and European rocketry societies came to over 2,300, not counting similar smaller groups in 27 other countries including Stephen Smith's contributions in India.[60] With the exception of the British Interplanetary Society, founded in 1933, which is still operating as an independent organisation based in London, by the late 1940s all the others had ceased to exist or had been subsumed by a unit of the national government.

Correspondence going back to the early rocketry societies of 1930s indicates this desire for international cooperation.[61] It did not happen then, but cooperation in space between multiple countries is now common and facilitated by the International Astronautical Congress. The establishment of the International Astronautical Congress (IAC) represents the culmination of the desires of those earlier rocketry groups.

The IAC, established in 1950, was largely due to the efforts of the then French group (Groupement Astronautique Francais) and the German society (Gesellschaft fur Weltraumforschung), supported by equivalent groups in Argentina, Denmark, Austria, Britain, Spain and Sweden.

The first IAC meeting in France was attended by over 1,000 participants. One of the unanimous outcomes was 'The creation of an international organisation for the study and development of interplanetary flight'. Of all the rocket mail experimenters, only Friedrich Schmiedl was present at that first meeting.[62] During the second meeting in London in September 1951, the International Astronautical Federation was established as a non-government space advocacy organisation. Since then, week-long IAC meetings have been organised by the IAF in a different country each year.

9.10 First meeting of The International Astronautical Congress 30 Sep 1950 in Paris. Credit International Astronautical Federation

The IAC has continued to grow in size and significance. It is an annual platform where the heads of national space agencies meet face to face and sow the seeds for future collaborative projects in space. The 69th IAC in 2018, meeting in the north German city of Bremen, was attended by 6,500 delegates from a record number of 83 countries. On the 50th anniversary of Apollo 11 in October 2019, the 70th meeting of the IAC was held in Washington, DC.

Since Sputnik, Gagarin and Armstrong more than half a century ago, the number of national space agencies has grown but a single International Space Agency remains elusive. International cooperation in space takes place on a project by project basis or through bi or multilateral arrangements frequently fostered through the IAC.

During the 1960s and 70s two countries, the USA and USSR, dominated all aspects of space including human spaceflight, investigating the earth and exploring the solar system with robotic spacecraft. Today there are 72 government space agencies, of which 14 have developed at least a basic in-house launch capability. However only six (China, Europe, India, Japan, USA and Russia) have a comprehensive space capability to design, build, launch and operate multiple spacecraft in various orbits.

India's space programme relied on international cooperation at the outset. In the early days, India sought help from France, Japan USSR and USA. International collaboration between all spacefaring nations is increasing and is essential to tackle projects that are big, complex or expensive. Today India has around 50 operational spacecraft including a space telescope in Earth orbit, a spacecraft orbiting Mars and another in lunar orbit. Through its space-based assets, India participates in the international satellite Search and Rescue and provides international civil aviation support through GAGAN. China (through the UN) has offered to take scientific experiments from several countries (including Italy, Spain, Peru, Mexico, Saudi Arabia, Japan and India) to its space station in 2021. The International Space Station is only possible through the collective effort of 18 countries.

Smith's vision of using rocket power to deliver medicine, food and communication is fulfilled today by the Indian Space Research Organisation. Rocket manufacturers in India have put into orbit satellites that are used to deliver medical assistance to small rural communities through a network of Village Resource Centres. Indian farmers and fisherman benefit from improved yields through data provided by remote sensing satellites. Indians across the country can now communicate almost instantly through a network of satellites much faster than the incredible speed Smith envisioned for rocket mail.

India has many active societies for science and space today, but Smith was alone when conducting his tests.[63] Had he received the support from others and especially from the authorities, India too could have played a role as a founding member of the IAC in 1950. In practice, this was a time when India was preoccupied with the transition to an independent nation. Smith himself weakened by the privations of World War II and a series of illnesses was nearing his end. He died in February 1951, just five months after the inaugural IAC meeting.

10

LEGACY

Smith and the Military

In 1946, following a decade of rocket experiments, Smith wrote to his friend Robert Paganini in Switzerland that he had received an offer 'for my services from a quite another quarter. Someday when I am permitted, I shall tell you'.[1] Apart from the certificate awarded to him in Sikkim by Mr C E Dudley from the Indian Civil Service in the presence of the King of Sikkim on 11th April 1935, this was probably the only other, albeit cryptic, evidence of a formal recognition of his work on rocketry. In the pursuit of spaceflight, Wernher von Braun in Germany and Sergei Korolev in USSR worked closely with their national military probably compromising their principles along the way. Schmiedl in Austria chose not to and destroyed his equipment and documents to prevent it. In contrast, Stephen Smith solicited military support in India but apparently in vain.

The twentieth century was a harbinger of new transformative means of transport. Trains, airships, airplanes and automobiles were transforming how people lived in the new century. Smith's motive for experimenting with rockets was to help develop a new revolutionary form of transport. His initial motivation was to use rockets for the transport of mail in India, as he saw it happening in the USA and Europe. Within months of starting out, he went further and showed that rockets could be used to transport more than just mail. By the summer of 1935, he had demonstrated the principle and practice of delivery by rocket of living creatures, medicine and food in addition to mail.

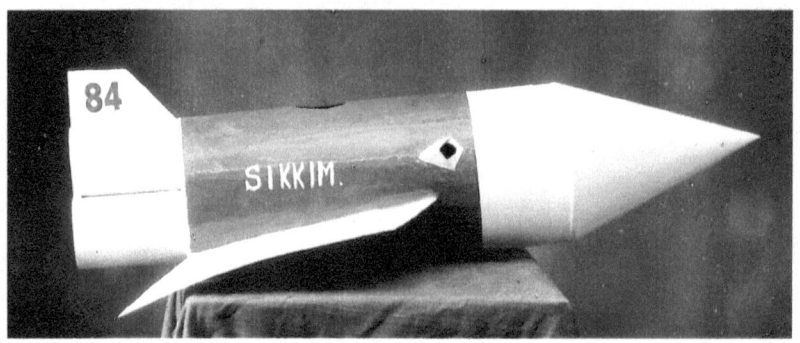

10.1 Close up of Rocket 84. This model carried the bird and had air holes on the side. 28 September 1935 Gangtok Sikkim. Credit Private collection of Leslie Johnson, Liverpool, England

Having lived in Calcutta for more than two decades, he was familiar with temperatures regularly exceeding 40°C in summer, eventually relieved by the monsoon rains. But the monsoon rains and the floods they triggered brought their own discomforts, hazards and destruction. It was probably this first-hand experience that motivated him to write in April 1938 to Paganini in Switzerland saying that the 'carriage of food and medicine is much more important than mail. People in distress want food and medicine before letters'.[2] This was his initial shift away from rocket mail.

But another much more significant change in direction was on the horizon. As a member of the British Empire, Smith was aware of the dramatic changes in geopolitics and the potential for war in Europe. As early as 1937, he knew about the military potential of rockets. Writing about the success of his Boomerang rocket to the BIS Secretary Leslie Johnson, he says 'when properly developed, it will be useful in time of war to fly over the enemy lines taking snapshots and returning with pictures of vital importance'.[3]

Through his contacts in high society and the key role of Calcutta as a central transport hub for the British Empire, Smith and his hometown could not escape the effects of World War II. Perhaps as a practising Christian, or because of his personal memories and experiences of World War I, he was at least for a time, against the idea of rockets for military use. However, working alone and unfunded, his progress was very slow. At this early stage, his rockets lacked the necessary range, capacity and precision for military operations. Engaging with the military offered an opportunity to accelerate their development, whilst doing his bit for the war and along the way realising his dream of developing a revolutionary high-speed transport system.

One innovation introduced by Stephen Smith and not replicated by anyone else was the idea of a Boomerang rocket. The 'Boomerang' was fired in Alipore (a southern district of Calcutta) on 11th October 1937. Carrying 170 printed missives, it was designed to demonstrate the ability of one rocket to travel to a specific location, drop its payload (of mail, food or medicine) and return to the point of launch. In 1937, a report in the *Star of India* recorded a successful flight, saying that the Boomerang 'true to its new name, after leaving the firing rack for about 200 yards, took a curve to the right, eventually gliding to earth back again about 25 yards from the rack'.[4]

Another attempt to launch the Boomerang rocket (number 163) on 25th April 1938 resulted in it getting stuck in a tree on the return journey. It was recovered and found to be undamaged. At the time, the declaration of World War II was more than a year away. However, a report in *The Star of India* emphasised its military potential, stating it was a 'formidable weapon for warfare, as it may be utilised for dropping bombs or spraying poison gas over enemy trenches and then returning to base for fresh supplies'.[5]

In September 1939, Smith approached the fifth anniversary of his first rocket experiment. Despite the global press coverage of his rocket experiments, the acknowledgement from high echelons of society of his achievements and the income he was generating from his flown covers, he had not made a significant breakthrough. His experiments in 1939 were not significantly different from what he had done in 1937. The outbreak of World War II presented an unexpected opportunity. Reluctantly he turned to the military, writing: 'I have placed all my knowledge and experience in rocket transport in the hands of the military authorities'.[6]

In the same month that war was declared, he conducted his first in a series of 'War Rocket' experiments. They were largely symbolic but through them he publicly affirmed his patriotism and then went further and reluctantly began to consider how the military use of his rockets could help defeat the Japanese forces approaching India.

In 1940, using rockets number 230 and 231, Smith attempted to take pictures of the ground from the air. This was a huge technical challenge, which required pointing the camera with precision, configuring a suitable exposure and recovering the camera on landing. These two rockets were launched on 17th July 1940 but both failed to acquire any photographs.

Since these tests were carried out after WWII had been declared, no press or public were invited to the launch. Only limited details of the attempt were recorded. Neither of the rockets carried any covers but each carried a single sheet inscribed by hand 'Carried by rocket No. 230 rocket to photograph test' and Carried by rocket No. 231 rocket to photograph No. 2 test'.[7] The locations of the single sheets are unknown.

By the summer of 1944, the war was approaching a conclusion. The Japanese air force bombed the Calcutta docks and as part of the Burma campaign Japanese soldiers crossed over to India. As part of the British Empire, India was involved from the very outset in the war. Over two million soldiers from India went to fight overseas and Smith, who had served in World War I, would have been aware of the physical and mental horrors for individuals as well as for communities.

From March to July 1944, the conflict arrived on Indian on India's north eastern border not far from where Smith lived. The two simultaneous battles of Imphal and Kohima, two cities 140 km apart, marked the end of the Japanese advance in India. As a major port city, Calcutta would probably have been the next objective had the Japanese forces not been defeated. This must have been a welcome relief to all in Calcutta including Smith.

Rocket development in Europe was progressing at a remarkable pace during the war. By late 1944, Germany's rocket development team in Peenemunde were building and launching the V1 flying bombs. By December 1944, the design and testing of the V2 rocket was complete and it could join the V1 in bringing death and destruction to several European countries. The prevailing secrecy and limited wartime communication meant that the information did not come to light until the war had ended.

Perhaps it was whilst watching this development of rocketry, accelerated by the political and financial investments at a time of war, that Smith engaged with his technically most challenging innovation. At the beginning of his experiments, his rockets were powered by dry powder as produced by commercial manufacturers. But in 1944, he described nine rocket launches that used two new forms of propulsion: compressed air and gas. He did not describe the technical details of either of these propulsion mechanisms, so it is not clear how he acquired the compressed air or which gas was used.

Date	Name	Type	Covers
10th September 1944	Hornet	Gas and Dry Fuel	0
11th September 1944	Black and Tan	Gas and Dry Fuel	10
20th September 1944	No name	Gas	13
25th October 1944	No name	Gas	15
31st October 1944	No name	Compressed Air	28
8th November 1944	No name	Compressed Air	19
21st November 1944	The Imphal	Gas	11
4th December 1944	The Kohima	Gas	78
4th December 1944	The Dimapur	Compressed Air	68

Some of the projectiles were first 'launched by compressed air, then carried by dry fuel and the journey completed by compressed air'. He explained that 'my reason for launching the projectiles first by gas or compressed air was that the enemy could not locate the place from where the projectile was launched. Gas and compressed air were noiseless and there was no smoke'.[8] Only some of the projectiles carried mail items and only some were given names. He completed these tests in December 1944 but did not communicate this information until after the war was over.

Despite his willingness to engage, Smith's letters illustrate his utter frustration when dealing with the military authorities in India. Writing in 1946, he says 'when the war first started, I offered my services to the authorities'.[9] This arrangement did not go well. He provided information on his rockets to the authorities until 1943 without any recompense, but then he was told that they were of 'no use'.

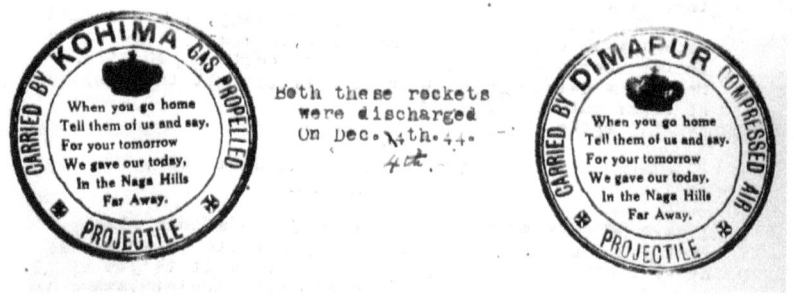

10.2 Gas and Compressed Air Propulsion Experiments. Credit Museum of Communication, Bern, Switzerland

In 1944, he was contacted again by the same authorities to take up work with them. This was probably motivated by the news of the success of the V1 and V2 rockets in Europe becoming publicly known. In the light of the poor treatment and lack of recompense for his earlier contributions, Smith expressed his feelings of being hurt, angry and cheated. Accordingly, he chose not to reply.

In contrast to his treatment in India, in 1944 he received an unsolicited letter from 'yankees from the Indo-Burma theatre' acknowledging his work and encouraging him to continue with it. On this unexpected interaction, Smith reflected on the adage 'a prophet is never believed in his own land'.[10] In December 1945, one of these 'yankees' visited Smith at his home in Calcutta to collect and take to America a set of his personal files and documents, including the letters he had received from the authorities.[11] This request was initiated by George W Angers, the founder of the Aero Philatelic Society of America in 1923. Smith was already familiar with Angers, having recruited him to join the Indian Air Mail Society as an honorary member when it was founded.

On one occasion, as a result of an accident in his workshop, Smith claimed to have stumbled across the phenomenon of invisibility. He referred to it only once and there is very limited information, so it probably was not a significant or an accurate observation. He claimed that his own hand 'turned opaque' and he would work on understanding this phenomenon as funds permitted.[12] Modern military vehicles in the air, ground and sea take advantage of stealth technology. Attributes of invisibility or stealth (although Smith used the word "opaque") are acquired through surface coatings that reduce the reflection of radio signals used to detect them from a distance. However, Smith did not work with radio and it is unlikely that this is what Smith had stumbled on.

The lesson most governments learned from the closing months of World War II was the critical role of atomic weapons and missiles that could travel at supersonic speed with remarkable precision in future wars. Was the offer 'from quite another quarter' an attempt to harvest Smith's talent and experience towards this end? Could it have been an offer from an external organisation, even a foreign government (Angers was a US national), looking to learn from his rocket experience? Precisely who made the offer for his services remains unknown.

There is no record of Smith leaving India. In 1949, he confided in Robert Paganini that 'my original intention in all my experiments was to help and improve the existing methods of transport. Now that I am compelled to cease my work, rockets are being improved only for war'.[13]

Distant Friendship

At a time when telephones were not common and long before email, Stephen Smith maintained a regular personal contact with individuals around the world through letters. Some of these contacts became friends or supporters and advocates of his work in airmail and rocket mail. With one of these, who he never met or spoke to, he developed a deep, sincere and profound personal relationship that lasted over a quarter of a century. Smith's correspondence with Robert Paganini (1866–1950), who lived many thousands of miles away in a small town in Switzerland, covered some of the darkest periods of the twentieth century: the Great Depression, World War Two, Bengal Famine and the post Indian Independence riots in Calcutta.

10.3 Stephen Smith with two of his rockets in Gangtok Sikkim 1935. Credit Private collection of Leslie Johnson, Liverpool, England

The two men were very different. Robert Paganini, twenty-five years his senior, was a trained professional scientist working in the chemical industry. Paganini had a PhD so was known as Dr Paganini. In many of his letters Smith refers to him as "My Dear Doctor". Smith had worked as a policeman, customs official and as a dentist. United by their interest in philately, they first made contact in 1925. On 24th December 1925, Smith wrote to Paganini saying 'personally speaking, I am indeed happy to learn that you have honoured the club that I have founded, by joining as an honorary member'.[14]

The hundreds of letters Smith wrote to Paganini over the next 25 years record not only the successes and failures of his rocket mail but also the details of the tumultuous period in the second quarter of the twentieth century through which they both lived.

Paganini is widely considered to be the father of philately in Switzerland, having started his collection in 1912 soon after airmail arrived in Switzerland. Smith sought Paganini's help to promote his work in India to the wider international philatelic community. As a recognised authority, Paganini could attract international attention to Smith's work, something that Smith himself could not.

Through his first-hand experience of India's challenging geography, climate and the lack of adequate transport infrastructure, he recognised the unique benefits of rocket transport for India. He confided in Paganini the limits of his capability as a rocket mail experimenter, telling him that 'I have discovered many many faults I have committed in the construction of my rocket, I am still a very big fool'.[15]

In Calcutta, Smith was at the forefront of global events. Against a backdrop of an emerging social unrest from the Great Depression, the independence movement grew in India. On 12th March 1930, Gandhi challenged the colonial British rule of India, using non-violent civil disobedience. In January 1931 Smith wrote to Paganini: 'we are having a bad time here in India' and by June he writes: "I regret to say that everything in India is getting worse and worse, business is very bad, everyday men and women are being thrown out of employment. It is almost a daily occurrence to hear that some patrons have been either shot, stabbed, or bombed. Thefts are taking place everywhere'.[16]

The Japanese Air Force attack on Pearl Harbour in 1942 was followed almost exactly two years later with an attack on the port of Calcutta.[17] Smith was a victim of the physical and emotional suffering resulting from a chain of events including lack of food, maladministration, a devastating cyclone in 1942, political infighting and a famine that killed around three million people among Bengal's rural and urban poor and the working class population.

On 14th April 1944, the SS Fort Stikine arrived in Calcutta docks with 1,400 tonnes of explosives. It was also carrying 50,000 tonnes of grain. An incident resulted in two huge explosions and a fire that took three days to bring under control. Seismic sensors recorded the explosion in Shimla 2,000 km away. Smith would have heard and felt that explosion and lived with its consequences of escalating prices and the dwindling availability of basic rations.

Whilst suffering from carbolic acid poisoning in March 1944, he wrote: 'I should have died by 13th March, I was very bad, nobody expected me to live. I was bleeding through my mouth, nostrils etc. I could not see and went deaf but then I made a miraculous recovery'.[18] In January 1949 he described a 'continuous chain of miseries' that he suffered in 1948. They included malaria, his son Hector contracting and recovering from typhoid, his wife suffering from fever, his four-month-old grandson contracting cerebro-spinal fever, costly repairs for two fans, and being robbed by his servants who then left suddenly.

The year 1948, the first year of India's independence, was a particularly bad one for him. He did no work nor did he conduct any rocket mail experiments. He wrote: 'illness and necessary finances have crippled me'.[19]

Paganini was central to Smith's limited international success. Smith sent him reports of his rocket experiments, asking Paganini to write about his work in the media in Europe and America. Later he sent his rocket and airmail items to sell on his behalf, partly because Paganini could secure higher bids from western collectors but also because he could help to develop Smith's international standing.

Christian Values

Working as a dentist and with a young son to support, Smith struggled to make sense of the events taking place around him. He concluded: 'Life to thinkers is a comedy and a tragedy to those that feel.' He had friends in high society but he knew his place, concluding 'all that glitters is not gold. Some of the cleanest and finest of hearts are found in persons of a humble station in life'.[20]

The primary purpose of Smith's correspondence with Robert Paganini was communicating news of airmail developments and later rocket mail, and also with sharing or selling airmail or rocket mail items. Although they never met or spoke to each other in person, over 25 years these two men developed deep bonds across very different cultures and vast distances.

Paganini collected and archived all of Smith's letters. What happened to the letters Paganini sent to Smith is not clear. Smith's letters to Paganini, now archived in the Museum of Communications in Bern, Switzerland, capture the deep personal views on what drove him: his Christian values, the insensitivity of wealthy individuals towards the poor and the harsh inequalities and poverty that surrounded him. In his letters to Paganini, he writes about his two adopted daughters, his small contribution in helping to educate a few of the street children in Calcutta and a friendship with a leper friend who has no fingers or toes.

The year 1931 was one of the first of many turbulent periods in Smith's life. It was the year that the Indian capital moved from Smith's home town of Calcutta to the newly built New Delhi. The Indian independence movement saw the execution of several leaders and Gandhi was released from another spell in prison. A meeting between the viceroy and Gandhi resulted in the Gandhi-Irwin pact. So started India's long journey to independence.

In July, Smith sent a letter to Paganini marked 'Private and Confidential'. It was a reply to a letter from Paganini who had offered to send Smith five pounds. In it, Smith struggles with his emotions.

He tries to hide his personal desperate state and the welcomed relief this money had brought. He describes his distressing personal situation, saying 'if you like Sir, send me a few pounds to help me to relieve the hardships of some poor people. Don't my good sir send it for my past actions (referring to airmail and rocket mail covers and stamps he had sent to Paganini) and my tokens of respect but send me anything you may care to send to help the forgotten, the trampled ones. I am begging on their behalf now, perhaps at some future date someone may intercede on my behalf, we never know, we do not what is before us' and 'I try to be good and ask for mercy, I am weak, Our Maker is strong, let Him have mercy'.[21]

Paganini did not only provide financial support to Smith near the end of their relationship but probably from the outset. In a letter in February 1949, Smith writes: 'the splendid pair of curtains which the late Mrs Paganini and your good self-presented to us in 1933 is almost in just as good a condition as when we received them'.[22] In this letter, he also acknowledges the receipt of a gift of £20 and explains that he will use it towards providing fifty children aged between six and ten years with half an hour of religious study in the form of pleasant tales and stories. He chooses to do this because he finds 'that all the stories that my mother told me about 50 years ago are still fresh'. A week later, he sent another letter listing a breakdown of how he had spent some of the £20 towards his charitable acts.[23]

Living in neutral Switzerland, Paganini experienced relative peace during the war, but would have been aware of the death, destruction and the extreme hardship forced on many in neighbouring Germany and around the world. Although Smith was privately educated and from a well-off family, while living under wartime conditions in Calcutta he admitted: 'I am struggling hard myself to keep the wolf from the door'.[24] Both men were humanitarians. It appears that Paganini supported Smith with occasional monetary donations several times over the 25 years they knew each other.[25]

In 1949, when recovering from a particularly difficult time, Smith thanked Paganini for the £49 that he had received. Smith had sent several postal items to Paganini, asking him to sell them on his behalf.

He was recovering from a series of illnesses and people in Calcutta was still getting to grips with post-war and post-independence recovery. The arrival of the cheque was timely. He tells Paganini 'You have a heart of gold. God bless you'.[26]

As the middle of the twentieth century approached, Paganini was nearing his eighty-fifth birthday and Smith his sixtieth. The world was dramatically different from the one in which they had first encountered each other in 1925. Between them, during the intervening quarter of a century, they had experienced profound shifts in population, famine, civil unrest, brutal effects of war and the rise of a new world order. Their mutual interest in philately had brought them together but a deep sense of human dignity, empathy and compassion had kept them together.

On 6th December 1950, Paganini died. In his will he left a quarter of his estate (worth at the time 38,780 Swiss Francs) to Stephen Smith. It was not a decision that Paganini made on his death-bed but in April 1946 just after the death of his wife. They had no children. It is not known whether Smith was aware before he died that his friend thousands of miles away had left him this gift.[27]

End of a Pioneer

Stephen Smith's adult life coincided with a revolution in transport. Cars, trains, airships and aircraft were coming of age during his formative years. He had started school in 1903 when the Wright brothers made their historic flight and left school in 1911, the year of the first official airmail flight. It was through his interest in collecting airmail that he learnt of another new development: rockets. He started off with rocket mail but was soon convinced that India in particular could be well served if rockets were used for the delivery of food and medicines at times of emergency.

Despite his success over a decade of experimenting with rockets, he never forgot his limitations. In 1937 he writes 'I am a novice and a man of limited education, in other words, I am a fool who has ventured where angels fear to tread'.[28] Ultimately, he was not successful in his primary objective of integrating rocket transport in India into the national infrastructure. In that respect, Schmiedl in Austria, Zucker in Germany, Pendray (founder of the AIS) and Hanna (founder of the Cleveland Rocket Society) in America also failed.[29] By the middle of the twentieth century, the accumulative advances in aviation supplanted the benefits of rockets.

At the time Smith was conducting his rocket experiments, transatlantic flights for passengers and mail were predicted to start as early as 1938, supported by a series of floating airports along the way: 'experts now confidently assert that transatlantic and transpacific aeroplane services will be inaugurated within a very short time, probably during 1938. These services are planned to run twice daily, east to west and west to east and will convey mails and passengers. They will be made safe and practicable by means of a chain of floating "seadromes" anchored to the seabed at intervals of 500 miles (800 km). The successful accomplishment of services of this kind will mark an epoch in the history of the world comparable with the opening of the Suez and Panama Canals'.[30]

Smith conducted his final rocket experiment on 4th December 1944, using compressed air. Since the war was not over, he kept a low profile; representatives of the press and the public were not invited. On 15th August 1947, India celebrated its independence, a political objective that had been in the making for decades. It was a cause for national celebration, but for many ordinary Indians it initiated another dark period of street riots, civil disorder and sectarian violence. In January 1948, that violence consumed India's man of peace, Mohandas Karamchand Gandhi.

On 23rd March 1949, Smith wrote to Paganini describing the shortage of rice, flour and clothes. Where these items were available, the black market prices were well beyond his reach. He described in graphic detail the brutal killings very close to his house. One of the victims in his neighbourhood was a man called Brennan, who was a widower and friend. His two daughters were now orphans.[31]

Most of the time his work was belittled, and he was marginalised. In

1937 he wrote: 'My experiments have stamped me as a suspicious dreamer who is only wasting money. Some have called me a LIAR... many hurtful remarks have reached Mrs Smith and sometimes we have had unnecessary family disturbances'.[32]

He is frequently portrayed as working as a dentist most of his adult life. In practice, philately is where he spent most of his time and it may have been his primary source of income during his adult life. His entry in to rocket mail experimentation may have been motivated by financial pressures. Soon after his first rocket mail test in September 1934, he wrote to Victor Pont, in England in November 1934, saying he was running low on cash "I am duced hard up at the moment, I spent six days under canvas at Dumdum".[33] A year later he wrote again to Pont saying "I need money badly to make my rockets, they are metal now. Had I the money I should make bigger ones of aluminium and better ones too. But I have no money."

In addition to the global coverage of his work by the media, in May 1938 he was contacted by the Keystone Press Agency Ltd asking for photos of his experiments.[34] After 1947, he wrote to Jawaharlal Nehru, the Indian Prime Minister of an Independent India, along with Dr Katju the governor of Bengal. These were heady times for a new government caught up in the early days of post-independence nation building. He never got a response.

10.4 Extract from a letter from Stephen Smith to Robert Paganini 3 November 1949. Credit Museum of Communication, Bern, Switzerland

In 1949, Smith concluded that it is 'very difficult for anyone born out of India to do anything'. So, he asked Paganini to write to His Excellency Dr Katju on his behalf, hoping that an external, independent western voice might solicit a response where he had failed. He asks Paganini to tell him 'of the great advantages of using rockets as a means of transport during floods, landslips and emergency conditions when and where it would be impossible to use airplanes. I have been working on these for over 12 years and my experiments were increasing more and more until the war when the military wrote to me on numerous occasions for aid. I am India's pioneer and premier rocket experimenter and that I am Indian by birth, having been born in Shillong, Assam. I have done lots of work in the Himalayas and my efforts have been recognised in the USA and the whole of Europe and yet in the land of my birth I am ignored. Thousands of my letters, cards and stamps are scattered about in collections all over the world. If His Excellency, Dr Katju should be interested he should send for me'.[35] But no one sent for him.

On seeing a jet plane over Calcutta for the first time in 1949, Smith reflected on this transition of air flight from one era to another and reassessed his accomplishments. He recalled that 'in my humble opinion, my boomerang rocket appears to me as very important'. He laments that despite his initial intentions to help improve methods of transport, now rockets are being improved only for war. Unwell and exhausted by the privations in the immediate aftermath of Indian independence, he recalled the memories of his hometown of Shillong. 'It's tucked away in the hills, clad in the pine forest, lovely flowers, orchids, ferns and beautiful butterflies'.[36]

In what was probably one of his final letters, in March 1950 Smith apologised to Paganini for not having written for a long time. He starts with a greeting for the new year and explains that he was 'taken severely ill on 10 December 1949 and unconscious of many days'. He had suffered from asthma throughout his life but now, older and frail, he was not able to recover as quickly as before. He continued: 'I was weak and could not speak or walk… an injection of Frystallin… saved my life… I wrote to Mr Cooper, the biggest Indian dealer and a great friend of mine.. He wrote back saying he was in serious financial difficulties... I could not write to you since I had no money for postage... Yes, Yes, I laugh at my fate".[37] He concludes this letter saying: 'I have not heard from H.E. Dr Katju, or Dr B. L Roy, or Pandit Nehru'. On the margin of the letter he added 'Please do not worry to reply'. This was March 1950, it is not clear if Paganini did reply.

Stephen Smith had started out working alone on rockets in 1934, and despite the worldwide interest in rocket mail, by 1946 in India he was still working in isolation. He recognised that he had no access to 'really interested people who would help me correct my mistakes and help me also financially, things would be very different'.[38] He had tried to find such 'interested people' but had not succeeded.

He contacted a former member of the Indian Air Mail society, Leon Victor Pont, a railway engineer. He wanted Pont's engineering input in designing and building rockets. Writing in 1935, he said to Pont, 'I need help very very badly from a person who has engineering skills and one who I could trust... I work alone. Zucker and Schmiedl, the other two rocket experimenters have a syndicate at their backs. I have none.' Although Zucker and Schmiedl had more funds than him, Smith was not aware that their progress too was hindered by lacked the funds.[39] Unfortunately, Pont had returned to England in 1933 and could not offer assistance from there.[40]

After his death, Stephen Smith's collection was dispersed widely.[41] Part of the collection was destroyed (according to his granddaughter), sold in India (to Jal Cooper) and around the world (to John R Dilworth). On 14th October 1953, some of his collection was put up for sale by the Normandy Stamp Studios in Los Angles, California. In part the description read 'For sale in three lots including a mounted collection of rocket mail experiments of Mr S Smith, of Calcutta, India, with picture of Mr Smith, the rocket constructor, reprints of newspaper stories on the experiments, short history of each experiment, number of stamps issued'.[42]

Today his work appears in a NASA publication, archived in the postal museums of England and Switzerland and the National Air and Space Museum in Washington, DC.[43] His covers are highly sought after by philatelists around the world.[44] Some of his flown covers are priced at around $12,000 and a few, that are extremely rare, at $20,000.[45] Victor Pont's daughter put up for auction her father's philatelic collection in Canada in February 2020. The 133 lots of Stephen Smith related items sold for $95,000 Canadian dollars to bidders around the world.[46]

He died on 15th February 1951, the day after his 60th birthday. Multiple obituaries were published amongst the international philatelic community.[47] One writer said that he was 'the greatest one-man campaign for rocketry'. Stephen Smith is buried at Circular Road Cemetery close to Elliot Road in Calcutta, an address still recognisable today by philatelists all around the world.

11
APPENDICES

GLOSSARY

Aerophilately: A branch of philately specialising in aerial transport.

Aerostat: Any structure, balloon or an airship that attains lift because of its lighter than air structure

Airship: Generic term for any manoeuvrable or powered air born vehicle, including blimps and zeppelins.

Astrophilatley: A branch of philately that records events in space exploration.

Balloon: A lighter-than-air vehicle devoid of power. Altitude is determined by controlling hot air and ballast.

Blimp: A non-rigid airship also known as a barrage balloon. It has no internal structural framework. The airship-like shape is maintained pressure of the internal gas or hot air.

Cachet: A stamp or a seal that adds a design, symbol or text to mark to a coverer card to record special events such as first-day covers.

Cancel: A marking over a stamp to show that it has been processed (or delivered) by the post office and cannot be used again. The marking usually indicates the date, time and location.

Catalogue: A compilation of comprehensive information to help describe, identify and assess the value philatelic items.

Catapult Mail: Mail that starts its aerial journey with the help of a mechanism to push it in to the air before the transport mechanism (aeroplane or rocket) engine engages.

Counterfeit: A philatelic item created for deception or imitation with intention to be represented or sold as a genuine.

Cover: A simple form of postal stationery, for example an envelop, postcard or folded letter. May also be referred to as missives, letters or postcards.

Dirigible: An airship that can navigate through the air under its own power.

First-day cover: An official cover with a stamp tied by a special cancellation showing date of release.

Mint: A stamp in its original unused state.

Missive: A letter or a message.

Overprint: Additional printing on top of the original stamp.

Par Avion: The French term meaning "By Air" Originally used to differentiate between mail transport by land/sea or Air.

Philately: Study and collecting of postage stamps, postal system and postal history.

Philately: The practice of collection and study of postage items as recorded in history.

Postmark: A marking provided by the official national postal service. As a minimum this includes a date and place as it passes through the postal system.

Rocket firing: The act of igniting a rocket which initiates the rocket's journey. May also be referred to as a rocket launch.

Rocket mail: Covers flown in a rocket. The covers usually have special stamps, cachets or cancels.

Tied: A stamp is tied to a cover when the cancelling mark extends over both the stamp and the envelope.

Vignette: The central part of a stamp design, usually surrounded by a border. In some cases the vignette shades off gradually into the surrounding area.

Zeppelin: A rigid airship developed by, Ferdinand Graf von Zeppelin (1838-1917). First developed in 1900 at Friedrichshafen in Germany. The common prefix LZ is short for Luftschiff.

PUBLISHED AND UNPUBLISHED WORKS

As the secretary of the Indian Air Mail Society, Smith was responsible for producing the regular society bulletins but his writing extended beyond that. This a summary compiled from various sources including Jal Cooper's *A Specialised Priced Catalogue of India Rocket Mail* and his correspondence with Dr Robert Paganini.

Published

1 1926 Indian Airways Part 1

2 1927 Indian Airways Part 2

3 1927 World Flyer's Danger Zone

4 1930 Indian Airways Part 3

5 1943 Rocket Mail Catalogue & Historical Survey of First Experiments in Rocketry

Not published

1 Details of flights - Chiefly illustrations

2 Aviation and what steps Indian government is taking on this matter

3 Indian Airways 100 years Ago

4 Rocket Transport in India

5 Queer Birds of Aerophilately

6 Rocketogrammes

7 Early Balloon Ascents in India

8 Indian Rocket Experiments (1938)

BRIEF TIMELINE

February 1891 - Born in Shillong, Assam.

December 1903 - Orville Wright piloted the first powered airplane. Smith arrived at St Patrick's school in Asansol in the same year.

February 1911 - First official airmail. Allahabad to Naini and back.

1911 - Leaves St Patrick's Asansol. The same year that first official airmail transport in the world. It took place in India.

March 1913 - Joins Calcutta Police as round Sargent with a salary of Rs. 100 per month. Resigned on 4 December 1914.

November 1918 - Marries Fay Gulnar Harcourt in Dhurrumtollah Street Catholic Church in Calcutta.

1925 - Founded the Aerophilatelic Club of India. Changed its name to the Indian Airmail Society on January 1930

September 1925 - First contact with Dr Robert Paganini in Switzerland which began a correspondence that lasted a quarter of a century.

September 1934 - First rocket experiment from a Ship on the River Hooghly to Saugor Island.

June 1935 - Conducts two rocket experiments at his former St Patrick's in Asansol

April 1935 - First visit to Sikkim. Receives certificate from the king of Sikkim asserting the utility of rockets.

June 1935 - First rocket transport of livestock.

February 1935 - Joins the British Interplanetary Society.

September 1935 - Second visit to Sikkim.

February 1937 - All-India Boy Scouts Jamboree in Delhi.

March 1937 - Girl Guides rocket display in Calcutta.

May 1941 - Experiments with "War" Rockets

December 1944 - Last rocket experiment. Used compressed air and gas for propulsion.

April 1946 - Paganini's wife, Martha deis and he draws up a will allocating 25% of his estate to Stephen Smith.

June 1948 - Grandson is born. On 3 October four month old Grandson contracted Cerebro Spinal fever.

December 1950 - Robert Paganini dies in Switzerland. Bequeaths 25% of his estate to Stephen Smith.

February 1951 - Stephen Smith dies in Calcutta and is buried in Circular Road cemetery

October 1953 - His personal philatelic collection is onsite in Los Angeles

October 1964 - His work was covered in a NASA Conference Publication *Essays on the History of Rocketry and Astronautics: Proceedings of the Third Through the Sixth History Symposia of the International Academy of Astronautics* held at Mar del Plata, Argentina,

10th October 1969. https://archive.org/details/nasa_techdoc_19770026086 p.64.

1989 - Inducted in the Hall of Fame by the American Airmail Society

February 1992 - The Indian government issues a stamp to mark the centenary of his birth. It was released a year after the centenary of his birth.

ROCKET LAUNCH LOG

This table is compiled from the various sources listed in the references and bibliography. Until the start of the war, Stephen Smith maintained a largely consistent approach in recording his rocket mail experiments. During the 1940s, the rocket launches were sparse, not witnessed by members of the press and perhaps the war time restrictions prevented him from publishing details of his activities. There are gaps in the sequence of his rocket experiments (especially from 1 to 264) between 30 September 1934 and 26th of September 1941. Some rocket experiments were conducted during these dates. If published details of a launch do not include and associated sequence number, it is not listed in this table.

Details of the final nine entries in the table come from a letter dated 11th April 1946 from Stephen Smith to Dr Robert Paganini.

No. Date Description No. of Covers

1 30/09/1934 "Rocket burst in mid-air about 100ft up and always from the "Pansey" The Diary of Stephen Smith by D.N. Jatia. 140

2 30/09/1934 "Rocket burst in mid-air about 100ft up and always

from the "Pansey. Burst almost immediately it was set alight. It did not leave its rack." The Diary of Stephen Smith by D.N. Jatia. 209

3 30/09/1934 "Burst almost immediately it was set alight. Rose about two feet. Got my face a bit burnt by the sparks." The Diary of Stephen Smith by D.N. Jatia.

4 30/09/1934 "Rocket burst in mid-air about 100ft up and always from the "Pansey. Burst almost immediately it was set alight. It did not leave its rack." The Diary of Stephen Smith by D.N. Jatia. 209

5 01/10/1934 "Got absolutely fed up." The Diary of Stephen Smith by D.N. Jatia.

6 02/10/1934 "Got absolutely fed up." The Diary of Stephen Smith by D.N. Jatia. Splendid Rocket. Fixed lightly in the frame." The Diary of Stephen Smith by D.N. Jatia.

7 02/10/1934 "The charge was far too great for the cardboard. None of the pieces of leather were damaged or burnt as they had been soaked previously in strong alum solution." " The Diary of Stephen Smith by D.N. Jatia.

8 03/10/1934 "Rotten luck." The Diary of Stephen Smith by D.N. Jatia. 135

9 03/10/1934 "Picked up by a country boat." The Diary of Stephen Smith by D.N. Jatia. 135

10 04/10/1934 "Rockets all bursting, very, very disheartened." The Diary of Stephen Smith by D.N. Jatia. 400

11 16/12/1934 "This was my 1st night firing. The rocket could be followed more accurately owing to the trail of sparks from start to finish. Very good." The Diary of Stephen Smith by D.N. Jatia. 220

12 16/12/1934 "Excellent, mails landed safely. Dreaded the rocket bursting. Carried miniature of the newspaper "The Statesman". The Diary of Stephen Smith by D.N. Jatia.

13 16/12/1934 "Excellent, mails landed safely. No bursting." The Diary of Stephen Smith by D.N. Jatia. 150

14 16/12/1934 The rocket after leaving the rack shot off beautifully till about 300 yards, then it went mad, see sketch, I cannot explain or understand what happened." The Diary of Stephen Smith by D.N. Jatia. 250

15 16/12/1934 "Thank heavens it did not burst." The Diary of Stephen Smith by D.N. Jatia.

16 17/12/1934 "Just a test as to height, no bursting." The Diary of Stephen Smith by D.N. Jatia.

17 17/12/1934 "Test as to height, no bursting." The Diary of Stephen Smith by D.N. Jatia.

18 17/12/1934 "Just a test to see if the wretched thing would burst. It fell into a tank." The Diary of Stephen Smith by D.N. Jatia.

19 17/12/1934 "Another test to watch for bursting." The Diary of Stephen Smith by D.N. Jatia.

20 17/12/1934 "No bursting? My own design". The Diary of Stephen Smith by D.N. Jatia.

21 17/12/1934 "The weight was too much, the rocket fell into the sea, picked by boat." The Diary of Stephen Smith by D.N. Jatia.

22 17/12/1934 "Cannot say anything further that that the rocket did not burst." The Diary of Stephen Smith by D.N. Jatia.

23 17/12/1934 "Gave a lot of trouble to ignite, then when it did ignite the wretched thing burst almost immediately. Burnt my right hand." The Diary of Stephen Smith by D.N. Jatia. 150

24 27/02/1935 "The rocket rose up from the rack and shot over some trees about 100 yards away then burst in mid-air about another 110 yards. Present: Messrs Winterton, Barber, Pouter & Hurst." The Diary of Stephen Smith by D.N. Jatia. 130

25 27/02/1935 "The rocket which was 3 inches in diameter 35.5

inches length after belching volumes of smoke rose up and after breaking the rack, landed about ten feet away. Very bad packaging I think. Present: Messrs Winterton, Barber, Pouter & Hurst." The Diary of Stephen Smith by D.N. Jatia.

26 27/02/1935 "Same as rocker no. 25, but this one did not even make an attempt to move. Heat intense." The Diary of Stephen Smith by D.N. Jatia.

27 23/03/1935 "Cartridge not properly dried." The Diary of Stephen Smith by D.N. Jatia. 180

28 23/03/1935 "Cartridge not properly dried. Addressed to Master Hector Smith. - Silver Jubilee." The Diary of Stephen Smith by D.N. Jatia.

29 23/03/1935 "No weight. Cartridge not quite dry." The Diary of Stephen Smith by D.N. Jatia.

30 23/03/1935 Test launch. No load carried.

31 27/03/1935 "Cartridge quite dry." The Diary of Stephen Smith by D.N. Jatia.

32 27/03/1935 "Cartridge quite dry." The Diary of Stephen Smith by D.N. Jatia.

33 30/03/1935 Test launch using 1 lb of dummy mail.

34 30/03/1935 Test launch using 1 lb of dummy mail.

35 30/03/1935 "Angle not correct." The Diary of Stephen Smith by D.N. Jatia.

36 30/03/1935 Test launch using 1 lb of dummy mail.

37 30/03/1935 Test launch using 1 lb of dummy mail.

38 07/04/1935 Fired from the grounds of the Gangtok post office. 200

39 07/04/1935 Fired from Sir Tashi Namgyal field. 410

40 07/04/1935 "Test No. 3 of Sikkim." The Diary of Stephen Smith by D.N. Jatia. 6

41 07/04/1935 Fired by the King who signed 2 of the 388 Gold cards. Smith acquired the Kings permission to make a block of his signature and duplicate it on the other cards. 388

42 07/04/1935 "First mail of Sikkim." The Diary of Stephen Smith by D.N. Jatia. 200

43 07/04/1935 "Second mail of Sikkim." The Diary of Stephen Smith by D.N. Jatia. 44

44 08/04/1935 "Mail rocket fired by His Highness the Maharajah of Sikkim." The Diary of Stephen Smith by D.N. Jatia.

45 08/04/1935 "Mail rocket fired by His Highness the Maharajah of Sikkim." The Diary of Stephen Smith by D.N. Jatia.

46 08/04/1935 "Ordinary rocket without mail fired by H. H. the Maharajah of Sikkim." The Diary of Stephen Smith by D.N. Jatia.

47 08/04/1935 "Mail rocket fired by H. H. the Maharajah of Sikkim." The Diary of Stephen Smith by D.N. Jatia.

48 08/04/1935 "Mail rocket fired by H. H. the Maharajah of Sikkim." The Diary of Stephen Smith by D.N. Jatia. The king signed 3 of the cards for Smith. 410

49 08/04/1935 The rocket carrying 388 gold cards, was launched on a vertical trajectory by the King. He also signed two of the cards. Smith acquired the King's permission to duplicate the signature on the other cards. 388

50 09/04/1935 "In alighting the rocket, which was fired by the British Political Officer, Mr. F. Williamson, struck a rock and was smashed." The Diary of Stephen Smith by D.N. Jatia. 175

51 10/04/1935 "First firing over a River." The Diary of Stephen Smith by D.N. Jatia. 158

52 10/04/1935 "First Parcel Mail in the world." The Diary of

Stephen Smith by D.N. Jatia. The parcel contents consisted of One bottle of Genaspirin; one bottle of Dimol; one tube of Phenosen, one packet of cigarettes, one box of matches, one cigar, one packet of tea, one packet of sugar, one toothbrush, one spoon, one handkerchief. 50

53 10/04/1935 "Mail from Ray to Surumsa, over the river Ranikhola." The Diary of Stephen Smith by D.N. Jatia.

54 10/04/1935 "This was a test to observe the strength of the rocket against the gale." The Diary of Stephen Smith by D.N. Jatia. 186

55 13/04/1935 "Test firing." The Diary of Stephen Smith by D.N. Jatia.

56 13/04/1935 "Mail over the river Sintam in Western Sikkim." The Diary of Stephen Smith by D.N. Jatia. 118

57 13/04/1935 Rocket mail flown over river Singtam.

58 13/04/1935 Rocket mail over the river Rungpo and last firing in Sikkim during this visit. 100

59 04/06/1935 "Test in preparation for Kolaghat." The Diary of Stephen Smith by D.N. Jatia.

60 06/06/1935 "Carried: rice, grain, gram, spices, biris; also 150 thin messages. First rocket parcel. Over River Roopnarain Kolaghat." The Diary of Stephen Smith by D.N. Jatia. 150

61 06/06/1935 "Carried: tint, bandages, medicines & 110 thin messages. O ver River Roopnarain Kolaghat." The Diary of Stephen Smith by D.N. Jatia. 110

62 06/06/1935 "Splendid. The rocket shot its way at a terrific speed through the still gale." The Diary of Stephen Smith by D.N. Jatia.

63 06/06/1935 "Swept away by the gale. See below (referring to diagram)." The Diary of Stephen Smith by D.N. Jatia.

64 29/06/1935 "The rocket rose up beautifully: at about 500 feet up it got caught in a stiff upper current and was turned round and

carried BACKWARD about a mile away." The Diary of Stephen Smith by D.N. Jatia.

65 29/06/1935 First transport of livestock by rocket." Livestock by rocket. Over river Damodar Luck with a capital "L". The wind and the soft sand helped me. These were in my opinion the greatest factors to the birds being alive." The Diary of Stephen Smith by D.N. Jatia. 189

66 29/06/1935 "Rocket dispatch over river Damodar. Addressed to Francis J Fields. Once again the wind and sand were of the greatest help." The Diary of Stephen Smith by D.N. Jatia.

67 29/06/1935 "The rocket accidentally got ignited by the backfire of R. No. 66. It almost laid out, flew round in circles here, there and everywhere till getting caught in a stiff upper current dashed off 300 yards away." The Diary of Stephen Smith by D.N. Jatia. 160

68 29/06/1935 "The rocket was fired empty to demonstrate to the boys that weight was required to balance the rocket." The Diary of Stephen Smith by D.N. Jatia.

69 29/06/1935 Demonstrated that an evenly weighted and well balanced rocket went a far greater distance than an EMPTY one.

========

83 27/09/1935 Contents included. 1. One dried Sea Horse (Hippocampi); 2. One glass tube of Carter's Liver Pills; 3. One tube Euthymol tooth paste; 4. One box of matches; 5. One tin of Rofein; 6. One cake of Soap (Nekko) 190

84 28/09/1935 Second experiment in life transport by rocket. Fitted with gliding vanes. One cockbird, and carried 155 messages. Fired by C E Dudley. Star of India report incudes a reference to him being "elected as a BIS member". 155

85 29/09/1935 Rocket fired by His Highness the Maharajah of Sikkim 170

86 29/09/1935 Rocket fired by His Highness the Maharajah of

Sikkim 260

87 01/10/1935 Fired by Mr R P Rai postmaster General. Captured in a picture. 200

88 01/10/1935 Also fired by Mr R P Rai postmaster Carried mail and a parcel of items including 1. One tube of Quinine; 2. One tube of President; 3. One tin of Butter; 5. One packet of Cigarettes; 6. One box of One tube of Iodine; 4 matches; 160

89 04/10/1935 Launched from the telegraph office and many of the covers were signed by princess Pemtsidon. 137

========

124 07/05/1936 Test launch of the telescopic rocket. Not open to the public. None of the covers were posted. 22

125 07/05/1936 Another test launch of the Telescopic Rocket. 33

126 09/06/1936 Flood Rocket dispatch using Telescopic rocket. 80

127 21/09/1936 Third experiment in life transport by rocket. Chringripotat to Malikpur. Rocket fitted with large wings had an unusual cargo. It included mail, a snake and an apple. Was he deliberately drawing a Biblical reference with the names of Adam and Eve for his the cock and hen test flight in June 1935. Here he is using the idea of a Snake and an Apple. 106

133

134 01/02/1937 Carried 87 covers - "Message of Loyalty. Indian Scouts offer their homage and Loyal Affection to their Imperial majesties King George VI and Queen Elizabeth". 87

135 02/02/1937 All-India Jamboree. Carried 1883 leaflets to be distributed in mid-air. 176

136 02/02/1937 Carried 132 official jamboree cards 132

137

138 03/02/1937 161 covers carried with the message "We scouts

gather together from all parts of India offer our loyal greetings and loving homage to his excellency chief scout for India and our beloved chief and lady Baden-Powel 254

139 03/02/1937 71

140 02/03/1937 Carried welcome message from Lady Baden-Powell. 2000

141 12/05/1937 Coronation Rocket. Addressed to Francis J Field Ltd. 7 foot Coronation Rocket carrying 200 cards bearing messages of loyalty to their Majesty King George V1 and Queen Elizabeth 454

142 22/09/1937 Cachet "Rocketgram. Indian Airways". 167

143 22/09/1937 Fourth experiment in life transport by rocket. Rocket Train - 4 compartments carrying mail, whisky and two mice (Mr & Mrs Mousie). Cachet "Rocketgram. Indian Airways". At 7 ft 2 ", this was probably his largest rocket.

========

162 25/04/1939 25

163 25/04/1938 Experimental Boomerang rocket but broke up in mid flight. 25

164 25/04/1938 Marianne Kronstein was the daughter of the philatelist Max Kronstein in New York. It "carried 102 special Rocketgram cards and a small consignment of James Carlton's cigarettes". From Billig's Specialized catalogue.

165 25/04/1938 This and previous rockets were designed to bring relief in an emergency. 102

166 "This rocket had sharp pointed wings and a tail fin fitted with a rudder; it carried in its mail chamber 166 special missives." From Billig's Specialized Catalogues: Rocket Mail Catalogue. 166

170

171 25/07/1938 "Rocket test at Alipore" in support of the

"Monsoon Flood Relief". 200

172 24/07/1938 Rocket named after the 19th century postal reformer of the postal service and accredited with the introduction of the adhesive postal stamp. 194

173 24/07/1938 "Rocket test at Alipore" in support of the "Monsoon Flood Relief". 102

========

189 25/12/1938 Martha Paganini was the wife of his friend in Switzerland Robert Paganini. Marked with "Peace on Earth. Good will to all men" and "Xmas relief Dec. 25th" 150

========

207 19/09/1939 First War Rocket. Two Cachets - "Au revoir" and "Carried by War Rocket the Liar No. 207" 91

208 19/09/1939 Second War Rocket. Two Cachets - "Au revoir" and "Carried by War Rocket Grog-Nee-Gin No. 208" 81

209

220 25/06/1945 A week after the fall of France in WW2, rocket 220 launched cards with a cachet "The Soul of France weeps. The bordeaux government have today put the life and liberty of France in to the custody of their enemies". 53

227

228 25/06/1940 Third War rocket." Park Street 25th June 1940" 53

229

230 17/07/1940 The rocket carried a brownie camera with the intention of taking pictures. It flew "300 yards to an altitude of 1500 feet". The photography attempt was not successful. 1

231 17/07/1940 The rocket carried a brownie camera with the intention of taking pictures. It flew 300 yards to an altitude of 500 feet. The photography attempt was not successful. 1

251

252 17/05/1941 4th War Rocket "War rocket A.A. Research" and "Par Aerienne" 4

253 17/05/1941 5th War rocket "War rocket A.A. Research" and "By rocket Par Fusee" 4

254

255 01/07/1941 The first parachute war rocket" and carried propaganda message. "Just a sting for the Nazi Gaolbirds" 10

256 01/07/1941 The second parachute war rocket." Another sting for the Nazi Gaolbirds" 10

257

258 07/07/1941 Sixth war rocket." War rocket A.A. Research" 7

259 10/07/1941 Seventh war rocket." War rocket A.A. Research" 8

260 03/08/1941 Eight war rocket." Per Razzo Espresso par Torpedo Aerienne" 2

262

263 26/09/1941 Ninth war rocket." War rocket A.A. Research" and "Villo Cooper No 263". Don't jump to conclusions". Large V for victory on each card. 8

264 26/09/1941 Tenth war rocket." Joanna Binns - No. 264" and "Villo Cooper No 263" 35

========

Details of the following rocket flights come primarily from correspondence between Stephen Smith and Dr Robert Paganini. After 1941, Smith appears not to assign unique numbers to each flight. This was probably due to either difficult living conditions in Calcutta as the end of the war approached or failing health. Perhaps both.

Date Description No. Covers

10/09/1944 Launched by gas carried on by dry powder.

11/0/1944 Launched by gas carried on by dry powder.

20/09/1944 Gas Propelled rocket. Cachet "For the blood thirsty Jappy" 13

25/10/1944 Gas Propelled rocket. A bread coupon stuck on the card. 15

31/10/1944 Compressed Air Projectile. Sub Sulentio" Per mark per terras. Pro rege. lege, et grege". (28 cards according to Ellington - Zwisler Rocket Mail Catalog by Jesse T. Ellington and Perry F. Zwisler. Published in 1967). 28

08/09/1944 Has a cachet in Latin "Lex Talionis" - The law of retaliation. (carried 11 cards according to Ellington - Zwisler Rocket Mail Catalog by Jesse T. Ellington and Perry F. Zwisler. Published in 1967). 19

21/11/1944 Gas propelled rocket. Cachet "For the blood thirsty Jappy". (Carried 11 cards according to Ellington - Zwisler Rocket Mail Catalog by Jesse T. Ellington and Perry F. Zwisler. Published in 1967). 11

04/12/1944 Lists the following location on the cover - Gun Spur Jail Hill, Naga Village Arudara Spur, April-May 1944 - Treasury Ridge, Hospital Hill, Garrison Hill. (Carried 78 posted plus 48 unposted according to Ellington - Zwisler Rocket Mail Catalog by Jesse T. Ellington and Perry F. Zwisler. Published in 1967) 78

04/12/1944 "When you go home, tell them of us. For your tomorrow, we gave our today. In the Naga Hills. Far away." (Carried 68 cards according to Ellington - Zwisler Rocket Mail Catalog by Jesse T. Ellington and Perry F. Zwisler. Published in 1967) 68

END NOTES

1. Origins

1. Hopferweiser, W, 2019, *Pioneer Rocket Mail & Space Mail*. See pages 115-169 especially pages 143, 147, 161 and 162.
2. This comes from a special 4-page large pamphlet entitled '*First Indian Rocket Dispatches*' (1934). In it, he summarises dates, times, individuals involved and gives his motivation for the first launch attempts.
3. Field, F. 20th September 1935, *Philatelic Magazine* Letters page.
4. Schmiedl, F. 22nd April 1969. Letter to Praemeso Titulo. In this letter Schmiedl says, 'I personally participated in the 1st Astronomical Congress in Paris'. National Air and Space Museum, Washington, DC.
5. 6th April 1946. Letter from Stephen Smith to Robert Paganini. Robert Paganini Collection, Museum of Communication, Bern, Switzerland.
6. Paganini's will dated 20th April 1946. In it he shares his estate equally between 4 parties: One quarter for the Luftpost Archive, the museum housing his collection; One quarter to be shared between the various airmail societies of which he was a member. One quarter to his nephews and nieces; One quarter to Stephen Smith. A copy of his will is part of the Robert Paganini collection, Museum of Communication, Bern, Switzerland.
7. 14th October 1953, Normandy Stamp Studio, Los Angeles California. A marketing letter addressed to 'Dear collectors'. National Air and Space Museum, Washington, DC.
8. India is one of the largest producers of tea in the world. Today, tea is grown in the South west, north west and north east of India. Renowned teas, such as Assam and Darjeeling, are grown exclusively in the North east of India. Since Assam is located in the far east of India, the sun rises about 2 hours earlier than over most of western India 2,000 km away. As a hangover from the colonial times, some there still observe a time zone an hour ahead of the official Indian Standard Time. https://zeenews.india.com/news/north-east/assam-tea-gardens-an-hour-ahead-of-india_659847.html
9. 18th August 2018 https://www.thehindu.com/society/how-chai-arrived-in-india-170-years-ago/article24724665.ece. Also see Alex Colvin and Robert Fortune, *Tea Thief: How to Break a Commodity Monopoly British-Style* (2018).
10. Charles William Bath Taylor was born on October 15th 1865. Email communication between the author and Smith's granddaughter.
11. http://www.andrewyule.com/about_group.php.
12. Mannan Mashhur Zarif, 8th March 2015, https://www.thedailystar.net/by-rocket-i-go-24615.
13. https://www.scotsman.com/news/travel-shillong-india-scotland-of-the-east-1-3481504.
14. The family history described here is very likely to be incomplete, given Smith's dark skin as seen in his pictures.
15. Personal communication between Smith's granddaughter and the author on 5th July 2016.

16. The book is dedicated to the memory of Engineer Arthur B Elliot who was flying with Alan Cobham. Elliot was shot in Baghdad during the England to Australia flight and all proceeds from the book were destined for his widowed mother.
17. The cemetery records show that he was buried on 15th February 1951. This is also the commonly quoted date of his death. Since it is unlikely that he was buried on the same day he died, his death was probably a few days earlier.
18. Based on this collection, John J Britt wrote this insightful piece: 'The Rocket Stamp Collection of Stephen H Smith'. APA_Volume_08_No_1_July_1960. Available at https://www.americanairmailsociety.org/resources/aero-philatelist-annals/.
19. 18th January 1949. Letter from Stephen Smith to Robert Paganini. Cerebrospinal fever is a form of meningitis. Robert Paganini Collection, Museum of Communication, Bern, Switzerland.
20. Personal communication between Smith's granddaughter and the author on 5th July 2016.
21. 2nd April 2014. Interview with Melvyn Brown, a writer on Anglo-Indian affairs and near neighbour of the Smith family. https://astrotalkuk.org/indias-forgotten-rocketeer-2/.
22. Cooper, Jal 1942, *Stamps of India*, p.151.
23. Ibid p.151.
24. Ibid, p.152.
25. Jatia, D N. 1980, *From the Diary of Stephen Smith*. p.61.
26. 27th January 1927, letter to Robert Paganini acknowledging his resemblance to one of his late masters at St Patrick's.
27. Kitson, S. 1992, *Policeman Rocketeer*, Indian Stamp Dealers Association.
28. Kronstein, Max *Rocket Mail Flights of the World to 1986* (The American Air Mail Society, 1986), p.80.
29. *India Post Journal of the India Study Circle for Philately* (No 101, Vol 23 No 3, July 1989).
30. Throughout pre-independent India, towns sprung up with names such as Youngpur, Barrackpur, Zaminderhat, Clarkabad, Severndroog, Abbottabad, Captainganj, Washermanpeta, Alphanagar and Dobbspet. The suffixes had an established meaning in the local language: Nagar and Abad are places or abodes; Pore, Pur Pura or Purrum means town; Gunge, Gunj, or Hat meant market.
31. Hans J Hillerbrand, Professor and Chair Department of Religion Encyclopedia of Protestantism. (Routledge, 4-volume set, 2004) p.72.
32. Dr Gloria Moore. 1988, article: 'A brief history of the Anglo-Indians' http://home.alphalink.com.au/~agilbert/jjean1.html.
33. Herbert Alick Stark, *Hostages To India: The Life Story of the Anglo Indian Race* (Simon Wallenburg Press, 2007).
34. James, Sheila, Pais. 'Anglo-Indians: The Dilemma of Identity' (2001), http://ehlt.flinders.edu.au/projects/counterpoints/PDF/A7.pdf. Accessed 10/2/2014.
35. In discussion with Stephen Smith's granddaughter, she stated that she believes he should be considered a British citizen, not an Anglo-Indian, as his birth was registered and domiciled in the UK.
36. Interview with the author, 2nd April 2013, http://astrotalkuk.org/2014/05/06/indias-forgotten-rocketeer-2/.
37. http://www.bharat-rakshak.com/IAF/History/1950s/Anglos.html.

2. Postal Services and Philately in India

1. Sir Rowland Hill and George Birkbeck Hill, *The Life of Sir Rowland Hill and the History of Penny Postage* (Vol 1 1880), p.486.
2. A blog post from the Postal Museum in Washington, DC: '100th Anniversary of the DC City Post Office Building' https://postalmuseum.si.edu/es/node/2085.
3. https://www.news5cleveland.com/news/originals/how-news-of-apollo-11-mission-traveled-from-the-surface-of-the-moon-to-the-prison-walls-of-the-hanoi-hilton-in-vietnam.
4. Clarke, G. 1921, *The Post office of India and its Story*, p.1. https://archive.org/details/postofficeofindi00claruoft/page/n8.
5. Information curtesy of Terry Hare-Walker
6. As the East India Company's trade and political power continued to grow, Lord Clive reorganised the postal service in 1766, requiring that all mail should go through Government House under the authority of the Postmaster or his assistants. A further reorganisation with expanded services came into effect in 1774 under Warren Hastings. He established a new position, the Postmaster General of East India Domain. Servants of the company were allowed to send letters without charge, and for the first time, private individuals were also allowed to use this service, but with a charge. In 1837 came a profound change, with the idea of post offices for local collection and distribution of letters and parcels across India and beyond. In 1852, the first adhesive stamp, the Scinde Dawk, was introduced in India in the Sind province (now in Pakistan).
7. Madras to Bombay is more than 1300 km, Bombay to Calcutta more than 2100 km and Calcutta to Madras more than 1600 km.
8. Prominent Indian philatelist Jal Cooper is a detailed source of Indian postal history. One of his many publications, *Stamps of India*, published in three editions, is a very readable source on Indian postal history, and the 1942 edition has information about Stephen Smith.
9. http://www.indianphilately.net/porg.html
10. Clarke, G. 1921, *The Post office of India and its Story*, p.26. https://archive.org/details/postofficeofindi00claruoft/page/n8.
11. Ibid, p.27. The list of individuals granted this right changed over time, but initially consisted of
    His Majesty's Principal Secretaries of State;
    The President and Secretaries of the Board of Control;
    The Chairman, Deputy Chairman and Directors of the East India Company;
    The Secretary, Deputy Secretary and Assistant Secretary at the East India House;
    The Governor-General;
    The Governors of Bengal, Madras and Bombay;
    The Governor of Ceylon;
    The Lieutenant-Governor of the North-West Provinces;
    The Chief Justices of Bengal, Madras and Bombay;
    The Bishops of Calcutta, Madras and Bombay;
    The Members of the Supreme Council;
    The Members of Council of Madras and Bombay;
    The Puisne Judges of the Supreme Courts of Bengal, Madras and Bombay;
    The Recorder of Prince of Wales Island, Singapore and Malacca;
    The Commander-in-Chief of His Majesty's Naval Forces;

The Commander-in-Chief of the Army in India;
The Commander-in-Chief of the Army at Madras and Bombay.
12. Cooper, J. 1952, *Stamps of India*, p.223.
13. The public website is available here: http://www.indiastudycircle.org/. The ISC also has a pretty active but closed group on Facebook.
14. http://fg-indien.de/index_E.html.
15. Cooper, Jal. 1952, *Stamps of India*, p.197.
16. Bulletin of the Indian Airmail Society, January 1931, Full text of the president's speech that opened the Philatelic Exhibition organised by the Indian Air Mail Society 17th December 1930.
17. The outward flight used Armstrong Whitworth Argosy 'City of Glasgow' (G-EBLF) to Basle, then train to Genoa, by Short S.8 flying boat 'City of Athens' (G-EBVH) to Alexandria, and by DH66 Hercules 'City of Jerusalem' (G-EBMZ) to Karachi. The return flight from India to England via the 'City of Baghdad' that left Karachi on 7 April and flew the mails to Alexandria 'G-EBMY'. My thanks to Terry Hare-Walker for this information.
18. Robert Paganini Collection, Museum of Communication, Bern, Switzerland.
19. Singh, 2017, *The Indian Space Programme* (2017), p.106.
20. *The Airpost Journal* (June 1933) p.9. https://www.americanairmailsociety.org/wp-content/uploads/2018/08/APJ_Volume_004_Issue_0038_No_09_June_1933.pdf. Some more interesting information can be found here: https://www.airindiacollector.com/blog/1932-london-stephen-smith-cover.
21. *Bulletin of the Indian Airmail Society* (January 1931), p.369.
22. Anstee, G,R. 'India at War in the Air – Part III', *India Post* (November 1967).
23. https://stampsofindia.com/readroom/IndiasStampJournal.html.
24. Cooper, Jal. 'The King's Stamps', in *The Illustrated Weekly of India* (5th May 1935), p.37.
25. In an obituary of Jal Cooper (*Stamp Digest*, April 1977, p.12), the author Hakuta writes about Cooper's abrasive relations with other philatelists in India. Cooper's criticism of other philatelists and especially contacts in the government lost him friends during his lifetime, so much so that he was denied a posthumous issuing of a commemorative stamp.
26. Cooper, Jal. *Stamps of India*, p.141.
27. Letter dated 4th December 1946 to Robert Paganini, The Paganini Collection. Museum of Communication, Bern Switzerland.

3. Mail Transport

1. https://en.wikipedia.org/wiki/German_occupation_of_the_Channel_Islands.
2. https://www.bletchleyparkresearch.co.uk/bletchley-park-pigeon/.
3. Personal letter to Robert Paganini dated 6th January 1931, Robert Paganini Collection, Museum of Communication, Bern, Switzerland.
4. 6th January 1931, Robert Paganini Collection, Museum of Communication, Bern, Switzerland. Stephen Smith was at the time the secretary of the Indian Air Mail Society.
5. 26th January 1933, Robert Paganini Collection, Museum of Communication, Bern, Switzerland.
6. http://flagsaudrapeaubandeirasandstamps.blogspot.com/2010/08/royal-indian-navy-pigeon-mail-service.html.

7. The first officially sanctioned mail in the USA by balloon took place on 17th August 1857. A balloon called Jupiter, flown by John Wise, carried 123 letters provided by the local postmaster from the town of Lafayette, Indiana, destined for New York. The absence of expected winds on the day forced the balloon flight to terminate after travelling just 30 miles; the mail was transported to New York by rail. https://postalmuseum.si.edu/collections/object-spotlight/balloon-jupiter.html.
8. The following source appears to confirm this assertion: (http://www.ballooninghistory.com/whoswho/who'swho-r.html).
9. https://books.google.co.uk/books?id=vJZeAAAAcAAJ&pg p.164
10. Lam, D. 1988, *To Pop A Balloon: Aeromedical Evacuation in the 1870 Siege of Paris*. Also see In Our Time, BBC Radio 4, 16 January 2020, https://www.bbc.co.uk/programmes/m000d8rv and Making History, BBC Radio 4, 21 January 2020.https://www.bbc.co.uk/programmes/m000dfpw
11. Hildesheim, Eric. *Stamps* (20th January1934, National Air and Space Museum, Washington D.C.).
12. Letter from Schmiedl to Robert Paganini dated 30th January 1933, The Robert Paganini Collection, Museum of Communication, Bern, Switzerland.
13. 1st October 1930, Letter from Stephen Smith to Robert Paganini, Robert Paganini Collection, Museum of Communication, Bern, Switzerland. Smith talks about this book and shares some details with Paganini on a 'Strictly Confidential' basis. Most of the details of this book come from this letter. I have not been able to track down the original manuscript.
14. Initially, India was administered by the East India Company, but after the mutiny, the British government took control.
15. Letter from Stephen Smith to Robert Paganini, 24th June 1930, Robert Paganini Collection, Museum of Communication, Bern, Switzerland.
16. Pringle, John, *Early British Balloon Posts*, (1928) p.52. This is a privately published book about early balloon flights in England and has a foreword by Robert Paganini. On page 52 of the book, the author refers to Francis J Fields of Sutton Coldfield, who indicates that a block used to generate the prints for the covers is in an 'Indian Collection'. He does not refer to Stephen H Smith by name, but given that Paganini, Field and Smith all knew each other, it is reasonable to assume that the 'Indian collector' was Smith.
17. http://www.guinnessworldrecords.com/world-records/highest-flight-by-a-hot-air-balloon.
18. Singh, G, 2017, *The Indian Space Programme*, p.69.
19. The use of Congreve Rockets at Niuafo'ou is probably the earliest attempts to use Congreve Rockets for Ship-to-Shore routine mail transport.
https://www.engadget.com/2019/02/02/the-history-of-rocket-mail-backlog/
20. A lovely Youtube video shows the Tin Cans being dropped overboard from by TSS Katoomba and swimmers collecting the mail. https://youtu.be/hs60SK-tCJA
21. 23rd January 1947 from Quensell to a friend in California. www.bettybillingham.co.uk/WalterGeorgeQuensell.html.
22. These numbers come from claims in a letter he wrote to a friend: http://www.bettybillingham.co.uk/TCM.html.
23. Earl R. Hinz, Jim Howard, *Landfalls of Paradise: Cruising Guide to the Pacific Islands (2006)*, p.166.
24. The full story, posted by a writer daughter of the recipient, is here: https://angelasavage.wordpress.com/2012/01/19/tin-can-mail/.
25. The advantage of using a ship as a launch platform is the ability for the whole ship to

turn in to wind further reducing the need for longer runways. https://wondersofworldaviation.com/catapults.html
26. https://www.flightglobal.com/FlightPDFArchive/1932/1932%20-%200217.PDF.
27. 17th December 1928 Letter between the White Star Liners Management company and General Williamson of the Post Office. The weight (in tonnes) and the cost (in £1000) breakdown look like this:
Seaplane = 3t/£6k
Catapult = 15t/£10k
Stump mast and derrick=7t/£4k
Extras (i.e. hanger) =£5k
Installation £2.5k excluding the compressed air for the catapult.
Postal Museum, London.
28. 9th September 1931. Letter to Mr Lister, Postal Museum, London.

4. Airmail

1. Letter dated 2nd December 1928, asking Robert Paganini to send him any duplicated Airmail items, if he had any, from the 'Isle De France' or Graf Zeppelin. Robert Paganini Collection, Museum of Communication, Bern, Switzerland.
2. Deighton, L and Schwartzman, A. *Airshipwreck (*Holt, Rinehart & Winston, 1979).
3. One of the earliest designs for an airship with a metal construction came from the Russian rocketry pioneer Konstantin Tsiolkovsky in 1890. He called it 'Small Metal Airship'. It had a volume of 6,000 cubic meters and was 64 m long, 17 m high and 12.8 m wide, able to travel at a speed of 32 km/h. It was never built. Rynin, N, A. Life, Writings, and Rockets, *Interplanetary Flight and Communication* (Volume III No. 7, 1931), p.18.
4. 5th November 1930. Volume 244, Parliamentary Q&A as recorded in Hansard. https://api.parliament.uk/historic-hansard/commons/1930/nov/05/airships
5. Keisler, K. *Airpost Journal* (May 1964), p.209.
6. Some interesting detail in the following sources https://www.airshipsonline.com/airships/r101/Crash/R101_Crash.htm
   https://www.airshipsonline.com/learn/R101%20Control%20Cable%20Bryan%20Lawton/control-response-and-crash-of-hma-r101-Bryan%20Lawton.pdf
   Journal of Aeronautical History Paper No. 2015/02
7. Roessler, A,C. a New Jersey based dealer engaged in some shady dealing practices, wrote a letter dated 20th October, asking the highly respected Swiss philatelist Robert Paganini, to engage with him in 'a little plan that I have for the Zepp mail'. His plan involved sending Paganini covers that would have flown aboard the first commercial transatlantic flight on an airship and asking Paganini to send the covers to himself, writing the address in pencil. Once they had a Swiss stamp and a Swiss cancellation, these covers would have been returned to Roessler in New Jersey. It is not clear if Paganini participated in this plan. Letter dated 2nd October 1928, Robert Paganini Collection, Museum of Communication, Bern, Switzerland.
8. Laufer, Berthold. 1928, *The Prehistory of Aviation*, p.52.
9. The following item has several pictures of Windham and his aeroplane and details of his visit to India. https://scroll.in/magazine/829185/the-story-of-the-first-men-and-woman-to-fly-in-india.
10. http://kbhargava.com/flyingtales/aviation-in-india-a-peep-into-its-early-history.html
    Also, it is unclear if the Maharajah's interest in aviation was motivated by the success

of Hardit Singh Malik. Malik had been studying in Oxford when WWI broke out. With some difficulty he joined the British Air Force and took part in several aerial battles, gaining the title 'Flying Sikh of Biggin Hill'. http://indiaww1.in/Flying-Sikh-Hardit-Singh-Malik-by-Somnath-Sapru.pdf.
11. http://www.flightglobal.com/pdfarchive/view/1911/1911%20-%200038.html Accessed 22/02/2014.
12. *The Air Annual of the British Empire* (1931), p.170.
13. Smith, S.1930 *Indian Airways*. Preface by H. A. Outhwaite.
14. Ibid, p.152.
15. Smith, S. 1930, *Indian Airways* p.157.
16. Hartley, J 'Airmail Historical Side Lights', *The Air Post Journal* (October 1959), p.14.
17. Kronstein, Max. *Air Post Journal* (May 1963), p.202.
18. *Ibid*
19. Ibid
20. Kronstein, Max. *Air Post Journal* (January 1972), p.109. In this piece, Kronstein acknowledges that he was in regular correspondence with Smith during that time.
21. 30th March1929 - First Airmail Service from Karachi to London. Reply from the Palace on 17th April 1929.

    4th November 1929 - Sent two copies (one for the King and the other for the Queen) of First Airmail Stamps in India. Reply from the Palace 22nd November 1929.

    27th December 1929 - First flight from Delhi to Croydon. Reply from the Palace on 11th January 1930.

    29th November 1934 - Sent four covers and a detailed report from his rocket firings at Saugor Island.

    Reply from the Palace on 7th December 1934, in which the King returned the covers.
22. This term was introduced in 1930s by Ary Sternfeld. It is known as cosmonautics in Russia and every year, 12th April (the anniversary of Yuri Gagarin's flight in 1961) is commemorated as Cosmonautics Day.
23. A letter dated 21st February 1934 to Robert Paganini. Robert Paganini Collection, Museum of Communication, Bern, Switzerland.
24. It was the supercharged engine that technically made this flight possible. Pegasus 8.3 engines manufactured by the Bristol Aeroplane Company were employed. In the absence of supercharging (forcing the air in the engines under pressure) the power of the engines would be about a third that at sea level.
25. P F M Fellowes, L V Stewart, Blacker, and P T Etherton, *First Over Everest! the Houston-Mount Everest Expedition*, 1933, (Robert McBride & Company, 1934) p.20.
26. *Air Post Air Journal* (May 1962) p.254. In response to his query, Max Kronstein received the following mail response from India cancelled at Srinagar, June 19, 1938: 'Dear Dr Kronstein: As far as possible we would like to respond to your request, even though we do not carry an actual airmail and have no special cachet of the expedition. But we are sending you here the flyer-greetings from the crew of the Airplane D-AvVBR of the German Nanga Parbat Expedition.'
27. *Air Post Air Journal* (Vol 4, Issue 0038, Number 9, June 1933), p.7.
28. 13th October 1938, *Flight Global*, p.321. https://www.flightglobal.com/FlightPDFArchive/1938/1938%20-%202831.pdf. An interesting sequence of images showing the first separation of the two aircraft whilst airborne is shown and described here: http://www.flightglobal.com/FlightPDFArchive/1938/1938%20-%200599.pdf. A nine-minute Youtube film summarises the achievements through

flight footage and audio recordings with the pilots. https://youtu.be/bYtazEBQ1K8.

5. Rocket Mail

1. *Air Force magazine* (Volume 74, April 1991), p.84.
2. Kronstein, Max. *Air Post Air Journal* (November 1978) p.48.
3. Staff Correspondent, 9th February 1958, *The Statesman*. National Air and Space Museum.
4. Hopferweiser, W, M. 2019, *Pioneer Rocket Mail and Space Mail*, p.173.
5. https://www.criticalpast.com/video/65675024389_Rocketry_Zucker-arranges-rocket-mail_test-launch-of-rocket-mail_rocket-comes-back-swirling.
6. The patent is available here: https://patents.google.com/patent/US1903303A/en.
7. Video of some of Tiling's flight from Cuxhaven with Angela Buddenboehmenr and Friedrich Kuhr, including the rocket with retractable wings, is available here: https://www.youtube.com/watch?v=MBqY99Qrzo8.
8. The following website includes unique video (originally silent cine film) of some of the launches https://www.criticalpast.com/video/65675024393_Rocketry_Drawings-and-models-of-rockets_rocket-inclined-on-stand_pictures-of-rocket-in-motion.
9. S Epstein and B Williams, 1955, *The Rocket Pioneers*, p.148.
10. From the Diary of Stephen Smith, 1980. Rocket 3: minor burns to his face on 30th September 1934 whilst conducting a ship-to-shore test off Saugor Island. Rocket 23: minor burn to his right hand on 17th December 1935 whilst at the Semaphore Station on Saugor Island.
11. Friedrich Schmiedl, *Early Postal Rockets in Austria: A Memoir* (NASA Conference Publication 1977). Essays on the history of rocketry and astronautics: proceedings of the Third through the Sixth History Symposia of the International Academy of Astronautics. Volume II https://archive.org/details/nasa_techdoc_19770026086.
12. Schmiedl and Smith corresponded with each other and with Robert Paganini in Switzerland. This is a quote from a letter dated 26th April 1938 from Smith to Paganini.
13. Schmiedl, F. 28th August 1937 letter to Francis J Field, 'Regarding your queries Re Distance and Time of Flight'. Stephen Smith collection, National Air and Space Museum, Washington, DC.
14. Friedrich Schmiedl, *Early Postal Rockets*, https://archive.org/details/nasa_techdoc_19770026086.
15. He goes on to say that not all his rocket tests went as intended. One problem that he never resolved to his satisfaction was deploying the parachute at the correct point. *Early Postal Rockets in Austria. A Memoir*, p.109.
16. Schmiedl refers to this as a bio-experiment in a letter to Beatrice Bachmann, who was in contact with him by phone and letter. This is an account of R1 from Schmiedl to Bachmann in a letter dated 6th December 1979. Bachmann shared a copy of this letter with the author via email on 16th May 2019.
17. An online forum called Austria-forum:https://austria-forum.org/af/Biographien/Schmiedl%2C_Friedrich. Kronstein, Max. *The Air Post Journal* (Vol 43, Number 3, December 1971), p.73. F Winter, *Journal of the British Interplanetary Society* (Vol 48, 1995), p.235. This obituary was published a year after Schmiedl died.
18. This is a three-page report written near the end of 1934 where he describes his first

rocket mail experiments at Saugor Island. The three-page typed report was found in a copy the book *From the Diary of Stephen Smith* in the procession of Brian Lythgoe. A copy is also located in the Stephen Smith collection. National Air and Space Museum, Washington, DC.
19. 11th October 1937, Letter from Stephen Smith to Leslie Johnson. Private Collection of Leslie Johnson, Liverpool, England.
20. 11th October 1937, letter from Stephen Smith to Leslie Johnson.
21. Stephen Smith wrote a piece entitled 'The World's first Boomerang Rocket Flight'. In it, he recalls a rocket flight on 22nd September which did not go as planned. He was surprised to see that on re-flying it without any repairs on 11th October, the rocket returned, gliding back to within 200 yards of the launch rack. He goes on to indicate that there were no invited members of the press to witness this flight, although there were many members of the public present.
    Authorised by Mrs S. H Smith. *Billig's Specialised Catalogue: Rocket Mail Catalogue*, (Volume 8, 1955), p.51.
22. Baldwin N,C. January 1938, Rocket Posts, Stamp Review.
23. During this time, his he recorded his rocket launches using various prefixes (FS = his initials, V=versuchen (experimental), K=katapult):
    1928 - FS1, V1-V6
    1931 - V7, R1, V8
    1932 - V9-V13
    1933 - V14-V18, K1-K2, K1-U
    1935 - N1-N6
24. Willy Ley, who chose to flee Germany as Hitler came to power, characterised Schmiedl's option as '"hardly less dangerous than taunting the Gestapo"'. Ley, W, 1960, *Rockets Missiles and Men In Space*, (1960), Pp.586
25. Schmiedl, F, May 1946, *Austria Philatelist* (National Air and Space Museum, Washington, DC, May 1946).
26. Kessler, F. October, *Air Post Journal* (Vol VII, No. 1. October 1935), p.12.
27. This comes from a special 4-page large pamphlet entitled '*First Indian Rocket Dispatches 1934'*. In it he summarises (dates, times, individuals involved) and his motivation for the first launch attempts.
28. Winter, E. *Prelude to the Space Age* (1983), p.109.
29. Turner, C. 'Letter Bombs' (2006). http://www.cabinetmagazine.org/issues/23/turner2.php.
30. Gotz, E A. 'The Rocket Post Trials in Great Britain', *The Stamp Collectors' Fortnightly* (Vol LIV, No. 1383. 27th March 1948, National Air and Space Museum, Washington, DC), p.73.
31. Turner, C. 'Letter Bombs' (2006). http://www.cabinetmagazine.org/issues/23/turner2.php.
32. Hansard records the following question and answer in June 1934., two days before Zucker conducted his test in Sussex. Mr Thomas Ramsay asked the Postmaster General in view of the use of mail rockets on the continent of Europe, if he has considered the possibility of their use in this country, especially in the case of islands where it is difficult to land the mail by ordinary methods when the sea is rough? Sir K WOOD Not yet; but I shall be prepared to consider their use, if such a method is found to be practicable. https://api.parliament.uk/historic-hansard/commons/1934/jun/04/mail-rockets.
33. https://www.scotsman.com/lifestyle/german-s-air-mail-idea-goes-up-in-smoke-1-465768

34. Macleod, J. *Scots Magazine*, July 1982 as shown on page 4 in Donald Malcolm's 1997 book *The Paisley Rocketeers*. This book provides a detailed and succinct account of this, the first rocketry society to be founded in Scotland in 1935 by John. D Stewart.
35. Stamp Review, January 1938, p.7
36. Gotz, E A, 'The Rocket Post Trials in Great Britain', p.74.
37. The Rocket in Britain 1900 to 1940: Part 1 – Postal and Amateur Rockets. *Chronicle: JBIS* (Vol. 62, Suppl. 2, 2009), pp.48-60.
38. Winter, F. from around the late 1970s or early 1980s during research at the Seeley G Mudd Manuscript Library, attributed to P E Cleator founder of the British Interplanetary Society: 'As a result of his rocketry experiments in England, the German mail rocket experimenter Gerhard Zucker was sent to prison'.
39. One report, at https://www.scotsman.com/lifestyle/german-s-air-mail-idea-goes-up-in-smoke-1-465768, raises suspicion on his motives. 'Was it really to improve mail services for people living on remote locales, or, as some residents believed, was he attempting to identify suitable ports to recharge German U-boats or to establish the grade of British-supplied explosives in the event of war?'
40. *The Rocket Post* Film - https://youtu.be/1HSIBo9NUJE
    https://youtu.be/qNPuOZ7dMhA.
41. https://www.pressreader.com/uk/scottish-daily-mail/20170923/282359744894768.
42. Letter from Stephen Smith to Sir Philip Sassoon, MP for Hyth, 17th September 1936. Postal Museum, London.
43. Some stills of Roberti are near the end of this short video: https://www.criticalpast.com/video/65675024395_Rocketry_Gerhard-Zuckers-rocket-mail_rocket-boosters-attached_rocket-explodes-in-flight.
44. Hopferweiser, W. 2016, *Pioneer Rocket Mail and Space Mail*, p.42.
45. *The Indian Airmail Society* (Quarterly Bulletin December 1936), pp.27-29.
46. http://users.belgacom.net/raketpost/english.htm.
47. APJ_Volume_006_Issue_0063_No_10_July_1935 p.15.
48. *Pushing the Envelope. Pioneer Rocket Mail, 1928-1959.* http://americanastrophilately.com/exhibits/PushingtheEnvelope.pdf.
49. *Philatelic Magazine*, 20th September 1935, Letters page.
50. One of the most vivid accounts of this event is by Art Lizzote, *Scribblings from the Rocky Mountain Philatelic Library* (Nov-Dec-2010), p.12. (https://www.rmpldenver.org/images/pdf/2010novdecscribblings.pdf)
51. This is from an unpublished work by Leslie J Johnson, *History of the British Interplanetary Society 1935 to 1945*, p.38. Willy Ley had arrived in Liverpool from Germany before going on to the USA.
52. https://www.bis-space.com/what-we-do/the-british-interplanetary-society/history/philip-e-cleator
53. 11th February 1935. *Daily Dispatch*, a local newspaper in Liverpool at the time.
54. British Interplanetary Society Journal *Spaceflight* (Volume 60 Number 08, August 2018) p.28.
55. Letter dated 22nd November 1936 from Willy Ley to Robert Paganini. Ley expresses his disappointment, having lost four months working on the rocket plane demonstration in Greenwood Lake. He is still optimistic that spaceflight is achievable in his lifetime. Willy Ley lived to see Sputnik and Gagarin but died four weeks before Apollo 11 landed on the Moon.

6. Rocket Mail in India

1. Singh, G. 2017, *The Indian Space Programme*, p.11.
2. This comes from a special four-page large pamphlet entitled *First Indian Rocket Dispatches 1934*. In it he Smith summarises the dates, times, and individuals involved and explains his motivation for the first launch attempts.
3. 17th September 1930. In a letter to Robert Paganini, he tells him about this incident and shares some covers flown on these flights. The Robert Paganini Collection, Museum of Communication, Bern, Switzerland.
4. Jatia, D N. 1980, *From the Diary of Stephen Smith*, p.6.
5. Ibid, p.11.
6. *The Mercury* (Pottstown, Montgomery, Pennsylvania, United States of America) (1st November 1934), p.9. Some of the other press reports included: Star of India, Calcutta 6th October 1934, Daily Telegraph, London 26th December 1934, Cleveland Palin Dealer, 26th December 1934, Statesman, Calcutta, 30th December 1934, The American Weekly, August 1936, The Philadelphia Enquirer, 29th November 1936, The Amrita Bazar Patrika, 6th February 1937, The Meccano Magazine, England, September 1937, Popular Flying, November 1938
7. 25th November 1934, The Sunday Times
8. Letter from the King's Private Secretary dated 7th December 1934. Royal Archives, Windsor Castle.
9. Letter from Stephen Smith to Robert Paganini, 2nd January 1935, The Robert Paganini Collection, Museum of Communication, Bern, Switzerland.
10. Smith, S. and F Billig, *Billig's Specialized Catalogues: Rocket Mail Catalogue* (Vol. 8. 1955), p.38. This issue was published after Smith's death. It was authorised by his widow and edited by Max Kronstein and J Dellenbag.
11. Jatia, D N. 1980, *From the Diary of Stephen Smith*, p.12.
12. *The length of the rocket of 18 feet comes from page 39 of Billig's Rocket Mail Catalogue Vol. 8. This is much larger than any of his rockets mentioned anywhere else. It is almost certainly an error.*
13. The state archives in the Sikkim capital Gangtok have a file on Stephen H Smith. He did not make his visit until April 1935, but the file is dated 1934.
14. Jatia, D N. 1980, *From the Diary of Stephen Smith*, p.42.
15. This detail can still be traced in an approximately 18 page file stored in the Sikkim State Archives in Gangtok. It contains many samples of Smith's handwriting and one rocket stamp used during his experiments in Sikkim.
16. *Billig's Rocket Mail Catalogue* Vol. 8. p.59.
17. 19/1/1934, An item in the Leon Victor Pont collection. A newspaper clipping signed by Smith clipping from the Advance Daily. Entitled Germ-Hunt by airplane. Signed by Smith. Supplied via email by Stephane Cloutier, Sparks Auction 12 February 2020.
18. 6th June 1935, rocket #65 called the 'Sir David Ezra' with a cockerel (Adam) and a hen (Eve) over the Damadoor River.27th September 1935, rocket #84 called 'Sikkim' with a single cockerel was dispatched in Gangtok by Mr C E Dudley, the General Secretary to His Highness the Maharajah of Sikkim.21st September 1936 rocket #127 called 'The John Winterton', with large wings, had an unusual cargo including mail, an apple and a snake called 'Miss Creepy'. 22nd September 1937 rocket #144 rocket called 'Saturn Express' .
19. *Billig's Rocket Mail Catalogue*, Vol. 8. p.41.

20. Jatia, D N.1980, *From the Diary of Stephen Smith*, p.57
21. *Ibid, p 56*
22. *The San Francisco Examiner*, San Francisco, California 9th August1936, p.83. https://www.newspapers.com/clip/25660342/the_first_rocketship_to_carry_living/. The experiment (R1 on 9th September 1931) conducted by Friedrich Schmiedl was the first to carry live passengers, beetles and butterflies, but was not widely known at the time.
23. 9th August 1936, *American Weekly*. https://www.newspapers.com/clip/25660342/the_first_rocketship_to_carry_living/
24. JBIS (Volume 2 No 2 10, 1935), p.13 Other international press coverage included: *Oakland Tribune*, 29th October 1939, p.28. https://www.newspapers.com/clip/25660295/havanas_attempt_to_send_mail_by_rocket/ *The San Bernardino County Sun*, San Bernardino, California, 9th May 1964, p.32. https://www.newspapers.com/clip/25662138/history_built_on_dreams_failures/
    The Ottawa Citizen, Ottawa, Ontario, Canada, 12th April1958, p.45. https://www.newspapers.com/clip/25660101/say_calcutta_scientist_pioneered_mail/
    His work was covered in a book published a year after he started his experiment. C G Philip, *Stratosphere and Rocket Flight*, 1935, p.66. Eventually, he was recognised in a NASA publication: NASA Conference Publication 2014 *Essays on the History of Rocketry and Astronautics: Proceedings of the Third Through the Sixth History Symposia of the International Academy of Astronautics* held at Mar del Plata, Argentina, 10th October 1969. https://archive.org/details/nasa_techdoc_19770026086 p.64.
25. A letter dated 6th December 1979 from Friedrich Schmiedl to Beatrice Bachman. In this letter Schmiedl says he conducted a Bio experiment on 9th September 1931 transporting beetles and butterflies. This was four years earlier than Smith's test with 'Adam and Eve' but appears to have been a one off. There are no other examples of Schmiedl's work involving any forms of life.
26. Hopferweiser, W, M. *Pioneer Rocket Mail and Space Mail*, p.69. This is one of the most comprehensive of recent publications documenting the work of several pioneers including Friedrich Schmiedl and Stephen H Smith. The author is someone who had personal interactions with fellow Austrian Friedrich Schmiedl prior to his death in 1994.
27. Beischer D E and Fregly A R , *Animals and man in space. A chronology and annotated bibliography through the year 1960* (US Naval School of Aviation Medicine, 1962), p.55. Available here: http://archive.rubicon-foundation.org/xmlui/handle/123456789/9288. The V2 flight was conducted on White Sands Las Cruces, New Mexico. A summary of each of these early high altitude/sub orbital flights is recorded in the book.
28. Siddiqi, A. *Beyond Earth: A Chronicle of Deep Space Exploration, 1958–2016* (Washington, DC: NASA History Program Office, pdf, 2018), p.80.
29. Royal correspondence. Response from the King to Stephen Smith's request to visit Sikkim, Gangtok Archives.
30. Seron, Z. 'The first Rocket Mail Parcel Post', *The Air Post Journal* (January 1981), p.134.
31. *Billig's Rocket Mail Catalogue*, p.60.
32. Billig's Rocket Mail Catalogue p.61.
33. Margaret D Williams and John Snelling, *7Memoirs of a Political Officer's Wife in Tibet, Sikkim and Bhutan*, (First Edition, London: Longmead, Shaftesbury, Dorset: Wisdom Publications, U.S. 1988), p.14.

34. Royal correspondence. Response from the King to Stephen Smith's request to visit Sikkim. Gangtok Archives.
35. Williamson, D, Margaret, 1987, *Memoirs of a Political Officer's Wife*, p.139.
36. Smith refers to his attempts to travel to Tibet and Bhutan in letters to Leon Victor Pont. Pont had been a member of the Indian Air Mail Society whilst he was living in Calcutta in the late 1920s. By the time of these letters (27 December 1934 mentions Bhutan and 5 March 1936 refers to Tibet) Pont had returned to England. Scans of these letters were sent to me by Stéphane Cloutier of Sparks Auction in February 2202.
37. Donen N, and Gillham, B. *India Post* (Vol 53, 53/3 No. 212, 2009) p.122.
38. *Billig's Rocket Mail Catalogue*. This issue was published after Smith's death. It was authorised by his widow and edited by Max Kronstein and J Dellenbag. p.40.
39. Stephen Smith was a Christian. Is he deliberately using biblical themes? For example, he used the names of Adam and Eve for his cockerel and hen test flight in June 1935 and here he is using the idea of a snake and an apple. Just a thought.
40. 5th August 1937. Letter from Stephen Smith to Leslie Johnson. Private Collection of Leslie Johnson, Liverpool, England.
41. 16th July1938, Letter from Stephen Smith to Leslie Johnson. Private Collection of Leslie Johnson, Liverpool, England.

7. Special Event Rocket Mail

1. Levinge, N and Prasad, R. *1935 Silver Jubilee Stamps*, p.214.
2. *Billig's Specialized Catalogues: Rocket Mail Catalogue* Vol. 8, 1955, p.8.
3. *Billig's Rocket Mail Catalogue*, p.48. The piece written by the editor of the *Star of India*, Mr L P Atkinson, who ignited both rockets, is duplicated here.
4. 9th September 1937, L J Johnson, 'Transatlantic Rocket Mails', *The Meccano Magazine*.
5. A goodwill flight from Tokyo to London was organised by Japan's most prominent newspaper 'Asaki Shimburn" to bring Japanese congratulations to the British nation for the coronation of King George VI. The aeroplane used was called "Divine Wind".
    On the return flight the "Divine Wind" left Croydon on 14 May and landed in Calcutta. Stephen Smith took the opportunity to ask the pilot via the Japanese Consulate to carry some cards that he had prepared to record the flight. He had some Coronation Rocketgram cards and put a Coronation Rocket Despatch stamp on them, crossing out the words "Rocket" and replacing it with the words "Divine Wind". He had prepared 54 cards which he numbered 1 to 54. These cards then had a 2As stamp affixed to them so that they could be flown from Calcutta to Rangoon and posted back to Calcutta. The cards were taken to the Japanese Consulate. A Consulate General stamp was applied and then they were given to the pilot to fly them to Rangoon.
    This information is curtesy of Terry Hare-Walker who has the card number 15 in his personal collection.
6. Cooper, J. *Stamps* (National Air and Space Museum, Washington, DC, 4th April 1964),. A journal established by Jal Cooper. This piece carries a report on the Boy Scouts and Girl Guides events. It includes copies of the letter inviting Smith to the Jamboree.
7. The use of the term propaganda here does not have the meaning we understand today, i.e. to manipulate opinion and to serve a predefined agenda. In the 1930s it

had a more innocent, neutral even positive meaning: something that is to be disseminated.
8. The Amrita Bazar Patrika, Saturday, 6th February 1937.
9. The rockets launched during the Jamboree were given names. No. 134 was the 'Dr R Paganini' (in Bern Switzerland), No. 35 was the 'Dr M Kronstein' (in New York), No. 138 the 'Princess Elizabeth' and no 139 'Lord Baden-Powell'.
10. *Billig's Rocket Mail Catalogue*, p.47.
11. *The Star of India*, (3rd Edition, Stephen Smith collection, National Air and Space Museum Washington, DC, 1st September 1939) National Air and Space Museum,.
12. Binns, A R. *The Aero Field* (Vol 7, April 1943), p.47. Stephen Smith collection, National Air and Space Museum, Washington, DC.
13. 23rd September 1939, Letter from Stephen Smith to Robert Paganini. Robert Paganini collection,.
14. Ibid.
15. 11th October 1937. Letter from Stephen Smith to Leslie Johnson. Private Collection of Leslie Johnson, Liverpool, England
16. 23rd March 1949, Letter from Stephen Smith to Robert Paganini. Robert Paganini Collection, Museum of Communication, Bern, Switzerland.
17. *The Aero Field* (No. 6, 1957), Postal Museum, London. An aerophilately magazine published by Francis Field in England.
18. Interestingly, in 1944, Lady Baden-Powell's apartment in Hampton Court was damaged by a V2 missile. She was not at home at the time and suffered no injury. https://en.wikipedia.org/wiki/Olave_Baden-Powell#Death_of_Robert_Baden-Powell.

8. Global Connections

1. https://www.americanairmailsociety.org/about/aams-awards/aerophilatelic-hall-of-fame/.
2. The Robert Paganini Collection, Museum of Communication, Bern, Switzerland contains possibly the largest quantity of correspondence with Stephen Smith, spanning over two decades. Other key resources used for this book have been the archives of Leslie Johnson in Liverpool, London Postal Museum, the Gangtok Archives in Sikkim and contributions from several philatelists who have generously shared parts of their personal collections.
3. Kronstein, Max. 'Foreign Pioneer Airpost Flights 1909-1914', *The Air Post Journal* (May 1962), p.246.
4. A French version of his original German document of the *Les Grandes Archives de la Posts Aerunne*, (Grand Archive of Airmail) founded in 1913, is kept in the National Postal Museum in Washington, DC. Dedicated by the author to the state of Switzerland. Robert Paganini Collection, Museum of Communication, Bern, Switzerland.
5. *Les Grandes Archives de la Posts Aerunne*. The document is mostly in French but has one page in English. National Air and Space Museum, Washington, DC.
6. This comes from a piece written in 1923 by Max Kronstein in the April 1941. Bulletin of *The Helvetia Society for Collectors of Switzerland*. http://s107851386.onlinehome.us/HB/HB0404.pdf.
7. *Bulletin of the Helvetia Society for the Collectors of Switzerland*. April 1941, Robert Paganini Collection, Museum of Communication, Bern, Switzerland.
8. Robert Paganini, *Geschickte der Luftpost Historischer Katalog samtlicher Luftpost*,

(Airmail history Historical catalog of all airmail, 1920). A copy is available in the National Postal Museum, Washington, DC.
9. *The Airpost Journal* January 1940, p.78.
10. Paganini, R. 'Philately and Rocket Mail', *Air Post Journal,* (December 1936), p.23.
11. Birch, B *Philatelic Translations* (January 2015). https://www.fipliterature.org/birch/A%20List%20of%20Translations.pdf P1027.
12. Kronstein, Max. *Rocket Mail Flights of the World to 1986*, 1st Print Edition (The American Air Mail Society, 1986). p.77.
13. Ibid, p.78.
14. The March 1963 issue of *The Air Post Journal* carried a profile of Max Kronstein.
15. *The Air Post Journal* Volume 016, Issue 0177, No 04, January 1945 p.139.
16. https://www.nytimes.com/1992/11/24/obituaries/max-kronstein-chemist-97.html.
17. *Billig's Rocket Mail Catalogue 1955*.
18. Kronstein, Max. *The Air Post Journal,* February 1961, p.123.
19. *Air Post Journal* (10, Issue 0109, No. 8, May 1939), p.10.
20. *Philippine Philatelic News* (Volume XI, No 3 Third Quarter, 1989). http://www.theipps.info/journals/PPN%20vol%2011%20no%203%20t%20q%2089.pdf.
21. *Air Post Journal* (015, Issue 0167, No. 6, March 1944,) p.10.
22. http://india.blogs.nytimes.com/2013/10/24/the-last-jews-of-kolkata.
23. The earliest Jewish community was in Kerala in the south of India. They arrived around AD 70 and have now completely integrated with the local community and speak Malayalam although they still practice Jewish rituals.
24. http://www.telegraphindia.com/1120103/jsp/frontpage/story_14955920.jsp
25. A more detailed account of David Ezra's many commercial interests is summarised here:
http://shodhganga.inflibnet.ac.in/jspui/bitstream/10603/164753/17/17_appendix.pdf.
26. 14th May 1938. Letter from Stephen Smith to Leslie Johnson. Private Collection of Leslie Johnson, Liverpool, England In his reply of 31st May, Johnson indicated that he would make time to see the Ezra family if he travelled to London while they were there. The BIS was looking for influential sponsors just as much as he was. There is no record to indicate that Johnson met with David Ezra.
27. 17th September 1936 Letter from Stephen Smith to Sir Philip Sassoon, MP for Hyth, Postal Museum, London.

9. Prelude to Space

1. Turner, C. 2006, 'Letter Bombs', http://www.cabinetmagazine.org/issues/23/turner2.php.
2. Ibid
3. 5th June 1902, Copy of Report by Captain A. P. H. Desborough, His Majesty's Inspector of Explosives, to the right Hon. the Secretary of State for the Home Department, on the circumstances attending an accident which occurred in the building for non-explosive ingredients at the factory of Messrs. James Pain and Sons, at Mitcham, Surrey, on Hansard, 16th October 1902. https://api.parliament.uk/historic-hansard/commons/1902/oct/16/explosions-accident-at-messrs-pain-and.
April 24, 1961 - The Orient Fireworks Company. An explosion in the factory in India. Lok Sabha debates Thirteenth Session. http://eparlib.nic.in/bitstream/123456789/55849/1/lsd_02_13_24-04-1961.pdf p.13745.

4. Not clear how often Smith was supplied with rockets by the two companies or how many they provided. https://enacademic.com/dic.nsf/enwiki/693438.
5. Letter dated 3rd April 1935 from Stephen Smith to Mr Leon Victor Pont who was a former railway engineer and member of the Indian Air Mail Society while living in Calcutta. Copy of the letter provided by Stéphane Cloutier from Sparks Auctions.
6. Cooper, J. 1952, *Stamps of India*, p.1.
7. Ibid p.142.In the June 1938 edition of the Indian Airmail Society's bulletin, Smith records that the 'famous French inventor M Robert Esnault-Pelterie is busy in Europe designing a special rocket for Air Mails at the moment'. It is unclear if Smith was in personal contact with Esnault-Pelterie.
8. A decade earlier: M Valier, an article entitled 'Berlin to New York in one hour' Science and Mechanics, November 1931, p.648.
9. https://www.newspapers.com/clip/25690033/rockets_to_carry_mails_of_future/.
10. Astronautics was a term coined by by J.-H. Rosny, president of the Goncourt academy, in France and was known in French as 'astronautique'. Given the overlap between air and space, the term aerospace is commonly used to include both aeronautics and astronautics.
11. Kessler, F. *The Air Post Journal* (May 1936), p.15. Interestingly, this same article entitled 'A review of Foreign Rocket Flights' covers Smith's work in India and states: 'There is no doubt that some of these flights were not necessary. But on the other hand, he has clearly demonstrated the utility of rockets'. Oddly, Smith was very troubled by this apparently reasonable statement. In a letter to Robert Paganini dated 7th October 1936, he asserts that testing was necessary because 'they have as yet not been studied and mastered'.
12. Robert Paganini joined the Cleveland Rocket Society on 6th June 1934, a year after it was formed and the BIS on 13th July 1936.
13. Robert Goddard was the first to transport rocket mail over international border. *Billig's Rocket Mail Catalogue*, p.68.
14. 17th September 1936. Letter from Stephen Smith to Sir Philip Sassoon MP for Hyth, Postal Museum, London.
15. Letter from H Napier, the Principal Private Secretary to the Postmaster General, request to advise Sir Philip Sassoon. 15th October 1936, Postal Museum, London.The following press report indicates that Sir Phillip Sassoon was present on the Island of Scarp to witness Gerhard Zucker's rocket launch on 28th July 1934. https://www.pressreader.com/uk/scottish-daily-mail/20170923/282359744894768.
16. Letter dated 3rd April 1936 from Phil Cleator (founder of the BIS) to G Pendray (founder of the American Rocketry Society). In this letter, Cleator is sending reports of Smith's work in India to Pendray and receiving reports of Goddard's work from Pendray. Archives Division. National Air and Space Museum, Washington, DC.
17. The following publications refer to Smith's work in the context of spaceflight:John J Britt, 'Stephen H. Smith Rockets and Space Missiles', *Aero Philatelist Annals* (Volume VII, No. 3, 3rd January 1960), p.67. NASA Conference Publication 2014, *Essays on the History of Rocketry and Astronautics: Proceedings of the Third Through the Sixth History Symposia of the International Academy of Astronautics*, Vol II, Symposia held at Mar del Plata, Argentina, 10th October 1969. https://archive.org/details/nasa_techdoc_19770026086 p.4. Winter, Frank. in his 1983 book *Prelude to the Space Age, The Rocket Societies: 1924–1940*, does not refer directly to Stephen Smith but references his work (*The Indian Air Mail Society Quarterly Bulletin*, 11th June 1937: 50-51), p.152.
18. Britt, J, 1960, *Stephen H Smith Rockets and Space Missiles*, p.75.

19. Staff Correspondent, *The Statesman* (National Air and Space Museum, Washington, DC, 9th February 1958). This is a typewritten early draft (it has some corrections) four-page document.
20. *First International Rocket Mail*, with a foreword by George W Wentz. This looks like a privately published book, with no page numbers and no named author. National Postal Museum, Washington, DC.
21. https://postalmuseum.si.edu/airmail/historicplanes/unusual/historicplanes_unusual_missile.html.
22. This is from an unpublished work by Leslie J Johnson, *History of the British Interplanetary Society 1935 to 1945*, p.38.
23. A detailed account of the both the 1st May and 8th June events in a document held in the Udvar-Hazy museum in Washington, DC.
24. Statement by Postmaster General Arthur E. Summerfield. Release No. 149.
25. June 1959, 'The First Official Missile Mail', Press release from the Postmaster general. Robert Paganini Collection, Museum of Communication, Bern, Switzerland. Museum of Communication, Bern, Switzerland.
26. Putnam, C, S. 'One Small Step for Mail. Damn Interesting'. 10th August 2007. http://www.damninteresting.com/one-small-step-formail.
27. Hopferweiser, W. *Astrophile* (March 1988), p.6.
28. Collins, Michael, 1974, "Carrying the Fire". There is also a typed and signed letter from Neil Armstrong to Dr. Joseph F. Rorke dated 15 January 1970. In this letter Armstrong confirms that the rubber stamp was carried to the lunar surface in the Eagle. https://www.19thshop.com/book/armstrong-letter/
29. In the final months of WWII, the US-initiated 'Operation Paperclip' to acquire German technology for the US. Many former Nazi members ended up as American citizens. The US government had adopted the policy of not permitting 'ardent Nazis' into the country, as many were deemed security risks, and at least some were implicated in war crimes. The applications of German citizens desiring to go to the US were sent by the US Army to the US State Department, where they were marked 'Ardent Nazi' and rejected, or 'Not Ardent Nazi' when the applicant's skills were deemed useful for the US national interest. The term 'Paperclip' came from processing these applications.
30. A list of (pretty much) all known V2 launches is available here: https://en.wikipedia.org/wiki/List_of_V-2_test_launches
31. Hopfweriser, W 2019. *Pioneer Rocket Mail & Space Mail*, p.473.
32. Johnson, L. 'Transatlantic Rocket Mail', *The Meccano Magazine* (September 1937).
33. For example: *American Weekly*, 9th August 1936. https://www.newspapers.com/clip/25660342/the_first_rocketship_to_carry_living/.
34. Hopferwieser, W, 2019. *Pioneer Rocket Mail and Space Mail*, p.475. Another source indicates that the nose cone also contained another letter from scientist Dr Kurt Debus. https://www.nasa.gov/exploration/thismonth/this_month_august07.html.
35. The primary recovery method was from an aircraft, to snag the parachute during descent. Alternatively, recovery by helicopter after splashdown was also an option. Once recovered, the film was chemically developed. This was long before the digital era.
36. This is a term coined by Margaret Morris in 1988 and has slowly grown as the space sector has evolved. http://venngeist.org/opsa2_morris.pdf.
37. Hopferwieser, M. *Pioneer Rocket Mail & Space Mail*, p.210.
38. https://bittergrounds.com/moon-mail-celebrating-the-anniversary-of-the-apollo-moon-landing/.

39. Apollo 13 commander, Dave Scott performed the cancellation in a live telecast from the surface of the Moon. The transcript: 'To show that our good Postal Service has deliveries any place in the universe, I have the pleasant task of canceling, here on the Moon, the first stamp of a new issue dedicated to commemorating the United States' achievements in space. And I'm sure a lot of people have seen pictures of the stamp. I have the first one here on an envelope. At the bottom it says, "United States in Space, a decade of achievement," and I'm very proud to have the opportunity here to play postman. I pull out a cancellation device. Cancel this stamp. It says, "August the second, 1971, first day of issue".'
   https://history.nasa.gov/alsj/a15 a15PostalKit.html (transcript). Available on Youtube at https://youtu.be/LR6SsDMlKrw.
40. Fishbein, L. *The Astrophile, Space Unit Bulletin,* ATA APS Unit 29, September 1972.
41. Ibid. The letter is replicated in full in this collection. National Air and Space Museum, Washington, DC.
42. Hopferweiser, W. 1988, *Astrophile,* p.6
43. A Christmas card with a photo of all the school members, signed by each one, was sent to Robert Paganini in December 1930. In addition, two works of philately were sent to the Library of Congress in Washington. The Robert Paganini Collection, Museum of Communication, Bern, Switzerland.
44. Hermann Oberth, through his 1923 book, *The Rocket into Interplanetary Space,* is considered to be the father of Astronautics. Like other German rocket engineers, he ended up working in the USA. Approaching retirement in 1958, he had not built a sufficient pension, so he faced a choice of either staying in the USA without an income or returning to Germany. He wanted to stay in the USA. To support this choice, Arthur C Clark wrote to the editor of the New York Times highlighting Oberth's dilemma. 25th February 1958, Arthur C Clarke collection. National Air and Space Museum, Washington, DC.
45. November 1934 BIS bulletin, a short article with the title 'Indian Rocket mail'. It goes on to record that 'In the lower reaches of the River Hooghly, India, has been inaugurated the first Ship-to-Shore rocket mail in the world'.
46. Journal of the BIS, October 1935, p.11.
47. 11th October 1937, Letter from Stephen Smith to Leslie Johnson. Private Collection of Leslie Johnson, Liverpool, England
48. Johnson, L, 'Transatlantic Rocket Mail', *The Meccano Magazine* (Vol XXXIL No. 9, September 1937).
49. Not something practiced today, but in the past many learned societies encouraged the use of society-headed paper for inter-membership correspondence. BIS Bulletin in October 1935 carried the following: 'The BIS Members are reminded that Society notepaper may be obtained from the Hon. Secretary at a nominal charge of 2/6 per 100 sheets, post free.'
50. Letter from Cleaver to Pendray, 3rd April 1936. In the letter, Cleaver refers to Smith's work as 'details of the East India experiments'. National Air and Space Museum Washington, DC.
51. Research notes written by Frank H Winter sometime during the late 1970s or early 1980s. Notes are entitled 'Misc. notes on the British Interplanetary Society. Email correspondence between the author and Frank H Winter, 18th December 2019.
52. Malcolm, D. *The Paisley Rocketeers* (1997), p.17. Letter from Phil Cleator to Edward Pendray 3rd April 1936. He tells Pendray that he is awaiting a 'considered reply' from the Home Office. National Air and Space Museum, Washington, DC.
53. Burgess, E. *Rocket Propulsion* (1952), p.225. Eric Burgess provides a concise summary

of the numerous rocketry organisations in Britain during the 1930s and 40s. He was the founder of the Manchester Interplanetary Society in 1936. In the following year a schism developed and the some members of the MIS formed the Manchester Astronautical Association. The MAA continued to operate during the war and was one of the organisations incorporated into the reformed BIS in 1945.
54. Some details here https://www.bis-space.com/what-we-do/projects/bis-lunar-spaceship.
55. Burgess, E. , *Assault on the Moon* (1966), p.30. Eric Burgess was a key player in the early days of rocketry in England. He founded the Manchester Interplanetary Society and was integral in re-establishing the post-war BIS. He reviewed the design of the BIS Lunar Spaceship a quarter of a century after it was published. He did this in 1966, by which time he had moved from the UK to the USA and the USA's Apollo mission was at an advanced stage of planning.
56. British Interplanetary Society Journal, Spaceflight Volume VII Number 4, July 1965
57. Ciancone, M, L. (Ed.) *History of Rocketry and Astronautics* (American Astronautical Society, 2010), p.53.
58. Clarke, A, C , Personal correspondence with H G Wells, 19th July 1939. Exactly 30 years later, Apollo 11 embarked on its historic journey to the Moon. Arthur C Clarke Collection, National Air and Space Museum, Washington, DC.
59. 31st May 1938, Letter from Stephen Smith to Leslie Johnson. Private Collection of Leslie Johnson, Liverpool, England. For a pdf of this story see https://astrotalkuk.org/tales-of-wonder-summer-1938-satellites-of-death-by-leslie-johnson/
60. Winter, Frank. *Prelude to the Space Age: The Rocket Societies, 1924-1940* (First edition, Washington D.C: Smithsonian Inst.), p.117. The American Rocketry Society 17,000 members; The BIS 3,500; Deutsche Gesellschaft fur Raketentechnik und Raumfahrt (the German Society for Rocket Engineering and Space Travel) 1,600; the French Astronautical Society 580; the Argentine Interplanetary Society 500; Osterreichische, Gesellschaft fur Weltraumforschung (the Austrian Society for Space Flight Research) 144 and similar groups in 27 other countries.
61. Cleaver, V. BIS annual Report on the first International Aeronautical Congress (1950), p.316. 'We have on file, at the BIS, some very interesting correspondence between Prof. Oberth, Herr Willy Ley (both then of the VfR), Mr G E Pendray of the American interplanetary Society (now the ARS), and our own P E Cleator; this dates back to 1931-33 and represents an early attempt at international co-operation, unfortunately destined to be fruitless.'
62. Cleaver, V. annual report of the BIS 1950, p.316.
63. One of the many new startups in New Space India is a Rocketeers. Set up in 2018, it provides solid rockets of the type that Stephen Smith used for education across India. https://www.rocketeers.in/.

10. Legacy

1. 6th April 1946. Letter from Stephen Smith to Robert Paganini. Robert Paganini Collection, Museum of Communication, Bern, Switzerland.
2. 26th April 1938. Letter from Stephen Smith to Robert Paganini. Robert Paganini Collection, Museum of Communication, Bern, Switzerland.
3. 20th October 1937. Letter from Stephen Smith to Leslie Johnson. Private Collection of Leslie Johnson, Liverpool, England

4. *The Star of India* article under the heading 'The World's First Boomerang Rocket Flight', 11th October 1937.
5. 25th April 1938. *The Star of India* article under the heading 'The Flights of "Miss Fortune" and the "T Kimball".
6. 22nd September 1939. Letter from Stephen Smith to Robert Paganini. The Robert Paganini Collection, Museum of Communication, Bern, Switzerland.
7. This information comes from a letter by Max Kronstein to Frank Winter dated 21st June 1973. Frank Winter was preparing a paper for the IAC in 1973 held in Baku, which at the time was in the USSR. National Air and Space Museum, Washington, DC. Also see https://www.paisley.org.uk/paisley-history/paisley-rocketeers-society-1935-2005/camera-rocket-rr53/
8. 11th April 1946. Letter from Stephen Smith to Robert Paganini. Robert Paganini Collection, Museum of Communication, Bern, Switzerland.
9. 6th April 1946. Letter from Stephen Smith to Robert Paganini. Robert Paganini Collection, Museum of Communication, Bern, Switzerland.
10. He writes this in a letter to his friend Robert Paganini in Switzerland. It is remarkably similar to a response made by K E Tsiolkovskii in *Works on Rocket Technology* (Moscow, 1947). NASA Technical Translation F-243, 1965, p7.
11. Letter from Stephen Smith to Robert Paganini. Robert Paganini Collection, Museum of Communication, Bern, Switzerland
12. 6th April 1946. Letter from Stephen Smith to Robert Paganini. Robert Paganini Collection, Museum of Communication, Bern, Switzerland
13. 23rd March 1949, Letter from Stephen Smith to Robert Paganini. Robert Paganini Collection, Museum of Communication, Bern, Switzerland
14. Smith invited Paganini to join on 1st September 1925 and wrote again acknowledging his acceptance on 24th December 1925. Robert Paganini Collection, Museum of Communication, Bern, Switzerland.
15. 23rd September 1937. Robert Paganini Collection, Museum of Communication, Bern, Switzerland.
16. 6th January 1931 and 9th June 1931 Robert Paganini Collection, Museum of Communication, Bern, Switzerland.
17. This account records that Dm Dum airport was the busiest in the world at he time. The target of the air attack was the Calcutta docks and specifically Howrah bridge https://www.bbc.co.uk/history/ww2peopleswar/stories/50/a5756150.shtml
18. 6th April 1946. Letter from Smith to Paganini. Robert Paganini Collection, Museum of Communication, Bern, Switzerland.
19. 29th January 1948. Letter from Smith to Paganini. Robert Paganini Collection, Museum of Communication, Bern, Switzerland.
20. 19 January 1927 Letter from Smith toPaganini. Museum o Communication, Bern, Switzerland.
21. 15th July 1931. Letter from Smith to Paganini, marked Private and Confidential. Robert Paganini Collection, Museum of Communication, Bern, Switzerland.
22. 10th February 1949. Letter from Stephen Smith to Robert Paganini. Robert Paganini Collection, Museum of Communication, Bern, Switzerland.
23. 16th February 1949. Letter from Stephen Smith to Robert Paganini. Robert Paganini Collection, Museum of Communication, Bern, Switzerland.
24. 15th July 1931. Letter from Stephen Smith to Robert Paganini. Robert Paganini Collection, Museum of Communication, Bern, Switzerland.
25. 9th June 1931 – Letter from Stephen Smith to Robert Paganini in which he talks

about his charity work. Robert Paganini Collection, Museum of Communication, Bern, Switzerland.
26. 7th November 1949. Letter from Stephen Smith to Robert Paganini. Robert Paganini Collection, Museum of Communication, Bern, Switzerland.
27. His will is dated 20th April 1946. In it, he shares his estate equally between 4 parties: One quarter for the Luftpost Archive (the museum housing his collection); One quarter to be shared between the various airmail societies that he was a member of; One quarter to his nephews and nieces; One quarter to Stephen Smith. A copy of his will is part of his collection. Robert Paganini Collection, Museum of Communication, Bern, Switzerland.
28. 11th October 1937. Letter from Stephen Smith to Leslie Johnson. Private Collection of Leslie Johnson, Liverpool, England
29. Johnson, L. unpublished Personal History of the BIS (Leslie Johnson Collection, Liverpool, England) p.47.
30. Philp, C,G. *Stratosphere and Rocket Flight* (1935), p.2.
31. 23rd March 1949. Letter from Stephen Smith to Robert Paganini. Robert Paganini Collection, Museum of Communication, Bern, Switzerland.
32. 20th October 1937, Robert Paganini Collection, Museum of Communication, Bern, Switzerland.
  Letter from Stephen Smith to Leslie Johnson. Private Collection of Leslie Johnson, Liverpool, England
33. Letter from Smith to Pont, dated 31/10/1934. Supplied via email by Stephane Cloutier, Sparks Auction 12 February 2020.
34. 14th May 1938, Letter from Stephen Smith to Leslie Johnson. Private Collection of Leslie Johnson, Liverpool, England.
35. 7th November 1949. Letter from Stephen Smith to Robert Paganini. Robert Paganini Collection, Museum of Communication, Bern, Switzerland.
36. 23rd March 1949. Letter from Stephen Smith to Robert Paganini. Robert Paganini Collection, Museum of Communication, Bern, Switzerland.
37. 2nd March 1950. Letter from Stephen Smith to Robert Paganini. Robert Paganini Collection, Museum of Communication, Bern, Switzerland.
38. 26th January 1938. Letter from Stephen Smith to Robert Paganini. Robert Paganini Collection, Museum of Communication, Bern, Switzerland.
39. 19 February 1935. Letter from Stephen Smith to Victor Pont when Pont had returned to England. Scan of letter supplied by Stéphane Cloutier, Sparks Auctions.
40. Telephone conversation 11th January 2020 with daughter of Noel Victor Pont. Pont was a member of the Indian Air Mail Society when he lived in Calcutta in the late 1920s and early 1930s. Smith continued to correspond with him once Pont had left India in 1933 to live in England.
41. Britt, J, J. The Rocket Stamp Collection of Stephen H Smith, *Aero Philatelist Annals* (July 1960), p.7
42. 14th October 1953. A marketing letter addressed to 'Dear collectors' from Normandy Stamp Studio, Los Angeles California. National Air and Space Museum, Washington, DC.
43. National Air and Space Museum historian Frank H Winter included a reference to Smith's work in India in his 1983 book *Prelude to the Space Age*. His personal archive contains letters, documents and photographs that indicate he had sought out details of Smith's work in India.
44. For example: INDIA 1937 SCOUTS JAMBOREE ROCKET EXPERIMENT KRONSTEIN SMITH SIGNED RARE COVER$1,000.00 From Singapore or Best

Offer+$5.00 shipping https://www.ebay.com/itm/INDIA-1937-SCOUTS-JAMBOREE-ROCKET-EXPERIMENT-KRONSTEIN-SMITH-SIGNED-RARE-COVER/123734837874
45. Hopferweiser, W. *Pioneer Rocket Mail & Space Mail.* See pages 115-169, especially pages 143, 147, 161 and 162.
46. Details supplied via email by Stephane Cloutier, Sparks Auction 12 February 2020
47. 1. The Aero Field, May 1951, P83,

    2. Stamps of India 2nd Edition, Jal Cooper, P209,

    3. The Air Post Journal February 1961 Max Kronstein P123 - "the greatest one man campaign for rocketry".

ALSO BY GURBIR SINGH

The Indian Space Programme

Yuri Gagarin in London and Manchester

www.ingramcontent.com/pod-product-compliance
Lightning Source LLC
Chambersburg PA
CBHW030105240426
43661CB00001B/24